DATE DUE

DEMCO 38-296

Models of Misrepresentation

Models of Misrepresentation

On the Fiction of E. L. Doctorow

Christopher D. Morris

UNIVERSITY PRESS OF MISSISSIPPI
Jackson & London

PS 3554 .O3 Z79 1991

Morris, Christopher D.

Models of misrepresentation

Copyright © 1991 by the University Press of Mississippi
All rights reserved
Manufactured in the United States of America
Designed by Sally Hamlin

95 94 93 92 91   5 4 3 2 1

The paper in this book meets the guidelines for permanence and durability of the Committee on Production Guidelines for Book Longevity of the Council on Library Resources.

Library of Congress Cataloging-in-Publication Data

Morris, Christopher D.
    Models of misrepresentation on the fiction of E. L. Doctorow / Christopher D. Morris.
      p. cm.
    Includes bibliographical references and index.
    ISBN 0-87805-524-X (alk. paper)
    1. Doctorow, E. L., 1931–   —Criticism and interpretation.
I. Title.
PS3554.O3Z79   1991
813'.54—dc20   91-3730
                                                                                                                      CIP

British Cataloguing-in-Publication data available

You want to do better and go on and develop and dig deeper and say things you haven't said before, and it's a terrible, awful struggle.

—E. L. Doctorow

For Martha

Contents

ACKNOWLEDGMENTS............................... xi

EDITIONS USED IN THE TEXT........................ xiii

INTRODUCTION..................................... 3

1. Construction/Destruction/Construction:
   Welcome to Hard Times........................... 25

2. *Big as Life:* The Dead-End of Hermeneutics.......... 41

3. "The Songs of Billy Bathgate":
   The Writer as Orphan, Killer, Performer............. 66

4. Ellipses and Death in *The Book of Daniel*........... 79

5. Illusions of Demystification in *Ragtime*............ 98

6. *Loon Lake:* The World as Fiction.................. 115

7. The Intertextuality of *Lives of the Poets*......... 133

8. Models of Misrepresentation in *World's Fair*....... 157

9. Selected Essays and Interviews..................... 176

10. *Billy Bathgate:* Reading as Larceny............... 199

AFTERWORD.. 216

APPENDIX: LANGUAGE AND DEATH IN HEIDEGGER......... 221

NOTES.. 225

INDEX.. 257

Acknowledgments

On several occasions, while researching this book, I read about E. L. Doctorow's cordiality, but these hints did not prepare me for the exceptional hospitality he showed me, both during my interview of him in New York City and afterwards. I discuss some of his responses at the end of chapter 9; the complete interview appears in *Michigan Quarterly Review* 30 (1991), 439–56. He and I represent his work differently; perhaps our differences make part of my argument manifest. In any case, they have not changed my lasting impression of his graciousness. I hope he will see this study as an appreciation.

My intellectual debt to J. Hillis Miller is formidable and, I hope, evident in the pages that follow; I am also grateful for his words of encouragement while I was writing. I owe thanks to Martin Jay for listening sympathetically to my ideas about Heidegger. Working with both men at the School of Criticism and Theory at Dartmouth in the summer of 1986 was an immensely rewarding experience for me. The person who first taught me respect for the work of Heidegger and Derrida was Joseph N. Riddel, in a stimulating seminar on William Carlos Williams at Buffalo. I also profited from the insights of Margot Norris and Jim Vickery. My brother David's good sense has always helped me, quite apart from his cogent comments on my introduction.

I am indebted to the committee on faculty development at Norwich University for generous support at many stages of this project. In addition, I have been fortunate in receiving advice and assistance from several valued colleagues in the university's humanities division: Judy Anhorn, Scott Fields, Keith Gould, Andrew Knauf, Rob McKay, and Floyd Stuart. I am very grateful for their help.

I read a draft of chapter 8 at the English Institute at the University of Warsaw, where I spent the 1988–89 academic year on a Fulbright; my colleagues, Wiasław Furmańczyk, Elżbieta Foeller-Pituch, Christopher Knight, and Andrzej Sosnowski, were supportive of this early effort. An expanded and revised version of that paper appeared in the December 1990 issue of *Papers on Language and Literature*. The present chapter was extensively revised from the published article; I thank the editors of *PLL* for permission to publish the new adaptation here.

The epigraph in the front matter is from Hillary Mills, "Creators on Creativity: E. L. Doctorow," *Saturday Review*, 7 October 1980, p. 47.

For editorial support I am happy to acknowledge the professional expertise of my copy editor, Gwen Duffey, and of Seetha Srinivasan, of the University Press of Mississippi. Without the hard work of Wilma Coon, interlibrary loan librarian at Norwich, my research would have taken much longer. For accurate, skillful secretarial assistance, I thank Andrea Adams-Pierce and Sharon Smith. My most profound debt is to my wife, Martha, for the gift of her love.

Editions Used in the Text

Welcome to Hard Times. New York: Random House, 1960.
Big as Life. New York: Simon and Schuster, 1966.
"The Songs of Billy Bathgate." *New American Review* 2. New York: New American Library, 1968, 54–69.
The Book of Daniel. New York: New American Library, 1972.
Ragtime. New York: Bantam Books, 1976.
Loon Lake. New York: Bantam Books, 1981.
Lives of the Poets. New York: Random House, 1984.
World's Fair. New York: Fawcett, 1985.
Billy Bathgate. New York: Random House, 1989.

Essays and Interviews Discussed in Chapter 9

"False Documents," *American Review* 26 (1977): 215–32. Rpt. in Richard Trenner, editor, *E. L. Doctorow: Essays and Conversations* (Princeton: Ontario Review Press, 1983), 16–27.
"The Writer as Independent Witness," interviewed by Paul Levine for Canadian Broadcasting Corporation (March 1978). Rpt. in Richard Trenner, editor, *E. L. Doctorow: Essays and Conversations* (Princeton: Ontario Review Press, 1983), 57–69.
"The Art of Fiction," interviewed by George Plimpton in *Paris Review* 28 (1986), 23–47.
"The State of Mind of the Union," *Nation*, 22 March 1986, 327–28.
"Braver Than We Thought," *The New York Times Book Review*, 18 May 1986, 1, 44–45.
"America's Sacred Text: A Citizen Reads the Constitution," *Nation*, 21 February 1987, 208–17.
"Fiction Is a System of Knowledge: An Interview with E. L. Doctorow," by Christopher D. Morris, *Michigan Quarterly Review*, 30 (1991), 439–56.

Models of Misrepresentation

Introduction

My title has two references, the first to the fiction of E. L. Doctorow and the second to the chapters that follow; the first reference is discussed on pages 3–18 of this introduction and the second on pages 18–23.

With regard to Doctorow's novels, the phrase "models of misrepresentation" is a trope, a paradox, for we ordinarily understand that a model is a representation of something, not a misrepresentation: a model airplane is a miniature version of its original; an architectural model shows what a future building will look like. How could novels, which traditionally are supposed to represent, also be models of misrepresentation? As with every paradox, or apparent contradiction, the resolution must be sought in the word "apparent." Especially on first reading, Doctorow's novels do indeed appear to represent the world in a variety of ways, but closer scrutiny of them shows that appearance to be a mirage. In some studies of Doctorow, this doubt as to the representational function has taken the form of challenges to the accuracy of the depiction of setting (like the old West) or characters (like the Rosenbergs or Henry Ford), or trends in history (like the immigrant experience or the cold war); indeed, on occasion critiques of Doctorow's accuracy have led to strictures against the ethical implications of such inaccuracy.[1] But it should be made clear at the outset that the word "misrepresentation," as it is used in the title and the book, does not denote an inaccuracy in this sense but, instead, an incapacity to represent. Doctorow's novels, which at first seem to teem with rendered life, eventually disclose the artifice that created this first false impression on plenitude. Before taking up this thesis, I want to stress that complaints about the accuracy of Doctorow's novels should not be ignored; in fact such critiques have helped me in defining other contradictions in the novels. The most important fact, however, is that they attest prima facie to the centrality of the problem of representation in Doctorow.

From the standpoint of American literary history, the larger issue of representation in Doctorow's works may merely repeat the long-standing dilemma of our writers' attempts to "represent America": from Bradford's *Of Plimoth Plantation*, through Emerson and Whitman, Faulkner and Fitzgerald, to Doctorow and his melting-pot novels, this duty has seemed inescapable. In *American Hieroglyphics*, John T. Irwin argued that in the attempt to represent America our great nineteenth-century writers followed an analogy from the deciphering of the Rosetta Stone, which meant the task of representation was understood on the model of hermeneutics: a translation of the world conceived as text. (It is of interest in this connection that the little boy in *Ragtime*, who may be its narrator, loves hieroglyphics.) Doctorow's novels—with their invocations of Hawthorne, Poe, Thoreau, Whitman, Hemingway—may be part of the tradition Irwin traces, accepting the imperative of representation-as-deciphering.[2]

At the same time, however, Doctorow's novels attest to the impossibility of fulfilling this imperative, hence my title's use of "misrepresentation." My understanding of the dilemma of representation in his texts is influenced by the work of five writers: Friedrich Nietzsche, Martin Heidegger, Paul de Man, Jacques Derrida, and J. Hillis Miller. These writers share this trait: they challenge the tradition in Western philosophy—often seen as beginning with Plato—in which truth is defined in terms of representation. They express the challenge variously: for Nietzsche, in the idea of eternal return; for Heidegger, in the link between language and death; for de Man, in the exploration of delusions seemingly necessary to reading; for Derrida, in the rejection of hermeneutics; for Miller, in the definition of literary works in terms of prosopopoeia and intertextuality. Over the past twenty-five years, these challenges have been widely discussed. From the perspective of intellectual history, they may be associated with related developments: in linguistics, Saussure's doctrine of the arbitrary nature of the sign; in psychoanalysis, Lacan's doctrine of the unconscious; in philosophy, Wittgenstein's interrogation of ordinary language. Considered from whatever vantage-point, the influence on literary criticism of the work of these five writers has been unmistakable.[3]

For the study of Doctorow, the single most important concept in the work of Nietzsche is popularly known as the eternal return or, more precisely, the "the unconditioned and infinitely reiterated circulation of all things."[4] Already critics have discussed this concept in Doctorow's works. For example, Richard King finds it in both *Drinks Before Dinner* and *Welcome to Hard Times:* "This nightmarish version of Nietzsche's 'eternal recurrence' obviously echoes *Hard Times:* the inevitable legacy of survival is the promise of repeated destruction. Some force, some impersonal will or desire, persists behind or within all our institutional arrangements."[5] King understands Nietzsche's concept as a statement about the past and the future, but the concept may also pose a challenge to representation. Heidegger's commentary on Nietzsche will clarify this less familiar sense of the concept.[6]

Nietzsche formulates it as an afterthought to *The Gay Science* (1882) and later develops it in *Thus Spake Zarathustra* (1884) and *Ecce Homo* (1888). In dialogues with sailors, Zarathustra illustrates the concept in a parable of a sleeping shepherd whose tongue is bitten by a blacksnake. Unable to help the shepherd by tugging at the snake, Zarathustra cries "Bite! You must bite!" ("On the Vision and the Riddle" in Part III). Now this story is interpreted by one of Zarathustra's listeners as espousing the doctrine of repetition in history, but Zarathustra angrily rejects that interpretation. The parable clearly recounts a crisis in articulation. According to Heidegger, the sailor-listener may be Zarathustra himself as a young man, and the true importance of the story is this insoluble dilemma at the heart of metaphysics: "[Nietzsche's doctrine] expresses the way in which the one who poses the guiding question remains enmeshed in the structures of that question, which is not explicitly unfolded; thus enmeshed, the questioner comes to stand within being as a whole, adopting a stance toward it."[7]

For Heidegger, Zarathustra's parable defines this moment of enmeshing or "the infinitely reiterated circulation of all things," by indicating that the answers to metaphysical questions are already presupposed in them, or, in Heidegger's earlier gloss, "everything that can in any way be must, as a being, already have been."[8] So in addition to describing history, Nietzsche's doctrine points to a circularity in philosophical inquiry: to represent a metaphysical position is already to reiterate or repeat. Nietzsche calls this "the most burdensome thought";[9] Heidegger's lectures on Nietzsche carry on this burden while seeking some way out of the quandary.

In Doctorow's novels both temporal and philosophic senses of Nietzsche's concept appear, much as they do in Zarathustra's parable. In *Welcome to Hard Times,* the action of the novel shows how future destruction seems latent in every new construction, as Richard King observed. However, this return in time is predicated on the much more burdensome return Nietzsche and Heidegger dare to think: that no new articulation—*of whatever content, even of recurrence in history*—can escape reiteration. As chapter 1 explains, the thought of this possibility haunts the narrator, Blue. Again, both senses of the eternal return are present in *Ragtime.* J. P. Morgan expresses and embodies the familiar Nietzschean doctrines of the *Ubermensch* and cyclical history, but at the same time, the novel's "duplicable events" are recounted by a "double narrator" of both first and third persons. As chapter 5 argues, the implication is that repetition is inherent in narration itself. Nietzsche's eternal return thus implies a linguistic impasse that is, indeed, a movement "beyond pessimism," as Heidegger notes, into a vastly more uncertain space. It turns pessimism on the expression of pessimism, doubt on the expression of doubt, because the essence of the return is found in the representation of concepts in language.

Of course, Heidegger's "answer" to Nietzsche's "burdensome thought" is to define it as a metaphysical position—the last one, according to Heidegger, possible in the West. By contrast, in Heidegger's own work the very possibility of metaphysics is interrogated. In *An Introduction to Metaphysics,* Heidegger makes his classic statement concerning the separation of Being and representation (*Vorstellung*),[10] but an equally powerful challenge to traditional notions of representation, crucial for Doctorow's novels, is implied in Heidegger's comments on death. That a philosopher and a novelist should share such a concept should not surprise; indeed, Gerald Bruns argues that the work of the late Heidegger, at least, warrants comparison with that of contemporary postmodern writers.[11] Because the evolution of Heidegger's thinking on death is too lengthy for inclusion in this introduction, it is summarized in the appendix. Here it is sufficient to note that for both Heidegger and Doctorow, death is finally related to language, and language—which is not in its essence a system of representation—is conceived as independent of the human.

In Doctorow's novels, death is conceived as a function of the failure of linguistic representation. In *Welcome to Hard Times* the narrator, Blue, seeks to comprehend the murderous Bad Man from Bodie, but his narrative account of the Bad Man's rampages undermines itself to such a degree as to show the futility of attempts to represent, especially to represent death. For Blue, bleeding to death from wounds as he writes, the failure of narrative coincides with mortality: "I'm trying to put down what happened but the closer I've come in time the less clear I am in my mind. I'm losing my blood to this rag, but more, I have the cold feeling everything I've written doesn't tell how it was, no matter how careful I've been to get it all down it still escapes me" (199).

Here the ambiguous "rag"—a talismanic term in Doctorow's lexicon—may be either a stancher or Blue's palimpsestic ledgers, in which he writes his narrative, but in either case the flows of blood and ink are concurrent and futile. Doctorow's works often explore this Heideggerian juxtaposition in scenes of high drama and ferocity. The following examples anticipate the link between misrepresentation and death which is explored in this study. In *The Book of Daniel*, Daniel savagely mocks his own efforts to understand death during his literary reconstruction of his parents' execution. In *Ragtime*, Houdini frightens audiences when his escape acts attempt to represent death with increasing accuracy. In "The Water Works" the narrator unsuccessfully pursues a deathly "black bearded captain," who carries off a dead child. In *World's Fair* the narrator, Edgar, recalls his youthful attempts to understand his grandmother's death through the Hebrew letters on her prayer candles. In these and other instances, Doctorow's scenes of death also announce failures of representation. When death enters these narratives—such as the Bad Man from Bodie in *Welcome to Hard Times*—representation is shaken.

It may be that death enters *because* of questions about representation. Paul de Man, extending Heidegger's thought, sees mortality as derivable from the moment prosopopeia is discovered: "As soon as we understand the rhetorical function of prosopopeia as positing voice or face by means of language, we also understand that what we are deprived of is not life but the shape and the sense of a world accessible only in the privative way of understanding. Death is a name for a linguistic predicament, and the restoration of mortality by autobiography (the prosopopeia of the voice and the name) deprives and disfigures to the precise extent that it restores."[12]

This passage captures the dilemma of Doctorow's narrators, beginning with Blue in *Welcome to Hard Times*. In his very attempt to represent the Bad Man from Bodie, to give him a face, Blue is cut off from "the shape and sense of the world," and it is from this predicament that death may be inferred. His illusion of representation (necessary to the creation of any text) is gained only at the cost of a forgetting of mortality that reappears, nevertheless, in every moment of rhetoricity. In *Welcome to Hard Times* and in other "autobiographical" fictions by Doctorow, oscillation between representation and death becomes a structural feature.

This oscillation is a special case of the more general dyad of blindness and insight which, according to de Man, lies at the heart of reading. In his essay "The Rhetoric of Blindness," de Man argues that "a certain degree of blindness is part of the specificity of all literature" and that a moment of blindness (variously placed in the system of text-reader-second-reader) is a precondition of interpretation.[13] Insights into literary meaning are facilitated by blindness to the rhetoricity of language. De Man amplifies this theme in *Allegories of Reading* in which he offers his model or "paradigm for all texts": "The paradigm for all texts consists of a figure (or a system of figures) and its deconstruction. But since this model cannot be closed off by a final reading, it engenders, in its turn, a supplementary figural superposition which narrates the unreadability of the prior narration."[14]

Therefore at least two misinterpretations—ultimately the series is infinite—are presupposed in an act of reading: the first, mistaking the arbitrary for the real; the second ostensibly "corrects" the first but in fact adds new figuration. Blindness and insight alternate redundantly throughout the process of interpretation. An "allegory of reading" traces this process in any specific text (as de Man traces in Nietzsche, Rousseau, and others) while helplessly and automatically recommitting the crime it set out to solve. For de Man reading is Nietzsche's "infinitely reiterated circulation of all things."

De Man's work is especially relevant to Doctorow's "autobiographical" fiction, which over the course of thirty years has taken many complex narrational forms. In *Welcome to Hard Times* the dying narrator's act of writing is, explicitly, a secondary interpretation, laid upon a prior text. Daniel, the narrator of the book that bears his name, repeats his parents' crime, the manipulation of documents, in his own narrative, which elides and suppresses information from his sources. In *Ragtime*—for the first time in Doctorow's ouevre—the final identity of the narrator is in doubt. According to one hypothesis, Father's little boy, now a historian of American culture in his sixties, narrates a story that implies history is fiction. In *Loon Lake* there is a convergeance of the identities of Joe, Warren Penfield, the "omniscient narrator," and even a nonhuman computer-narrator; the congeries undermines distinctions between narrators and characters. In *World's Fair* the narrator Edgar is an oral historian blind to the false models he builds as he writes. In *Lives of the Poets* the reader must analyze several fictive narrators and their indeterminable creator. These works put the existence of "the author" at issue. In them reading and writing often compound error. De Man's concept of an "allegory of reading" offers a way of evaluating their writing dilemmas.

De Man's writings share at least one characteristic with Derrida's: a general challenge to the validity of hermeneutics.[15] "Hermeneutics" is defined here as the art or science of interpretation, as that activity is understood to follow the model of the deciphering, sending, and retrieving of messages. This rudimentary definition of the word is faithful, I believe, to its etymology, which traces it to the Greek god Hermes, conveyer of messages that are dispatched by a sender and delivered to a recipient. By hermeneutics, then, I understand the interpretive activity of meaning-making or representation that takes for its paradigm the deciphering of a text. Doctorow's novels challenge this conception just as decisively as do the theorists discussed in this section.

Derrida's most famous critique of the hermeneutic project is in the essay "Structure, Sign, and Play in the Discourse of the Human Sciences," in which he poses the alternatives of interpretation and free play:

> There are thus two interpretations of interpretation, of structure, of sign, of play. The one seeks to decipher, dreams of deciphering a truth or an origin which escapes play and the order of the sign, and which lives the necessity of interpretation as an exile.... The other, which is no longer turned towards the origin, affirms play and tries to pass beyond man and humanism, the name of man being the name of that being who, throughout the history of metaphysics or of ontotheology—in other words, through his entire history—has dreamed of full presence, the reassuring foundation, the origin and the end of play.[16]

Developing this description of the delusory dream of interpretation-as-deciphering, Derrida in "Sending: On Representation," makes his most explicit rejection of traditional hermeneutics. That essay exposes unnoticed metaphysical assumptions in the very concepts of "sender," "message," and "receiver," claims that promote the privilege of the Cartesian subject as the origin of messages.[17] Instead of man as speaker or sender of messages, Derrida argues, he is himself the construct of a language that precedes (or may even be said to "send") man.

It is true that in reaction to the work of Derrida, there have been numerous recent attempts to redefine hermeneutics, some of which shift to a different paradigm or defend the validity of the traditional paradigm.[18] Judgments as to the efficacy of these innovative hermeneutics must await an intellectual history of the future that can weigh their merits as responses to challenges like Derrida's. It is enough, for the purposes of this study, that the definition of hermeneutics be understood as the more circumscribed notion of deciphering and representation. By understanding the word in this way, for the duration of this study, we can situate Doctorow's novels in the same milieu that Derrida's revolt against representation foregrounds.

Doctorow's fictions participate in this revolt, too. Beginning with Blue, his first narrator, Doctorow's storytellers are most often hermeneuts, readers and writers (like Daniel, Edgar, Jonathon, Billy Bathgate) whose most conspicuous activity is their engagement in the process of deciphering history and, in the most crucial moments, its verbal representations (documentary trial evidence, oral history, letters, deathbed monologues). Even in *Big as Life* and *Ragtime*—novels whose narrators are less obviously meaning-makers—the hermeneutic task is pursued by principal, sympathetic characters, such as Creighton or Tateh, who nevertheless remain deluded to the end about the world they confidently interpreted. The dream of these characters, like that of Derrida's exile from the truth, is a representation of the world that fits their experiences—of suffering, of political repression, of childhood. So the first step in reading Doctorow's novels is to demystify these hermeneutic dreamers, but, following de Man, the second step is to see that even this insight can be achieved only at the cost of the reader's blindness.

These two steps in reading are noticeable in understanding personification (prosopopoeia, or mask-making), a process analyzed at some length by J. Hillis Miller. Amplifying upon de Man's argument in "Autobiography as De-Facement," Miller sees prosopopoeia as the essential trope for narrative, a rhetorical and linguistic fiction constitutive of all discourses—even of philosophy—which aspire to illustrate, to bridge the gulf between abstraction and experience, in short, to represent. For example, Miller sees prosopopoeia functioning in the attempt to rescue from internal collapse Kant's formulation of the categorical imperative. Miller finds that narrative is omnipresent and inevitable. (Doctorow himself arrives at this conclusion in his essay "False Documents.") Miller finds in the stories of Kleist and Kafka meditations on the function of prosopopoeia. For Miller, allegories of reading dramatize the dilemmas that de Man saw in literary and philosophical texts. Thus, prosopopoeia and story-making temporarily fill a void left by the failure of hermeneutics; they are then exposed in criticism as delusions. Finally even such an exposure can never be regarded as definitive, because it always remains open to new reading. Miller calls this endless process "varnishing."[19]

Three complex narrational instances of varnishing are discussed at length in chapters 5, 6, and 7 in the interpretation of *Ragtime, Loon Lake,* and *Lives of the Poets;* in each case, the attempt to name the narrator results in error, but, of course, some identification of the narrators is essential to the reading of these novels. The result is an interpretation that cannot succeed but must be made.

For Miller this open-ended process that exposes the groundlessness of hermeneutics also attests to the inescapably intertextual nature of interpretation:

> The critic is not able by any "method" or strategy of analysis to "reduce" the language of the work to clear and distinct ideas. He is forced at best to repeat the work's contradictions in a different form. The work is . . . incapable of being encompassed in any single coherent or homogeneous interpretation. [It is] open to other texts, permeable to them, permeated by them. A literary text is not a thing in itself, "organically unified," but a relation to other texts which are relations in their turn. The study of literature is therefore a study of intertextuality.[20]

Texts, prior texts, and interpretations indistinguishably cohabit and vitiate every new reading, as the hosts and parasites that seem to comprise an organism actually destroy its unity.[21]

The intertextual dimension of Doctorow's novels is obvious in titles (*Welcome to Hard Times, The Book of Daniel, Lives of the Poets*) and in formal properties (for example, epigraphs and internal titles) that allude to specific works. Of course, the numerous articles devoted to the subject of Doctorow's use of Heinrich von Kleist's story "Michael Kohlhass" in *Ragtime* attest to the explicitly intertextual aspect of that novel; however, Doctorow's celebrated literary borrowing is only a more conspicuous instance of the permeability of Doctorow's works to many others: Salinger's *The Catcher in the Rye* in *The Book of Daniel;* Thoreau's *Walden* in *Loon Lake;* Wordsworth's *The Prelude* in *World's Fair.* Situating works within such intertextual matrices calls into question the idea of "sole authorship." In fact, in *Loon Lake* this very questioning is depicted in the narrative, which is, undecidably, written by Joe, by Penfield, by a computer, or by some combination of these. The fact that its last page reveals Joe's "true surname" to be Korzienowski, the surname of Joseph Conrad, raises the issue of intertextuality to major importance. I conclude chapter 6 with the idea that *Loon Lake* dramatizes empty intertextuality.

As we shall see, the interpenetration of authors and works is repeated *within* Doctorow's works, where individual texts often seem linked by identical features. Both outer and inner filiations contribute to the open-ended quality of Doctorow's work, the sense in which each of his fictions undermines closure and, instead, takes its place in a larger literary and philosophical network.

The common denominator among the five writers discussed here is a refusal to presuppose that texts necessarily represent a signified, extratextual presence. In this respect all undertake the activity of writing without the prospect that a representable, paraphrasable idea, set of ideas, or "theme"—what Derrida sometimes calls a philosopheme—will be its result. It is the argument of this book that in similar intellectual austerity, Doctorow's novels share and repeatedly illustrate this refusal. The distinction between this argument and more traditional hermeneutic studies of Doctorow's novels will become more evident when they are contrasted in the following pages.

Most criticism of Doctorow's works is hermeneutic in regarding them as representations, not misrepresentations, of particular ideas, which it is the critic's business to elucidate: for example, radical Jewish humanism, or a left-wing, existentialist critique of American history and capitalism.[22] There can be little doubt that Doctorow's novels are preoccupied with the subject of American politics. In *Welcome to Hard Times* the American frontier ethic is shown to be a dangerous delusion; in *Big as Life* the military-industrial-academic complex is depicted as founded on principles of destruction; in *Ragtime* the patriotic pieties of prewar America conceal racism, sexism, and economic exploitation. Almost every piece of fiction depicts some fraudulence at the heart of American life, and yet this political satire is only a seeming demystification, since the novels never rest in any "truth" that might serve as the alternative to the political illusions they condemn. For example, Blue, in *Welcome to Hard Times*, shows the contradiction at the heart of the phrase "enlightened capitalist," but the novel shows us no alternative to Blue, whose actions seem fated. In other works, the putative opponents of the mystified political establishment—characters like Red Bloom, Billy Bathgate, Coalhouse Walker, Joe Korzienowski—are readable only in terms of other texts. This study argues that such characters do not represent truths by which political illusions are to be judged; instead, their potential for heroism becomes, after all, part of a more universal delusion. In the words of the epigraph, each seems like an articulation of the new, of "things you haven't said before," but in the end each becomes part of an eternal return.

A second problem in such criticism is the silent assumption that the political themes or ideas represented are especially readable in the novel's endings. Sometimes this trait results in contested, even contradictory critical positions, disputes that are detailed in the chapters and notes that follow. However, discussion of a few examples here will distinguish my own approach from such readings and suggest that this unacknowledged assumption of hermeneutics may be a kind of "varnishing." It may be a strategy similar to the one that de Man analyzed in Nietzsche's attempt to make Greek tragedy serve this thesis in *The Birth of Tragedy:* "[Nietzsche] moves instead, with sure hermeneutic instinct, to the sensitive points of imitation, the *beginning* and the *end* of the works, the points where the validity of the genetic pattern is at stake."[23] In a like manner, Doctorow's critics often read the novels' endings as validations of themes elaborated in their essays. I believe, on the other hand, that Doctorow's endings warn critics from just such a practice, as part of a more general warning against hermeneutics itself.

Chapter 1 proposes that the ending of *Welcome to Hard Times* makes precisely this warning; other chapters reach similar conclusions. *The Book of Daniel* has three endings as well as two unannounced codas, all of which put the question of authorship in doubt; *Lives of the Poets* ends in mid-sentence, with the narrator giving up the act of authorship to a child ignorant of English. Everything in *Ragtime* seems to point to the assassination of Archduke Francis Ferdinand as the novel's climax, but after that news is known, we read of Houdini performing another, repetitive stunt. The novels often and powerfully denounce the error of privileging endings. It becomes the subject matter of *Billy Bathgate*: there, the "final words" or deathbed monologue of Dutch Schultz become the occasion for Billy's criminal, profitable misinterpretations. In these works, endings warn us against hermeneutics while at the same time conceding its inevitability. To paraphrase de Man, they realize a blindness in the delusion of insight.

As noted earlier, a hermeneutics of closure may also be discouraged by the intertextuality of Doctorow's oeuvre, its filiations to works both within and outside it. For example, different works sometimes share nearly identical features, a fact that inhibits efforts to restrict representation to only one text. The character Billy Bathgate is a folk-rock singer in "The Songs of Billy Bathgate" but a gangster in *Billy Bathgate*. Conversely, "the same character" sometimes appears in separate works under different names: the Edgar of *World's Fair* becomes the Jonathon of "The Writer in the Family," who reappears in "Lives of the Poets." "Leather men" are Latin American peasants ("The Foreign Legation," 59) and security administrators ("The Leather Man"). "The same events"—the death of a crazed Jewish grandmother and a childhood trauma induced by the sight of a dead woman who had driven her car through a chain-link fence—befall the narrators of *The Book of Daniel* and *World's Fair*. To Evelyn Nesbit, in *Ragtime,* and Edgar, in *World's Fair,* Hebrew letters look like "arrangements of bones" (48, 125). Finally, the titles of Doctorow's works sometimes separate parts of the works as well; such synechdochal titling is evident in *Big as Life,* "The Songs of Billy Bathgate," *Loon Lake,* and *Lives of the Poets*.

In breaking down the boundaries within and among Doctorow's works, these coincidences problematize the attribution of represented meaning to single texts, and intertextual uncertainty deepens with the recurrence of more general plot features. For example, the exhibition of freaks and a fat lady is a feature of both *Ragtime* and *Loon Lake*. As we shall see, the idea of the "grotesque show"—discoverable at Disneyland in *The Book of Daniel* and at the pavilions in *World's Fair*—becomes yet another figure for the false demystifications of art, but the repetitions perhaps most familiar to readers of Doctorow are his street scenes, depictions of teeming immigrant life amid pushcarts, greengroceries, and storefronts. These first appear in "The Orphans' Home" in "The Songs of Billy Bathgate." They recur in *Ragtime, World's Fair,* and *Billy Bathgate*. In fact, these set pieces are almost transferable from one text to another.

Other common features include punning, allusive titles, and character names that call attention to the arbitrary character of naming. These techniques unsettle referents. In addition, many of Doctorow's novels also employ "false chronologies"; that is, they are narratives that give a first impression of chronological precision that later collapses in insoluble contradiction. A similarly self-referential technique is the one Joseph Turner identifies as the "elaborate game of hide-and-seek" in *The Book of Daniel* whereby Daniel's "true name" is withheld.[24] This technique was first used in *Welcome to Hard Times* and later in *Loon Lake* and *World's Fair*. Of course, all of these techniques reinforce the more general pattern of blindness and insight in reading letters on a page: a first attribution of a referent to a sign is shown—only in retrospect—to have been illusory.

The reader's belated discovery of error often follows the revelation of blindness shared by Doctorow's first-person narrators. Blue omits from his narration evidence of his own complicity in the fate of the frontier town. Daniel suppresses material from his sources that would indicate moral culpability in his quest to learn the truth about his parents. Billy Bathgate, the gangster, interprets events so as to preserve his own innocence. Of course, the structural device of the "unreliable narrator" has received attention in the past, but Doctorow's narrators shift the issue from reliability to decidability. We cannot know whether his narrators' self-serving omissions are "deliberate" or "accidental." In the end, these suppressions suggest that the fabrication of a self with debatable motives may be the simple rationale of narrative.

Of crucial importance to the issue of representation are two figures for the artist often encountered in Doctorow's works. The first links the impossible object of the artistic quest with the tradition of the "white goddess"—Aphrodite or Artemis—first sketched by Robert Graves. In Doctorow's texts this quest takes many forms. In "The Songs of Billy Bathgate," Lovegirl, Billy's woman, is compared to Venus who arose from the sea. The goddess-figure with "hair like a helmet" appears as Evelyn/Diana in *Ragtime* (131) and Drew/Aphrodite in *Billy Bathgate* (46). Moreover, Clara, in *Loon Lake*, shares features with each goddess-figure: like Evelyn, she recapitulates the story of Diana and Actaeon; like Drew she is a magnet for gangsters. These goddesses also lure narrators, like Joe and Billy, who fill the role of the artist. The goddess-figures hold forth to them the false lure of truth, but not only do the goddesses elude capture, they also draw murderous instincts out of their votaries. Billy the singer imagines killing Lovegirl; Mother's Younger Brother becomes a terrorist; Joe contemplates the murder of Bennett; Billy the gangster becomes complicit in Schultz's orgy of killing. In these cases the writer, or interpreter, is likened to a killer; not only will he fail to win the prize of truth, but he must needs destroy in the very effort. Doctorow notices the importance of killing in Hemingway's life and works; his appreciation of Hemingway's work is discussed in chapter 9.

A second important recurrent figure in Doctorow's oeuvre likens the artist to a clown or performer-on-view. Of course such a figure is not new; in Kafka's parables a hunger artist or aerialist portrays the writer's dilemma. In Doctorow's texts this figure appears as a menacing confidence man in "The Songs of Billy Bathgate," as the death-defying Houdini in *Ragtime,* as an acrobat disguised as a clown in the essay "False Documents" and in the novel *World's Fair,* and as the juggler in *Billy Bathgate.* In each avatar the writer is seen as a technically accomplished performer, well aware of his own powers of deception. Yet at the same time, the audience understands a futility in the creation of artifice that becomes, on occasion, almost equally evident to the performer. In this way the drive to represent in art is seen as an act of desperation, a search for some "true performance," some escape from the eternal reiteration of the same thing in the face of the knowledge of its impossibility.

Doctorow's most astute critics have already shown that his novels struggle against repetition; however, they interpret that agon as an engagement with the events of history, not with the act of articulation. At the end of his perceptive, well-researched book *E. L. Doctorow,* John G. Parks writes: "One of the major struggles in Doctorow's fiction is the quest for a historical consciousness that avoids the fate of endless repetition and meaningless sequence." As this passage implies, Parks sees the novels' problem and solution in historical terms. He continues: "Doctorow's heroes of perception are in a struggle to wrest history from myth. And the essential tragedy in Doctorow's fiction is the sustaining of myth at the cost of history. The refusal to belong to history spells both spiritual and social disaster."[25] This thesis enables Parks to evaluate the novels' endings in the light of their characters' achievement of historical consciousness. From Parks's hermeneutic perspective, the threat of repetitious loss of meaning that plagues ahistorical characters like Joe Paterson or Billy Bathgate is balanced by the varieties of acceptance and maturity exemplified in Daniel and Edgar. For Parks, the prospect of endless reiteration never threatens writing itself.

By contrast, the coincidences, common features, and recurrent figures analyzed here imply a different, perhaps more menacing "eternal return," one that raises the issue of representation in fiction. These repetitions break down the boundaries of individual works and pose questions of signification and authorship: To what do the signs of Doctorow's texts refer? Is a single, stable, continuous narrator, or even author, inferrable from the accumulation of coincidences in texts? This book addresses these questions that are raised from the beginning of Doctorow's career, that arise from a reading of *Welcome to Hard Times*.

If Doctorow's works are models of misrepresentations, then certain questions about the present study naturally arise: Why is it organized as a series of chapters, each devoted to a single novel? Why does it persist in errors, for example the error of analyzing the novels' endings? Before addressing the full contradiction raised by these questions, a discussion of the organization and limitations of the book is in order.

Each chapter starts with a short summary of the plot of the work under consideration; these are included for readers who may not have recently read particular works, but readers impatient with this rhetorical *narratio* may easily skip to the conclusion of the summary, where the thesis of each chapter is presented. (Of course it is plain, too, that plot summaries directly raise the issue of representing texts. In the field of literary criticism, plot summaries are almost universally considered incorrect representations of texts. So the following chapters, opening with such misrepresentations, imply the same inevitability as the texts they study.) The introductions differ with each work: sometimes the thesis takes up an interpretive problem evident in the criticism of Doctorow, sometimes a general topic, like narratology. Chapters often analyze the most accessible matters first: formal questions involving narrative, titles, epigraphs, and chapter divisions. Then major characters are examined. Key concepts from the five writers discussed earlier in this introduction are taken up. Sometimes tropes and rhetorical devices are studied. I make no apology for the extended scrutiny of small as well as large elements. So rich is Doctorow's prose that single sentences often require extensive commentary; an example is Geoffrey Galt Harpham's superb analysis of a sentence from *The Book of Daniel*.[26] Endings are also studied, as they bear on controversies in criticism and on the larger issue of the hermeneutics of closure.

Withall, it is evident that large portions of the works themselves remain undiscussed and other issues slighted, although occasionally seeming neglect may be explained by my method. One example is the subject of genre—for example, the genre of the western, in *Welcome to Hard Times,* or of science fiction, in *Big as Life.* The generic classification of texts often begs the question of representation. As Derrida observes, it is impossible for a work *not* to have a genre.[27] In any case, some of Doctorow's texts—"The Songs of Billy Bathgate" and *Lives of the Poets* are good examples—flaunt a status unclassifiable by ordinary conventions. Others show the breakdown of such distinctions as those between prose and poetry or short story and novella, to say nothing of that between fiction and nonfiction. Nevertheless, readers for whom generic distinctions are crucial will find references to more traditional discussions of this issue in the notes.

I have not surveyed all of Doctorow's works. I have omitted consideration of his play, *Drinks Before Dinner,* and the film versions of his novels *Welcome to Hard Times, The Book of Daniel,* and *Ragtime.* I excluded these works because consideration of them would require exploration of the problem of representation in theater and film, a subject that would entail treatment of such length as to be prohibitive here. In addition, I selected only a few of Doctorow's many essays and interviews. I was guided by various aims. "False Documents," uniquely among Doctorow's nonfiction, concentrates on literature. Doctorow's reversal of opinion on Hemingway, in *The Paris Review* interview and in "Braver Than We Thought," is of importance for the study of both writers. My own interview with Doctorow took up key issues considered in this study. Some of his replies are discussed at the end of chapter 9; interested readers will find the complete transcript in *Michigan Quarterly Review* 30 (1991), 439–56.

Those parts of Doctorow's essays that oppose deconstruction are also discussed at length in chapter 9, but the general subject deserves comment here as well. First, the word "deconstruction" and its derivatives are often misleading today. Their original senses, in de Man and Derrida, have been largely effaced, to such a point that the term is often made synonymous with "critique." For that reason, I try to limit the word's application to certain general ideas of the writers discussed here. Second, it should be noted that a writer's opposition to a critical approach cannot exclude it. Feminist critics must be free to interpret writers who disapprove of feminism; Marxist critics must be free to interpret bourgeois literature. Of course, no attempt to sequester literary work from particular analysis can succeed, and Doctorow's strictures against deconstruction never seek such an immunity. More generally, opposition to deconstruction on the part of writers is natural and understandable, and Doctorow's is based on the insistence on meaning in life and art. This is also the cry of his most powerful characters and narrators. Beginning with Blue, in *Welcome to Hard Times*, Doctorow's heroes cannot tolerate the thought of a world, or a text, without meaning. And so in Doctorow's essays that attack deconstruction, the familiar wish of his protagonists is repeated.

The characters in the novels, however, just like the various "I's" of the essays and interviews, are constrained to express this wish in language that reveals, at every turn, the difficulty of the seemingly simple aspiration. And here the issue is joined: Doctorow's texts, novels and other writing, could not be written without some hope of signification that nevertheless may, on analysis, turn out to be misplaced. The same is true of this study. It is the burden of the chapters that follow to demonstrate the continuing dyad of illusion/disillusion.

The chapters that follow imply no "development" in Doctorow's career, no movement toward "greater clarity" or "greater depth of vision." These ocularcentric metaphors for learning conceal the assumption that a prior illusion can be replaced by a greater approximation to truth, rather than by a new illusion; however, this assumption is called into question in all of Doctorow's texts. A related subject may illustrate the danger of such generalizations. It is true that between 1975 and 1985, Doctorow introduced into his work major narrational experiments. *Ragtime* and the three works that follow it employ unconventional modes of narration that are ultimately undecidable: that is, the very act of attributing a narrator to these works involves the reader in error. Now, criticism concerned to trace "development" in a writer's career might interpret these experiments as a stage in a process of intellectual maturation. However, the chapters that follow indicate that these are precisely the assumptions challenged by the novels.

I must now return to the questions asked on page 18 concerning the format and scope of this study. The unsatisfying answer to each question is that decisions regarding these were adopted in the expectation that their arbitrary character would become sufficiently clear in the course of the text: for instance, each discussion of an ending notes a concluding warning against hermeneutics, such as Blue's last words. Each chapter includes discussions of a novel's intertextuality which indicate the mistake of attempting to claim for it a univocal meaning, but I concede that these disavowals do not fully respond to the questions for the simple reason that they are my own illusions. They mask the more fundamental problem, the sense in which my title must refer to its own chapters as models of misrepresentation. If the hermeneutic project is doomed from the outset, how can a book about novels hope to "represent" them at all?

The question is important. The remarks that follow will also be unsatisfying. First, it is clear that traditional hermeneutic criticism of Doctorow has sought to represent his texts; however, these representations have not settled crucial matters of interpretation. On the contrary, basic questions still dog criticism: Who is the narrator of *Ragtime* and *Loon Lake*? Is the ending of *Welcome to Hard Times* pessimistic or not? Does *The Book of Daniel* endorse Daniel's efforts as a writer? My text and notes describe deep, irreconcilable differences on these questions. They also show that traditional hermeneutic criticism has neglected the intertextual dimension of Doctorow's works and their tropes. There are other shortcomings. Critics have paid no attention to "The Songs of Billy Bathgate" and very little to *Big as Life, Lives of the Poets,* and *World's Fair.* No one has noticed the abuse of sources in *The Book of Daniel* or "False Documents." In this situation, a new attempt—one that seeks to survey and account for critical divergences and to begin discussion of neglected areas—may be justified.

In retrospect my own errors are obvious. In too many instances, my readings are cast in the metaphors of ground and support, darkness and clarity, that my study of Doctorow has shown to be fallacious. Thus I sometimes say that my examples illustrate ideas, discuss evidence as supporting contentions, and find that parts of novels clarify other parts. In all such instances, I rely on conventions of academic writing that easily betray themselves. These are "varnishings," to borrow Miller's term, which I did not know how to avoid. But even worse, de Man believed that writers may be by definition incompetent to understand their own blindnesses.[28] If this is true, then a retrospective effort to locate them will only create new error.

But I am encouraged by Doctorow's works themselves, each of which takes seriously the possibility of some alternative to the cul-de-sac of hermeneutics. In *Big as Life,* the characters Red Bloom and Sugarbush seem to offer some new way of existence—musical, dialogical, playful—that might confound all enigmas of misrepresentation. In *Ragtime,* Coalhouse Walker confronts a world of total mystification, demanding that it yield meaning. In *Billy Bathgate,* Billy's feckless, derelict mother seems to stand outside the world of rapacious reading and writing—"the rackets"—that he cannot leave. These and other elements of Doctorow's novels seek to say "things you haven't said before," in the words of my epigraph. They constitute challenges to the pervasive dead ends, the eternal returns, of the hermeneutic circle. The novels test the validity of such alternatives. That the tests' results are negative has not deterred Doctorow in the attempt to represent; it should not daunt his readers.

The last, related "answer" reflects an idea shared by de Man, Derrida, and Miller: it may be that interpretation, or hermeneutics, is foredoomed to failure, but *this cannot be known in advance;* that is, there is no way the invalidity of an interpretation could become apparent except through the act of attempting one. The point may seem elementary, but it must be reiterated. To know or, better, to be able to say in advance that an interpretive project must fail would be equivalent to finding a "true performative" in language—a statement that could actually, automatically perform work in the world. As must be obvious from the discussion above, I share the questions regarding the possibility of a true performative raised by all three writers.[29] Looked at from one perspective, this debility in discourse frees criticism from charges of negativity or nihilism, since errors and blindnesses in discourse could never serve as dogmas. Each new start is a new start. Looked at from a different perspective, the odds may seem never to favor "successful" interpretation, but steep odds cannot deter discourse. In short, I may accept the application of the title, "Models of Misrepresentation," to the text I have written, but for others that application must await the end of their own reading of the pages that follow.

One of the first problems studied in chapter 1 is the significance of the title, *Welcome to Hard Times*. But before arriving at that discussion, I will suggest a sense, pertinent to Doctorow's career as a whole, that may be permissible if we understand that *Welcome to Hard Times* was a first novel, by a writer certain of his vocation since childhood. In this light, the title can be understood in an inaugural sense as the announcement of a career, the "hard times" describing the difficult, grave, even desperate endeavor to come, of coming to terms with a pessimism and doubt so deep as to challenge, often, the fundamental principles of reason. Doctorow's later works continue the reading experience of his first: they offer little but "hard times" to readers who come to them with expectations of traditional literary consolation. Perhaps in this way the paradox of his title is resolved if we construe it as a warning.

Chapter 1

Construction/Destruction/Construction
Welcome to Hard Times

E. L. Doctorow's first novel tells of the fate of a Western frontier town, Hard Times, in the treeless Dakota Territory and of its inhabitants. The simple, shocking story is narrated by Blue, the town's record-keeper and de facto mayor. Before Hard Times is even officially founded, it is suddenly devastated, for no reason, in a violent rampage by the Bad Man from Bodie. He kills two men and seriously injures others, including the prostitute Molly, before burning the town to the ground; in the fire, Blue's first set of ledger books is destroyed. After most townspeople flee, Blue, Molly, and Jimmy Fee, the son of one of the Bad Man's victims, live together. Molly and Jimmy nurse a hatred for Blue; they consider him cowardly for not standing up to the Bad Man. With the help of the newcomer Zar, a saloon-keeper and whoremaster, Blue painstakingly rebuilds the town, using wood from the ruins of a nearby ghost city, Fountain Creek. Soon, others are drawn to settle because of the town's proximity to a gold mine and the possibility of new road construction. The profit motive drives small merchants as well as the remote, mysterious mining company. For a short while the town enjoys a superficial harmony and prosperity. Blue decides to begin keeping town records in new ledger books. Molly is still vengeful and instills in Jimmy her own obsession of one day retaliating against the Bad Man. Soon the mine boss receives an ominous letter; the mine is subsequently abandoned by its owners, and it is learned that the road will not be built. Hard upon this discovery, the Bad Man from Bodie, also called Clay Turner, reappears in Hard Times to devastate it a second time. Blue manages to wound the Bad Man, but during a struggle in which Molly tries to kill him, both Turner and Molly are killed by Jimmy. Jimmy leaves the burning ruins of Hard Times; it is understood that he will now become another Bad Man. Blue is mortally wounded. The sight of Zar's corpse prompts him to write the history of the town—across the ledger books containing his town records—the history we have just finished reading.

Criticism of the novel has focused on two major themes. First, the novel has been interpreted as a critique of American civilization, especially capitalism, from a tragic perspective, one which depicts the struggle between civilization, embodied in Blue, and evil or irrationality, embodied in the Bad Man.[1] The novel also has been interpreted as modernist, in its concern to illustrate, in Blue's narration, the debility of writing in the contemporary world.[2] The obvious problem is that these themes contradict each other. If the novel espouses a political critique, then the modernist view of Blue—that his narrative questions the validity of truth—becomes less plausible. In fact, critics sometimes quote Blue in support of the argument that the novel espouses a tragic sense of history.[3] These critics raise the issue central to this book, the issue of hermeneutics: whether a fictional text, like *Welcome to Hard Times,* represents or espouses ideas.

The title of Doctorow's first novel—like the titles of most of his works—is a trope, in this case, paradox: for who would want to welcome or be welcomed to hard times? Titles that are tropes flaunt rhetoricity. Here the primary meaning—an invitation to the reader to become acquainted with a fictional city—is reflexive, rather than descriptive; it evokes the image of the author as directly present-at-hand, even speaking orally to the reader, outside or around the text. Of course the author is not there; instead, that image is a construction derived from the syntax of the title, which resembles a speech-act, but this is only the first instance in which a construction or interpretation was elicited only to be destroyed, belatedly, as illusory. The title also accomplishes this effect in other ways. For example, it alludes to another title, *Hard Times* by Charles Dickens, a text also concerned with economic exploitation of the poor during the nineteenth century. The allusion to a work of English literature is initially disconcerting. (Doctorow later reproduces the effect in *Lives of the Poets*.) It raises the question of whether the title refers to present places and events or to other texts. Is Doctorow's text original? Can any text be original? These questions will also arise in connection with Blue's narration, but in order to continue the reading process, they must be temporarily suppressed. A third sense of the title raises still more questions. After reading two-thirds of the novel the reader learns that WELCOME TO HARD TIMES is a sign, stretched across the main street of the town. In other words, the title of Doctorow's first novel names, like all titles, a text, *but it also refers to a sign*. At the outset of the novel, then, the reader is confronted with the question of referentiality, of representation: do titles, textual signs, refer to "signifieds" or to other signs? Again the reader must suppress the question and instead make an assumption, or construction, that signs refer to a signified, but the suppressed question of referentiality will return again, will perhaps return eternally, as the Bad Man threatens to, after every new construction the reader makes.

Just as the title does, character names in *Welcome to Hard Times* call into question their seeming referents. The examples of Bert Albany or Swede confound self with place or ethnicity; the Indian's name, John Bear, problematizes totemic naming and even translation. The narrator is Blue, a name perhaps first apprehended as appropriate for a Western. However, the reader later learns that it also denotes the shotgun Jimmy brandishes: "That new oily double-barrel glinting blue was in my hands" (159). This shotgun becomes the instrument of Blue's mortal wound, so even in Blue's dying the arbitrary nature of his name is recalled. (This effect is also created continuously in the novel, in the townspeople's practice of calling Blue "Mayor," when it is made clear that Blue assumed that title unilaterally. Narrators with two names or "false names" occur frequently in Doctorow's fiction.)[4] Finally, the name "Blue" may also be construed as a trope, a grim understatement for the suffering the melancholic narrator constantly feels. This disengagement of the name from necessary reference to the narrator as Cartesian self is presaged in Blue's own recollection of his first journey West: "When I came West with the wagons, I was a young man with expectations of something, I don't know what, I tar-painted my name on a big rock by the Missouri trailside. But in time my expectations wore away with the weather, like my name had from that rock, and I learned it was enough to stay alive" (7).

Like the names themselves, this passage suggests the fallacy of "proper names,"[5] and it likens the existence of names to hopes inevitably blasted, constructions destroyed. It is as if Blue knows the outcome of his story before beginning it: one day his arbitrary name (like all others?) will be effaced into nothingness. His "learning" remains tautological, however, since he is left with only the Heideggerian alternatives, like without signification and death. In this light, Blue's most remarkable faculty may be his persistence despite the foreknowledge of failure, a trait he repeatedly exhibits in the novel. It is also a trait of each successive Doctorow novel.

Blue's "understanding" of his name's evanescence is thus insight achieved only with accompanying blindness: his stoicism may consist of repeated acts of insight-blindness. We can see this eternal return in the fates of the merchants Ezra and Isaac Maple, characters whose surname also calls attention to the alienability of supposedly proper names. Ezra is lured West by false signs—rumors that there were trees in the Dakota Territory. After Turner destroys his store, Ezra leaves town, only to be replaced, later, by his brother Isaac, who is lured in his turn by a tangible misleading letter, his brother's premature paean to life in the town. In this way, heedless and deluded people succeed one another. There may be grim humor—of the sort evident in the understatement of Blue's name—in the idea that Maples from Vermont left trees behind in pursuit of trees that did not exist. But, more gravely, Blue's persuading Isaac Maple to stay in the recently devastated town that his brother had fled shows once more his blindness to what he "learned" long before from his name, from language: that the West holds forth to its settlers only the alternatives of illusion and death.

These stark alternatives are embodied—and, portentously, the root of that word is in his name—in the Man from Bodie. This menacing character raises the question of referentiality as he enacts the drama of *Sein-zum-Tode*, that language ushers in death, in the text. Consider the novel's first words, "The Man from Bodie." The character is presented in such a manner as to emphasize the rhetoricity of his name, spelled with a capital "M," as in allegories or children's stories. Throughout his first rampage, this character has no other name. As a result, the destruction wrought on the town is committed by a shadowy entity about which the reader must speculate, from the outset, "generically." Is he representative of all men in Bodie? Representative of "Man" in general? In other words, before this character raises issues of nature, of violence, of evil, and the like he raises issues of representation. The reader must "construct" the Man from Bodie. At first simply "The Man from Bodie," he becomes next the Bad Man from Bodie, then Clay Turner. Through this technique the novel insists on the continual conferral of presence on arbitrary signs in the act of reading.

Critics have shown that this character's "apparently true name," Clay Turner, has, itself, many referents. For example, Arthur Saltzman points out that it is a "remarkable name for someone with so absolute a capacity for sending folks to their graves."[6] Marilyn Arnold finds an echo of the name in the novel's images of turning earth and cyclical history.[7] These comments confirm that the Bad Man's "real name"—like Blue's or the Maples'—refers to something other than himself. A third critic, Frank W. Shelton, suggests that the name may be "an ironic reference to frontier historian Frederick Jackson Turner."[8] Both intratextually and intertextually, then, the name "Clay Turner" functions as the novel's title does, to emphasize the rhetoricity of language. These features of the character—his shadowy first appearance, his association with "Bodie," and his ambiguous "true name"—prompt consideration of *Welcome to Hard Times* as an allegory of reading in which the Bad Man serves as an example of embodiment or personification itself. Turner reveals what transpires in the act of reading and writing, when absent becomes present and a text seems to create a person.

Blue may be blind to his own motives in narrating. Of course, he uses his story to justify his actions, but his apologia founders: the reader's efforts to find a "true" motivation for his actions end in contradiction. One knows, for example, that the survival of the town depends on the continuation of its status as a stop on the stagecoach route. Over Zar's protests, Blue pays Alf Moffet a bribe of $40 to protect the franchise, a seemingly selfless act; on the other hand, Blue thereby succeeds Ezra Maples as the local Express agent, a position that provides him with a steady stream of commissions. Is Blue's construction of the town for his own or others' benefit? Is his care for Molly and Jimmy selfless generosity or a self-interested act of reparation? Toward the end of the novel, in an apparent effort to quell growing social unrest in the town, Blue lowers the fee he charges for water from his well; but Zar quickly points out that this act preempts future competition in the sale of water of the sort he himself had planned. Blue's role as the "enlightened capitalist" calls attention to the contradiction inherent in that concept. When action may be interpreted as both selfish and selfless, the assignment of motivation, like any other conferral of presence, becomes arbitrary.

Moreover, Blue's narration conceals, to the point of undecidability, his own complicity in the events, and this concealment of the narrator's culpability will become a recurrent feature in Doctorow's first-person novels. Blue's complicity is evident in his delay in handling the letter for Archie Brogan, the mine boss, the letter that apparently tells of the mine owners' decision to close the mine. In his capacity as Express agent, Blue receives this letter for Brogan; however, he waits for days before notifying Brogan of its arrival.[9] During this time he considers delivering the letter but rejects the idea. He explains: "I was tempting myself to ride up to the lodes with Brogan's letter to see if I could commit someone to a hiring date" (176). When he finally does get around to notifying Brogan, he does so only indirectly, through the miner Angus Mcellhenny, who waits a week before informing Brogan and later claims to have known for weeks that the miners were not digging ore (183). Taken together, both men's delays suggest the desire to postpone as much as possible, for reasons of self-interest, news of a disillusionment that seems inevitable.

In fact the figure of the "Express agent" whose complicity delays the news of "the inevitable disillusionment of the letter" may be one of the novel's tropes for the writer of fiction.

Here, indeed, are hard times. This trope's implication of the utter futility of writing is echoed in another, when Blue's narrative is seen as palimpsest. Blue writes his account in ledger books; there are three, which correspond to the novel's three parts. He says, "I'm writing now, across the red lines, over the old marks" (185). The old marks in question are the town records Blue kept in his capacity as de facto mayor of the town: records of citizens' identities, of property ownership, of his commissions, of a marriage, and the like. Blue's story is thus a palimpsest, a narrative presupposing the existence of previous marks, a crucial figure for writing in general. (Doctorow returns to it in *World's Fair.*) Now the palimpsest has already received some attention in discussions of postmodernism. Generally the palimpsest has been linked to intertextuality, to the contemporary revision of the New Critical position that works of art are autonomous.[10] But in addition to intertextuality, a palimpsest implies a blindness at the heart of reading; because both texts cannot be read simultaneously, the palimpsest implies that the reading of one text is possible only through the suppression of the other. Therefore reading will always be misreading—insight achievable only through blindness. In the case at hand, Blue's narrative of the destruction, rebirth, and destruction of the town is possible only if his prior text is ignored, the supposedly straightforward or factual rendering of town transactions over which the narrative account has been written.

The metaphor of the palimpsest clarifies the novel's intertextuality. For example, Frank W. Shelton's remark that Turner's name may be an allusion to Frederick Jackson Turner suggests how the metaphoric palimpsest works: we can attend to Clay Turner as an ironic commentary on Frederick Jackson Turner only if we ignore, temporarily, Turner's intratextual values and vice versa. Yet another part of the palimpsest is the novel's relation to Dickens's *Hard Times.* Another is its relation to the genre of the Western.[11] Another is its relation to the Bible.[12] And so on. Each "intertextual insight" comes at the expense of blindness to the "text," and this is only another way of saying that textual and intertextual matters cannot be separated.

It would be incorrect to conclude that Blue's narrative account—full of introspection and emotion—is a false "overlay" on top of a "true" first text, the putatively more representative original ledger. In fact the original ledger is also a misrepresentation. When Blue writes that among the town's many "dealings" he had entered was the marriage notice of Bert Albany and his girl-bride, he remarks: "He could write, but all she did was put a mark down" (133). Here the mark of the anonymous girl-bride forms an analogy to naming and writing in general, which is composed of marks and, like them, is arbitrary and nonrepresentative. The figure of the palimpsest, then, suggests that narration be conceived not as fiction atop truth but as fiction enmeshed in fiction, like the "burdensome thought" that Heidegger read in Nietzsche. The girl-bride's mark is only more conspicuously misrepresentative than "proper names"; her mark is as representative of her as Blue's name on the rock is of him. Blue's ledgers show writing as the palimpsest of the arbitrary.

If this is the lot of the writer, what can be said of the decision to write? Blue begins to write on two occasions: when the town begins to prosper, he resumes keeping its records; and as he lies dying, Blue begins to write his narrative. For his first decision to write, Blue offers two conflicting, but not contradictory, explanations. The first links writing with delusions of hope and love. Blue's original ledgers had been burned during the Bad Man's first rampage. After painful rebuilding and near starvation during the winter, spring comes, and Blue allows himself to hope. Even Molly seems temporarily reassured after she voices to Blue her recurring fear of the return of the Bad Man:

> "I keep hearing his voice: 'I'll be back,' he says. It's what he said to me."
> "Well then, if that's so, I doubt it but if it's so, if he does come back then we'll be ready for him. We'll all be ready."
> She was quiet for a minute. "We've both suffered," she said. And I was holding her hand in my hands. It was enough to start me keeping the books again. [132]

Here the decision to write is linked with the hope of survival. The passage seems delicately balanced; only in retrospect is one aware how deceptive the moment is. According to this explanation, the decision to write is born out of a momentary delusion of hope.

After a gap in the narration, a literal blank spot on the page, Blue provides a second explanation of his decision: "No, maybe I'm not telling it right. When I dipped my pen in the ink it was not just for celebration, it was something that had to be done" (132).

Blue now wonders if there was any alternative to writing to boost the business of the town. According to this new explanation, writing is a matter of necessity. Blue's two motives do not cancel each other; instead, they suggest two components of writing: as the conferral of meaning on arbitrary signs, writing is a delusion; as articulation, it is also necessary.

Blue's second decision to write—this time his narrative—comes as he lies dying, and it is inspired by death. It was the sight of Zar's dead body, according to Blue, that "got me to take my books out here and sit down and try to write what happened" (211). The attempt to understand death is, like hope, the writer's formative delusion.

Like the title and character names, the assessment of Blue's narration brings to the fore certain dilemmas inherent in narrative. He is a figure for the writer as deluded delayer of disillusionment or as Express agent, "receiving and forwarding letters" in a wasteland. The letters do not originate with him, and his only function is to delay, temporarily, the "truth" they might contain, namely the eternal return, the inevitable destruction of all constructions. The futility of his function informs Blue's despair over the fated nature of both writing and reading:

> Of course now I put it down I can see that we were finished before we ever got started, our end was in our beginning. I am writing this and maybe it will be recovered and read; and I'll say now how I picture some reader, a gentleman in a stuffed chair with a rug under him. . . . Do you think, mister, with all that settlement around that you're freer than me to make your fate? Do you click your tongue at my story? Well I wish I knew yours. Your father's doing is in you, like his father's was in him, and we can never start new, we take on all the burden: the only thing that grows is trouble, the disasters get bigger, that's all. [184]

There is nothing new. Reading and writing are fated alike; in retrospect, the knowledge that "we can never start new" should have been obvious to the reader, if not to Blue, from the metaphor of writing as palimpsest, but instead, Blue's narration demonstrates the necessity to repeat this empty "learning" in every "new" act of reading and writing.

Blue's career as narrator exemplifies the fated character of writing in another way, too; by equating writing with deluded hope, Blue implies that such hope, however quixotic, is the only alternative to death. For Blue, existence requires some attribution of significance to the arbitrary, mute world. He expresses this connection near the end of the long, bitter winter, when he looks at Molly and Jimmy and thinks he perceives in them some gratitude: "These were strange quiet moments. We didn't have much to be proud of but I had to allow we were better off than we might have been. . . . A person cannot live without looking for good signs, and I thought these signs were good" (89).

Of course, a moment later Blue acknowledges he had deceived himself about Molly and Jimmy, but the interesting point is that he considers self-deception *necessary*. As he says, "I had to allow" for such signs, even misleading ones. It is as if survival depended on an acquiescence in misinterpretation, or, put another way, as if the only "true" interpretation, or model, could be a representation of death. As pure absence, however, death is the entity that can never be represented truly; all attempts to render death are metaphors, substitutions for an unknowable absence. This is the Heideggerian paradox of *Sein-zum-Tode:* that death confirms a condition of ontological inauthenticity also attested to in language. For Heidegger, the inability to represent death is the exemplary instance—if that paradox be allowed—of the universal condition of idle talk.

As narrator of *Welcome to Hard Times,* Blue is the first in a series of Doctorow's narrators who embody this Heideggerian paradox; their work is made possible by the deluded construction of "good signs," but they also concentrate fiercely upon death in an attempt to interpret it truly. Like his successor-narrators, Blue hopes to render death clear-sightedly, to dispense with all consolation in the apprehension of it, but at this point the aspiration to represent, to create a "true model," breaks down. The murderous deeds of the Bad Man from Bodie can be narrated, but death itself eludes all mimesis. With

Turner's death, a new Bad Man, in the form of Jimmy, springs up and runs away. The truth of death cannot be truly represented, but only "embodied" or personified in a fictional character. This necessity already occludes the truth, already removes the writer, once and for all, from his goal. The closer Blue comes to his own death, the more he senses that this ultimate contradiction has always been embedded in the heart of writing:

> I'm trying to put down what happened but the closer I've come in time the less clear I am in my mind. I'm losing my blood to this rag, but more, I have the cold feeling everything I've written down doesn't tell how it was, no matter how careful I've been to get it all down it still escapes me: like what happened is far below my understanding beyond my sight. In my limits, taking a day for a day, a night for a night, have I showed the sand shifting under our feet, the terrible arrangement of our lives? [199]

As the introduction explained, this passage connects the futility of the flow of blood and ink, but it should be noted, too, that this final admission of failure culminates a narrative inspired by the sight of Zar's corpse. For Blue, the endeavor to represent death in narrative results only in personification, while the truth of what happened remained "far below my understanding beyond my sight." Such is the empty lesson of death. Because the Bad Man from Bodie synthesizes personification and death, he becomes a model of the process of narrative misrepresentation.

It is now appropriate to explore how the Bad Man from Bodie may be read as "embodiment" or personification itself. As narrator, Blue makes the absent present by creating this figure (as well as all other figures in his text) out of nothing; the act of narrative construction thus implies an eventual destruction, a seeming imperative that the Bad Man enacts. It may be, as J. Hillis Miller has argued, that personification (prosopopoeia or mask-making) is inherent in any narrative.[13] This novel's first words, "The Man from Bodie," imply that he is essential to the story. But the equation between the Bad Man and prosopopoeia is also suggested by details that stress the spectral quality of the character's appearance, especially his face. These remind the reader of the "constructed" nature of the Bad Man and hence of Blue's artistry. In Marilyn Arnold's perceptive observation, we come to understand Blue as a "man who is creating fiction as he attempts to write history."[14]

In the novel's opening the reader is made aware of Blue's artistry by his active imagination, the *Einfuhlung* through which he asserts the ability to know the feeling of his created characters: "The Man from Bodie drank down a half bottle of the Silver Sun's best; that cleared the dust from his throat and then when Florence, who was a redhead, moved along the bar to him, he turned and grinned down at her. I guess Florence had never seen a man so big" (3).

It is instructive that one of the Bad Man's first gestures, turning, suggests his name (Turner); notice, too, that the man is characterized here by his grinning facial appearance, as if he is literally a mask; later he laughs to himself repeatedly (14) and grins and laughs as he sets up drinks (17). In Blue's first detailed description of the man, his mask-like face is rendered: "He was a younger man than I expected but his skin was shot red under the stubble, there was a blaze on one cheek and he had the eyes of a crazy horse" (18). By the time of the Bad Man's return, Blue identifies the Bad Man with his face: "It was justice to kill him, the single face, the one man" (202).

In his first appearance the man says nothing, merely grins and laughs; his taciturnity adds to his spectral function as a kind of "pure mask;" this sense is reinforced in Blue's narration of the uncanniness of his second appearance: "Looking over the doors I could see only his shoulders and his hat. But then he raised his head and there was his dark reflection in Zar's fancy mirror behind the bar. Two Bad Men, the Man multiplied. I remember feeling: He never left the town, it was waiting only for the proper light to see him where's he's been all the time" (195).

The Bad Man's return is here accompanied by values suggestive of "pure" return and repetition. The mirror image marks the man's return with a literal duplication. This time Turner does speak, but only to repeat himself: "'Hey, honey,' he said softly but there was no other sound now. 'Hey honey'" (195). Of course Blue himself acknowledges the principle that destruction is inherent and inescapable even when ostensibly dormant. It is only later, only belatedly, when "proper light" returns, that Blue, or the reader, can become capable of understanding an earlier blindness. Blue's blindness is demonstrated throughout his narrative by his rational remonstrances against Molly's fierce intuition concerning the man's return. The reader also experiences Blue's blindness. As a result, the process of reading *Welcome to Hard Times* confirms the idea encountered earlier in the figure of the writer as Express agent; with its necessary personification (of characters by the narrator, of the narrator by the reader), writing is only the temporary delay of disillusionment.

Of course such a judgment might seem to imply that Molly's point of view is the "correct" one, endorsed by the novel, for unlike Blue she perceives the imminence of destruction behind all constructed facades: her preternatural foreknowledge exposes, in retrospect, the naivety of Blue. At the height of the town's prosperity, for example, just as it has been (*because* it has been?) given an official name, Molly tells Blue, "if this town stretched four ways as far as the eye could see, it would still be a wilderness!" Blue's reaction suggests the way in which blindness and insight oscillate: "For one chilling moment I knew what Molly meant. A shudder ran down my back. But then the true sight of our town returned to me" (144). The point is not that Molly's view of "destruction' is true and Blue's hopes for "construction" false; instead, both coexist simultaneously, but to comprehend one is possible only through blindness to the other. Therefore, Blue, also, is "correct" to say that "the true sight of our town returned to me." If the town is simultaneously flourishing and dying, the attempt to interpret it "truly" will only result in the substitution of a new construction, a new metaphor, equally mistaken, for the old one.

The idea that learning is only a potentially infinite chain of substitutable metaphors occurs in the novel's peripeteia or "reversal and recognition scene," in which it is understood that the mine will be abandoned. It is worth remarking that this scene is itself an "allegory of reading"; the fate of the town is disclosed in a letter, but the letter itself is never revealed. The constructed purport of the letter is that the long anticipated "signified"—ore—does not exist. This disclosure leads to an interchange between Mcellhenny and Blue, one that is often cited as containing the novel's ultimate theme: "'As long as the payroll kept coming, Blue, we kept diggin' that rock. But I knew weeks ago that it wasn't ore we were diggin'. 'Twas only the color.' Like the West, like my life: The color dazzles us, but when it's too late we see what a fraud it is, what a poor pinched-out claim" (183).

Without question this is, as many have urged, a statement of profound disillusionment; the West is a fraud, a model of misrepresentation, but *this* "learning" is *also* fraud—an empty exchange of tropes. Mcellhenny utters synechdoche and ellipsis (It was only color we were digging). Blue replies with two similes (the second of which identifies his very life with the trope). In other words, the construction Blue puts on the allegory of reading he has just experienced *is itself new figuration*. His repetition of simile dramatizes the eternal return, the open-ended substitutability of tropes in interpretation. And, of course, the novel does not end here; instead, the next chapter opens with Blue's writing about writing and engaging in prosopopoeia (imagining his reader). "Learning," as defined by Blue's interchange with Mcellhenny, is only the exchange of tropes.

This sense of the novel's "learning process" explains why its apparently nihilistic, apocalyptic conclusion subverts the hermeneutic attempt to find meaning—even nihilistic meaning—in endings. Blue is dying; Hard Times has been destroyed; the Bad Man from Bodie has been killed only to be reborn in Jimmy Fee, who seems to inherit the Bad Man's function as pure personfiication. Toward the end of the novel, Jimmy appears to Blue as nothing but a pure, even sexless face: "[Jimmy yells at Blue:] 'You better not talk that way about my Pa—' Lord, it made me faint-hearted, it was Fee's face with no lines, a young hairless face with a frown of anger and no understanding at all. 'You better not talk that way,' it said pursing its lips, 'you better not!'" (165).

The pessimism of the ending seems unrelenting. The buzzards will soon descend on the carrion in the town. It occurs to Blue that he might scatter the birds by setting the street afire. Almost as an afterthought, he writes his final words: "And I have to allow, with great shame, I keep thinking someone will come by sometime who will want to use the wood" (212). Hermeneutic criticism focuses on these words as expressions of varying degrees of hope and despair, which in turn may comprise the novel's "final view" of its subject, but at the same time, these critics do not agree. For example, John Clayton sees in them "Blue's hope" and "the voice of quiet courage [which] conveys a vision of life's possibilities that stands as a critique of the bleak cycle contained in Blue's record."[15] Similarly, J. Bakker concludes that "though desperate, it is not a despairing novel," because Blue is depicted as a man who refuses "to give in to Hobbes's dictum that life is brutish, nasty, and short," even though the novel's events prove just that.[16] Other interpretations differ. Stephen L. Tanner thinks the novel is "essentially empty of hope and human affirmation,"[17] and Carol Ianone faults Blue for "his refusal to make an unequivocal stand for life."[18] The contradictions in these hermeneutic studies may derive from the assumption that a novel must end in a univocal, representable meaning, but if this assumption is faulty, then contradictions in interpretation would be natural.

It is important to recognize that Blue's last words express no emotions of hope or despair at the prospect of reconstruction, which he sees as a logical possibility ("I have to allow"). Thus before they begin to express feelings, Blue's words are constrained to admit a logical contingency, the possibility that the wrecked remains of the town might one day be used to form a new town (just as Blue rebuilt Hard Times from the ruins of Fountain Creek).

In continuing to suggest the novel as an allegory of reading, Blue's last words may also be understood as a warning against hermeneutics, against reading endings, as a forced admission that the process of interpretation is interminable, in other words, that later "construction" will be made, even from apparently obliterated construction. Eternal reiteration. In fact, all "new" readings of Blue's ledgers, or Doctorow's novel, like the one now in progress, are such subsequent, redundant constructions. The "shame" Blue feels is at the prospect of unavoidable future constructions, future interpretations that will only commit once more the errors he has involuntarily committed. The fact that "wood" is the traditional source of the paper used both in his ledgers and in his written interpretations makes Blue's expression of logical necessity at least defensible in the modern world; at some demystified level, reading and writing as redundant processes can be considered as "making use of the wood."

However minimal a statement about writing, Blue's neutral last words seem uttered in some Nietzschean manner removed from the "human, all too human" emotions of hope and despair. In the words of Paul de Man: "However negative it may sound, deconstruction implies the possibility of rebuilding."[19]

CHAPTER 2

Big as Life
The Dead-End of Hermeneutics

In *Big as Life* two humanoid giants, male and female, appear standing in New York harbor, where they remain motionless. The novel traces the public's reaction, especially the response of the four main characters: Red Bloom, a jazz bassist; Sugarbush, his girlfriend and, later, wife; Dr. Wallace Creighton, a professor of history; and General of the Army, Retired, Hugh D. Rockelmayer. For almost a year the government attempts to maintain public order through its agency NYCRAD, New York Command, Research and Defense. After initial panic, order is restored, but despite superficial normality, worry about the giants continues, for the male emits sounds that are interpreted as cries of pain. Religious panic and social dereliction (unemployment, alcoholism) increase; the general public is not mollified by NYCRAD's public-relations efforts. In response, the government reinstitutes curfews and travel restrictions in the city, measures that anger the religious groups that had made pilgrimages to see the giants. General Rockelmayer leads massive, violent demonstrations against NYCRAD and other considered blasphemers. On Easter Sunday, Red Bloom's jazz quartet is attacked by a mob of religious fundamentalists. After being severely beaten, he makes his way back to his apartment. The military can barely contain growing anarchy in the city. While Red is on his way home, Rockelmayer enters Red's apartment. In a delusional monologue, he frightens Sugarbush, who fears she will be raped. When Red finally arrives, he finds Dr. Creighton and his colleagues, Putnam and Kahn, as well as Rockelmayer. The NYCRAD officials believe it is inevitable that plans to destroy the giants will soon be put into effect.

Critical discussion of *Big as Life* has emphasized evaluation rather than analysis;[1] nevertheless, two critics have concurred that the function of the giants is to exhibit the arbitrary character of civilization. Arthur Saltzman notes that the giants "serve to lay bare the uncertainty and indeterminacy that underlie our social principles."[2] Paul Levine finds the giants "challenging the system of assumptions on which ordinary life is based."[3] Neither critic fully elaborates his theme, but their similar assessment of the giants' role provides a useful starting point for discussion. This chapter argues that the subversion of the social order effected by the giants is one part of a broader critique that challenges not only society but all systems of representation, including writing.

There can be little doubt that in NYCRAD the full import of contemporary hermeneutics and its concomitant principle of reason conceived as representation are exhibited. This sense of the organization becomes evident when Putnam, the physicist-administrator, leads Creighton on a guided tour of the facility (104–23). Creighton visits a tracking station that monitors the giants' movements; he watches biochemists using techniques of extraction, distillation, gas chromatography, bioassay. He learns of NYCRAD's computerized library, its pigmentation studies, its attempts to predict the giants' slow movements. The tour seems to confirm Putnam's boast that NYCRAD has "the best men in the country—from campuses east and west, and quite a few industries as well—a university in the true sense of the word" (108), but Putnam understands only his own contemporary conception of a university, one in which research is wholly oriented to the application of a representation. This presupposition is made clear in Putnam's explanation to Creighton that electricity for the researchers' elevators comes from the giants' body heat. He exclaims: "Once the idea of *using* them established itself, it turned out to be a theory with many practical applications" (109). The presupposition that knowledge is "applied theory" characterizes not only NYCRAD's natural scientists but all of its assembled intellectuals, whatever their disciplines. Thus Creighton's colleague Kahn, the sociologist, conducts surveys with the object of refining techniques of social control. Thus Father Justin, the Roman Catholic priest, works for the Human Relations Team, whose mission is to engineer social tranquillity. Throughout NYCRAD, then, Putnam's presuppositions about knowledge as applied research—including the hermeneutic belief in representation—prevail.

In "The Age of the World View," Heidegger argued that a definition of knowledge or science as research is inseparable from a particular presupposition about representation:

> Understanding as research holds the existent to account on the question of how and how far it can be put at the disposal of available "representation." Research has the existent at its disposal if it can either calculate it in advance, in its future course, or calculate it afterwards, as past. Nature—in advance calculation, history, in retrospection, calculation—is, as it were, held at bay. Nature and history become the object of expository representation, while the latter counts on nature and reckons with history. Only what thus becomes an object *is*, is recognized as existent. Science as research occurs only when it is in this objectification that the being of the existent is sought.[4]

Heidegger's essay is rich with implications for the study of *Big as Life*. In pursuit of its hermeneutic goal of representation, NYCRAD does seem to hold nature at bay and make both nature and history the object of research. (Heidegger's likening of the historian to the research scientist is obviously pertinent to the characterization of Creighton.) And in numerous details of NYCRAD's operations, the scientists' blithe confidence in representation—their dependence on it—is undeniable. For example, when Putnam wants to explain to Creighton the operation of NYCRAD, he first points to a scale model of lower Manhattan and New York harbor which has color-coded buildings. Research teams study the giants' eyes on four separate TV screens. In the tracking station, numbers flash "on large electronic boards like the scores of incomprehensible games" (119). The obsession of research with representation is evident in NYCRAD's determination to find the giants' exact color. Cardiographs and oscilloscopes produce other representations. Three charts—diagrams of human figures—illustrate the predicted movement of the male giant's arm. Audio engineers make their own "models" by miniaturizing the giant's cry, translating it with electronic gear into human terms (154). All of this model-building or attempted representation serves the effort to dominate reality as it is figured forth in the official response to the giants.

Following Heidegger, Derrida sees the modern university's misplaced confidence in representation as the attempt to master the world; as the transformation of reality into an object; and as the source of the illusion of the self as autonomous Cartesian subject, face-to-face with the truth-as-presence: "The modern dominance of the principle of reason had to go hand in hand with the interpretation of the essence of beings as objects, an object present as representation [*Vorstellung*], an object placed and positioned before a subject. This latter, a man who says 'I,' an ego certain of itself, thus ensures his own technical mastery over the totality of what is".[5]

The image of NYCRAD's researchers, gazing at the giants they strive to master, can serve as an allegorical picture of the modern delusion Heidegger and Derrida denounce: belief in the existence of a subject face-to-face with its represented object, in short, the radicle of hermeneutics. Oriented toward the object of their research with the goal of dominating it, NYCRAD's researchers study representations, or signs, which they assume have a necessary relation to some referent. Of course, their confidence in the represented object also provides researchers with comforting certainty of their own egos. Putnam's brusque self-confidence and eternal smile correlate with the scientific optimism driving his belief that, as long as NYCRAD's research continues, the truth of the object eventually will be found.

Hermeneutic research is half of NYCRAD's mission. It follows the principle of reason—Heidegger's *Satz vom Grund*[6]—by which confidence in constructions or models of reality (NYCRAD's endless papers, reports, measurements, data) is an illusion, one that is essential, however, to the very continuation of the research enterprise. Allied with hermeneutics, however, is NYCRAD's defense function, an ominous corollary that implies—as *Welcome to Hard Times* did—that some ultimate destruction may be inherent in the process of forming interpretive constructions. Such inherence is made visually obvious in the acronym in which signifiers for both functions, R and D, are always present; the constant repetition of NYCRAD across the pages of the novel suggests that both functions may be implicit even at the level of the word, in language itself. In any case, the inevitable coexistence of construction and destruction is demonstrated in this novel's action in much the same way as it was in *Welcome to Hard Times*. Paul Levine observes one parallel: "Both begin with the sudden appearance of a disruptive stranger and both end with scenes of apocalyptic violence."[7] Extending Levine's discussion, it can be observed that, while both novels are framed by overt anarchy and destruction, the seeming peace of their central portions is fraudulent: just as Blue comes to believe the Bad Man from Bodie never left Hard times, so the depiction of NYCRAD indicates that its defense component never disappears during the supposedly "normal" period of the research effort. In what follows, the destructive potential latent in hermeneutics is analyzed not only in the secular intellectual mission of NYCRAD but also in its fundamentalist opponent General Rockelmayer, who unwittingly shares its presuppositions.

On their tour of the facility, Putnam makes clear to Creighton the essential quality of the defense component of NYCRAD. The "cream of the cream," from Rand and the Institute of Naval Research, work in the Justification Lab. Their mission is to develop the PSD's (Practical Systems of Destruction) and thereby to ensure continuation of government appropriations (122–23). Research is self-perpetuating, and its survival is predicated on destruction. On the day of the tour the Justification Lab has produced five PSD's; only a few months later, seventeen have been approved. Thus the destruction component of the think-tank works continuously, inextricably with its research component. Although on the tour Putnam appears to consider the defense function intellectually inferior to scientific inquiry ("We keep the uniforms happy"), he comes to admire, at the end, the technical brilliance of the final total of seventeen PSD's. At the end, Putnam is convinced that the plans' mere existence ensures their eventual implementation. Obviously the novel's depiction of the self-perpetuating and self-fulfilling nature of NYCRAD's defense enterprise bears analogies to the field of nuclear-weapons research; however, at NYCRAD research and defense bond indissolubly because both are orientation- or application-driven. Both naively suppose that intellectual inquiry is "justified" only in some representable result in the world. Again, Derrida, discussing Kant's privileging of "architectonic" over "technical" knowledge, provides an excellent context for understanding the novel's embedding of defense within research:

> Today in the orientation or "finalization" of research—forgive me for presuming to recall such obvious points—it is impossible to distinguish between [Kant's] two sets of aims. It is impossible, for example, to distinguish programs that one would like to consider "worthy," or even technically profitable for humanity, from other programs that would be destructive. This is not new; but never before has so-called basic scientific research been so deeply committed to aims that are at the same time military aims.[8]

Derrida sees the modern use of "orientation" as a euphemism—one that holds forth, as Putnam does, the prospect of some untainted, worthy end—for the older term "application." For Derrida such euphemisms mystify; research conducted under the auspices of either term is based on an "instrumental determination of a calculable language" (14), and it presupposes that language is an instrument capable of unequivocal representation.

That the defense component is based on such hermeneutics is also made plain in the description of NYCRAD's war room, where Creighton observes the army's attempt to quell Rockelmayer's insurrection. Like the research labs, the war room is full of models and seeming representations. On a large Plasticene map are circles of green, orange, and red, apparently denoting trouble-spots in the city. The clashes between army and demonstrators are televised. Communications between units are broadcast over speakers. As Creighton listens to the disembodied voices, the necessary lie of prosopopoeia, familiar from *Welcome to Hard Times,* takes effect: "The exchanges of orders and tactical information came through . . . so that visions of the voices, the faces they belonged to—this one whiny, that one bitter, another stubborn or brutal or righteous—immediately came to mind" (179). Creighton's imagining faces from voices is his own model-making, his conferral of presence, an arbitrary extension of authority. But it is consistent with the principle by which both the research and defense components are executed.

Misleading conferrals of authority are identified with the defense component of NYCRAD from the very beginning. For example, Creighton's curiosity regarding the municipal reaction to the giants can be satisfied only when he puts on the disguise of a civil defense authority, the Red Cross workers' helmet; even his own, unofficial research is possible only by a construing himself as part of a defense network. In a like manner, General Rockelmayer's initial exercise of authority in the hotel is made possible by his uniform, which does not disclose his retired status. In both cases spurious authority is literally "put on," created by entry into a world of signs. But such supposed authority continually remains vulnerable to exposure; the necessary illusion always harbors the prospect of its imminent destruction. This vulnerability becomes apparent when Creighton accepts a second fictional role, his disguise in the general's uniform, in order to take Red and Sugarbush home in a military car. The dead-end of hermeneutics is dramatized in these examples: the fictional assumption of authority that enabled it to proceed in the first place requires continuous "defense" against exposure.

Thus it is not surprising when Creighton learns that satisfaction of a defense requirement is a prerequisite for his official research. His medical examination culminates in a security interview conducted by a man who Creighton at first believes is a psychiatrist. The identity of the interviewer, who effectively suggests the arbitrary character of defense authority, is never disclosed. Creighton's acceptance of the arbitrary and the inevitable defense of it is the price he pays at the threshold of research hermeneutics. Later, when his work is continually interrupted, he tells himself he must temporarily forget about his bizarre enlistment in NYCRAD and "wear the ID card on his lapel as if he had been born to it" (92).

This latent annihilation of all its constructions is, however, the ultimate dead-end of hermeneutics. In *Big as Life*, General Rockelmayer manifests this threat, just as the Bad Man from Bodie did in *Welcome to Hard Times*; Rockelmayer exposes the emptiness of

NYCRAD's interpretive efforts much as Turner's return exposed the futility of Blue's writing. Like the Bad Man from Bodie, Rockelmayer appears in scenes of social anarchy at the beginning and the end of the novel; also like the Bad Man, his appearance is spectral. For example, when he steps off the elevator, he seems an "apparition" (31). When he stares at Sugarbush "it seemed to be his picture looking at her" (25). But Rockelmayer is no innocent buffoon: he also harbors Turner's urge to rape in his threatened assaults on Sugarbush; and when he leads bands of religious fanatics in rebellion against NYCRAD's authority, he repeats the Bad Man's apocalyptic violence. From the beginning, Rockelmayer's claim to authority rests only on his now-dysfunctional uniform—truly a model of misrepresentation—and on his own word. So, like Turner, Rockelmayer shows how official systems of representation, built on lies, must collapse.

Rockelmayer also articulates the contradictions in NYCRAD's hermeneutics by parodying their foundationism. He becomes a spokesman for "Americanism," loosely defined as the values of the Founding Fathers, and for theological "fundamentalism," as those values might be associated with the Redemption Army band he comes to lead. Of course the reliance on such "foundations" by a character whose first appearance subverted claims to authority also unsettles the foundations of NYCRAD's enterprise. The patent groundlessness of Rockelmayer's messianism may make NYCRAD's rationality appear sane by contrast; however, on close examination, Rockelmayer's aberrancy derives from the same principles as NYCRAD's supposed normality. As Rockelmayer holds the terrified Sugarbush prisoner in her own apartment, he delivers a rambling autobiographical monologue that discloses the original motive for his military career: "Oh, you know, it has been a blessing, life, it really has. The greatest joy is organization, the superb brick by brick ordering of wanton life. The construction from a million disparate souls of a smooth, oiled engine of purpose. There are not many men who have had the good fortune to work with such vast materials" (186-87).

In fact Rockelmayer shares with NYCRAD belief in the efficacy of organization and construction oriented toward a hermeneutic end.

The end Rockelmayer pursues is religious and chauvinistic rather than scientific. He defends the fundamentalists' right to interpret the giants as religious icons, whereas NYCRAD interprets the giants as empirical objects, but in both cases the enigmatic figures standing in the harbor are destinations of quests or pilgrimages. They are *archons,* foundation concepts, or "signifieds" that offer validation of existence to those oriented toward them. Therefore it is no wonder that at the novel's end, its three main examples of hermeneuts—Putnam, Rockelmayer, and Creighton—are drawn together in Red's apartment, gazing at a television, a representation of the violence that was already inherent in the "construction" of their work.

Rockelmayer's bull-like aggression serves as a foil for the unacknowledged ways in which NYCRAD's research science and Creighton's research history also imply eventual destruction. As the intellectual-as-humanist, Creighton is a stand-in for the reader, condemned to assume a signification in every act of reading that must nevertheless, in the end, collapse. The historian-as-reader/writer must at first present himself in the uniforms of civil and military defense; correspondingly, at the end of the novel, Rockelmayer is able to escape only by exchanging his uniform for Creighton's civilian clothes. This symmetry suggests a troubling analogy between the discipline of history and the crazed delusion of defensive, fundamentalist hermeneutics.

In the character of Creighton, the reader may observe the failure of hermeneutics in contemporary history, which is described by Heidegger as a discipline governed by the need for explanation and for the reduction of the unique to the intelligible and the comparable. Thus contemporary history is depicted as sharing the presuppositions of scientific research. Of course Creighton thinks of his discipline as embracing perspectives broader than those of positivism. For example, on his tour of NYCRAD with Putnam, Creighton bridles inwardly at the physicist's hubris, his obliviousness to the human dimension (evident in his insensitivity to his co-workers), his failure to perceive the bureaucratic absurdities of his own administration. In these ways Creighton embodies a traditional humanism that would interpret scientific research within a larger social and political context. Yet at the same time, without realizing it, Creighton shares the same presuppositions about representation that Putnam and NYCRAD hold; as a result, despite its apparent detachment from scientific endeavor, his work as a historian is actually a part of it. Just as Creighton is given an office and a function within the bureaucracy of NYCRAD, so history is conceived in the novel as a discipline ancillary and subordinate to the larger research effort, whose presuppositions it silently shares.

A passage from Heidegger's "Age of the World Picture" will detail the way in which the contemporary idea of history has become absorbed into the same system of thought that governs research:

> In the historical disciplines just as in the natural sciences the procedure aims at representing the permanent and making history an object. The permanent in history, that with reference to which historical explanation assesses the unique and the diverse in history, is that-which-has-always-already-happened-once, the comparable. In the constant comparison of everything with everything the intelligible is figured out and is indicated as the ground plan of history. The sphere of history extends only as far as historical explanation reaches. . . . Nor is there any other historical explanation as long as explanation means reduction to the intelligible, and so long as history remains research, that is, explanation.[9]

Certainly *Big as Life* tests the historian's reaction to "the unique and diverse" in history, and just as Heidegger supposed, that reaction reduces the unique to the comparable. During his interview with the anonymous security official which concludes his physical examination, Creighton is asked, "What event in history, in your opinion, can compare to this? I mean in effect." The full import of Creighton's reply is revealing: "'Well, of course there have been plagues, wars, religious revolutions all through history.' Wallace felt peculiar speaking professionally without any clothes on. 'But I should think,' he said, clearing his throat, 'if there is any occasion from the past quite as totally and permanently disruptive, it is Copernicus writing the proof in his notebook that the earth turns around the sun'" (90).

Creighton's professional response immediately accepts the questioner's presupposition that history explains the unique in terms of the comparable. Creighton's essentializing (his selection of an occasion "quite as totally and permanently disruptive") is a remarkable instance of Heidegger's contention that the contemporary historian is bound by the reduction of history to the permanent-as-comparable. Creighton's choice of Copernicus reveals him as the historian of paradigm shifts, the interpreter who cannot articulate his subject without first having recourse to classifications of systems. The importance of the novel's link between history and science is evident in the fact that the question and reply are part of a screening process; they are prerequisites or literal prolegomena to the undertaking of history in the modern world. It is as if contemporary historians cannot write without first subscribing to the hermeneutics of history as explanation, as representation, as repression of the unique.

There is also simple irony in Creighton's reply, which may show the arrogance of history as conceived as hermeneutics; as he answers the interviewer's question, with sweeping historical evaluation, Creighton is naked. The fact makes him feel "peculiar" and injects a certain ludicrousness into the hermeneutic enterprise. But another effect is created, too: at this moment Creighton most resembles the naked motionless giant who to the end baffles scientists and historians. Both instances of nakedness contrast that state with hermeneutics-conceived-as-clothes; in many ways the simple contrast works as it does in the child's tale, "The Emperor's New Clothes," juxtaposing the universal mystification of hermeneutics with an otherness all the more conspicuous for its nakedness. That such nakedness becomes an affront to the hermeneutics of empiricism is suggested by the canvas loincloths draped on the giants. Humanity and the giants may be equally inexplicable, but in his reply at the physical exam and throughout the novel, Creighton speaks for a contemporary discipline whose presuppositions exclude this possibility.

A related error of the historian-as-hermeneut is the premise that history is only represented history. The mistake of such an assumption is made clear in Creighton's discussion with Mr. Giotto (or "Pinkeyes"), the fence for Red's diamonds, who has obvious connections to organized crime. At Big Al's club, Creighton listens to his explanation of his operations: "'Years ago I learned how to get along with cops,' the old man said. 'I've never had a bit of trouble, not even with the feds. I never argue, and I never rough anyone up. I meet my payoffs. I have never been sent away. In all these years I have nothing on my record'" (137).

Never for a moment does Creighton consider how a "record-less" criminal would escape the domain of historians who define truth as representation. In a similar vein, it never occurs to Creighton or Kahn "to do any work on the survival of the criminal element in the city" (134). The equation between history and represented history blinds Creighton to the sense in which history shares the same procedures as fiction. Revealingly, Creighton is an expert on the period of the Reconstruction (40); that word also describes the redundancy of writing in general, to which Creighton, like Blue before him, must remain blind.

Part of that blindness is Creighton's belief that rationality can be confirmed by representation; this is the same error Foucault finds in Descartes.[10] This is exposed in an early scene. First, as he gazes at the giants, Creighton poses to himself what he takes to be the only two alternatives available to historical hermeneutics—"explanation," in Heidegger's terms, or madness. Indeed, Creighton introduces these alternatives with the familiar, presupposed axiom of history: "What this means, he thought, is that all this time, in the whole history of the world, we have been nothing but a deluded swarm of insidious little vermin. The city is a patch of dirt in someone's garden. Either that, or I am simply mad" (40). Having posed the alternatives of meaning and madness, Creighton tests the second, his sanity, by means of a representation; he grabs a Polaroid camera and takes a picture of the giants. This reaction gives the lie to the assumptions of hermeneutics: "Somehow, with the picture in his hand, he expected the models to disappear or move on. But they didn't. Then the picture itself became frightening. There were now four creatures. He imagined a race of them proliferating in every harbor of the world. Creighton turned on the TV set" (40).

Creighton's belief in representation is matched here by his need for it, to confirm his sanity, but the photograph is only another dead-end. It frightens Creighton with the prospect of endless redundancy—the possibility of infinite new representations. That possibility—what Derrida calls iterability[11]—is the condition of representation. Here it appears in the moment Creighton's Polaroid snapshot transforms the giants, for him, from enigmatic others to photographic "models." Creighton suppresses the fear, the threat to his own sanity, in the vertiginous prospects inherent in representation, but as a historian he has, after all, no alternative. Without realizing the contradiction, he turns to another representation, his television set. Instead of confirming his sanity, the representations that Creighton consults only reinforce a delusion already mandated by his profession as historian.

Creighton's most cherished illusion is the one he shares with all of the other characters: belief in his own selfhood. Recall Derrida's idea that a false confidence in representation provided those who felt it with the comforting illusion of an ego face-to-face with a represented object. It is apparent how the egocentric Putnam, Creighton's superior at NYCRAD, exemplifies that illusion. But Creighton, too, falls victim to this universal ruse. Tellingly, this occurs when he decides to lend his help to NYCRAD. Creighton had been listening to the president's speech of reassurance to the nation, which praised the unsurpassed intellectual and military resources assembled for the purpose of dealing with the giants. He reacts to the speech in two ways, first by taking a representation as an article of faith: "'Why, I believe that,' said Creighton, addressing the TV set. 'I've never doubted it for a moment.'" In the next moment, the representation reinforces Creighton's belief in his ego: "Creighton had stopped paying attention. He was thinking of the President's words. He was thinking that among the intellectual resources of the nation were her historians. In the bright blue light of the television screen his face had the pallor of revelation" (68).

Creighton's work for NYCRAD affords him the contemporary historian's illusion that a single, autonomous writer can master the meaning of events constituted as present before him, but the proud historian's illusion is no different than the physicist's. Both succumb to the lure of an arrangement of arbitrary models—of records and data, photographs and instruments of technology—that hold forth the all-too-human promise that significance and presence may be conferred on those who arrange them.

The most prominent model-making in *Big as Life* concerns the giants: NYCRAD's quest to discover who or what they are. But the meaning of the giants eludes NYCRAD's hermeneutics; by the end of the novel, the creatures continue to loom as mute challenges to signification, and all human attempts to name and define them—to read them—are exposed as arbitrary. As in *Welcome to Hard Times*, these attempts come to a dead end. The fruitless effort to interpret the giants becomes a repetitive process, another eternal return in an allegory of reading.

The giants are first referred to as "they" (12, 13, 14); this pronominal usage encapsulates the entire problematic of naming to follow. Pronouns are categorized as linguistic shifters; their function is to indicate in binary terms the place in which discourse is put into practice or language becomes parole.[12] In the novel the giants function as a kind of permanent "they," never achieving a "true antecedent" or name and thereby calling into question the validity of naming elsewhere in the novel. As in *Welcome to Hard Times*, characters and their names often suggest the aribtrary nature of the sign in their multiple references.[13] From this vantage point, the giants, identified at first only with the name "they," ought to demystify naming in the human world.

On the other hand, research cannot proceed unless the giants are given names; Putnam calls them "honeys" sometimes, or Tarzan and Jane. A name-the-giants contest is held, in which suggestions such as Adam and Eve, Jack and Jill, or Pelleas and Melisande are proposed (177). The linking of these three sets of names—from Genesis, fairy tale, and opera—unsettles "canonical" names and emphasizes the arbitrary but necessary step in NYCRAD's research. Sometimes the giants are called simply "creatures"—also a redundant term when used in a novel. More often, characters revert to the original pronomial usage, as in Red Bloom's response to the owner of a newspaper stand devastated by riots: "'I don't know any more. I don't know what to think. Look at what they've done to me.' 'They didn't do it. They haven't done a thing'" (182).

It is worth noting that in this passage the "they" becomes ambiguous and refers both to the giants and the rioting crowds, a blurring of reference that suggests an underlying homology between the human and the nonhuman, as if the "they" would be a less mystified name for humanity than its welter of "proper names." This analogy between the giants and the anonymous crowds is extended to the figuratively anonymous bureaucracy of NYCRAD by Kahn, who reassures Creighton: "'You're making the mis-mistake of personalizing NYCRAD,' he said to Wallace. 'Forget the pa-people. You're not going to get by unless you deal with the organization. It has its own la-life. Like our friends in the harbor'" (89).

Kahn's stutter in this passage emphasizes the key terms of the paradox it expresses: prosopopoeia is a mistaken attribution of life. On the other hand, it is necessary, as necessary to the operation of NYCRAD as to the understanding of the giants.

The humanization of the giants is essential to NYCRAD's most important research goal, the prediction of what the giants will do. Of course, the nonhuman giants "express" only through gesture and sound: the male's hand gesture is followed by his arm reaching, his contorted face, bared teeth, and unearthly cry; the female turns to look at the male. To these movements NYCRAD attaches human signification: the male is making a benediction; he is in pain; the female is concerned. But to the last the giants' signs remain ambiguous. NYCRAD's interpretation is a human construction of a mute reality that is never confirmed. As in *Welcome to Hard Times*, personification (or, the human construction of reality) seems to be the inevitable precondition of articulation; whether as "they," "honeys," or "Tarzan and Jane," the giants—who in fact represent nothing—must be accorded a will that represents human understanding. So it appears impossible for hermeneutics to proceed without personifying the giants in arbitrary acts of naming and interpretation. From this perspective, NYCRAD's researchers merely repeat the dilemma inherent in the ordinary act of reading. If the giants resemble authors in one respect, in the emission of enigmatic signs that can be interpreted only in human terms, then NYCRAD's project resembles hermeneutic literary criticism, positing behind such signs an intending author.

Through many analogies, the novel implies that the same dead end to the interpretation of the giants also awaits the interpretation of humanity. In addition to the scene in which Creighton, naked at his medical exam, renders his professional judgment on the significance of the giants, there are other scenes that show parallels between the inexplicable giants and the humans' faulty conviction of their powers of explanation. A striking instance occurs when Creighton watches a television comedy produced by HRT, the Human Relations Team, which is NYCRAD's public-relations arm. The mission of the HRT is to mollify public opinion, a goal that "orients research"—for example, that of the sociologist Bernie Kahn—toward the maintenance of public order. To this end, the uniqueness and otherness of the giants are repressed—as they are in Creighton's comparison of them to Copernicus—in favor of the domestication of the giants. The television program succeeds in fully achieving this end through its "modeling" of the giants:

> [Creighton] sat back to watch one of television's most familiar comedians. The comedian and his guest star, a girl singer, were having great fun dressed in striped, floppy, turn-of-the-century bathing suits. They were standing in back of a pasteboard model of the New York sky line, making topical jokes about the city below them, making domestic jokes about *his* troubles with *her* mother, *her* pique with *his* conduct at last night's bridge party. The comedian and his guest star were breaking themselves up, much to the delight of the studio audience. [167; emphasis in original]

The show is a model of a model; it accomplishes its objective of domestication by humanizing the giants. Through its emphatic pronouns (which mimic comic intonation but also stress the prosopopoeia), the humanization process is constituted, but now the new issue arises of how, fundamentally, humanity distinguishes itself from the giants. If personification of them is the fiction necessary to academic research, then what of "common sense" or "normal" assumptions about reality made by the man in the street? Once again, confidence in representation carries with it the covert self-congratulation of the masses, of a collective ego willing itself present-at-hand. The very idea of *extending* the human principle to the enigmatic other presupposes the validity of the human. Viewers of the television comedy can be reassured of their existence as they domesticate the world.

This reassurance is tenuous, however, because humanity is shown, at base, to resemble the giants. Before leaving Red and Sugarbush, the drunken Creighton imitates the male giant's gesture by lifting his arm slowly, "as if blessing the darkness" (144). At another point the giant's cry of pain—if that hypothesis is allowed for a moment—blurs into the cries of the rioters. Running home to Sugarbush, the wounded Red hears chaotic sounds and tries to think of them as music. He "listened to the fearsome music, the screams, the sirens, the shouting, the soft whoomphs of tear-gas grenades. Everything was taking off from the pedal point A, which was today's giant note of pain. 'Easter Day Improvisations,' I'll call it, he said to himself" (177). The "giant cry of pain" from the other has become indistinguishable from the noises and cries of humanity. In this situation the process of humanization extends in both directions, from human to other and from other to human. In each case the construction of humanity is being put on arbitrary sounds, and the giants function to expose this illusion.

Late in the novel, a fleeting thought of this function occurs to Red as he gazes at the giants after waking up from his long sleep: "They were still there. They looked the same as yesterday, but at the same time they looked cooler. Less tortured. As if they were big mirrors for what went on below. 'That's stupid,' he told himself. But he was glad they were still there. It proved something. It proved they were what they were and nothing else" (204).

To consider the giants as mirrors, for a moment, is to accept that they serve the traditional function as art, as demystifiers of the world. This interpretation would be consistent, to a degree, with the account of their function advanced here (that they point up the illusions implicit in the humanization of the world), but no sooner does this thought occur to Red than he rejects it, or seems to reject it, in a double movement. He dismisses his own analogy, with its implicit claim for the representative function of art; but at the same time, he concedes the giants' authority. This double movement is surely a paradox, for either the giants can teach humanity or they cannot. Red does not resolve the paradox but replaces it with a tautology: "It proved that they were what they were and nothing else." At this moment the novel comes closest to elaborating the dilemma of art: that it seems to represent, that it seems to teach, but, after all, the most that can be said of it is, simply, that it is. The giants are this novel's most fully drawn models of misrepresentation; the tautology they inspire is the dead end of hermeneutics.

In Red Bloom and his relation to Sugarbush, *Big as Life* entertains a serious alternative to the world of permanent misrepresentation, of necessary errors, that seems to define hermeneutics; they are the first of several characters in Doctorow's novels in which some prospect of living authentically, free from the circular delusions of hermeneutics, is held forth. Such characters test the universal applicability of the novel's pervasive indictment of language and the world. It is as if the novel turns on itself, confronting its own skepticism with a newly imagined possibility for affirmation. In fact the relation of Red Bloom and Sugarbush depicts a mode or style of existence sometimes valorized by the very same philosophers (Nietzsche, Heidegger, Derrida) whose unrelenting assaults on any such "metaphysical" alternatives—metaphysical to the extent they may imply representable presence—seem to be seconded in the novels. Discussion of this putative alternative may thus reveal contradictions in the very philosophers whose work Doctorow's often resembles.

Red Bloom is a musician, a bassist, whose life has two passionate purposes, his music and Sugarbush. His virility and virtuosity set him apart from Creighton, the ascetic intellectual. Red's thoughts are the novel's first and last words, and although the narrative line switches between his life story and Creighton's, in many other ways the musician's life seems to "contain" or surpass the scope of the historian's. It is fecund, at least, in its promise of offspring, whereas Creighton's life seems sterile; it is committed without hesitation to the discipline of music, whereas Creighton regards his profession with some irony. This broad contrast is evident when they meet at Red's debut at Big Al's jazz club. There, Creighton becomes so drunk and maudlin that Red and Sugarbush, like Samaritans, drive him home (143–44). This incident reverses the roles, to Red's advantage, of an earlier scene (47–55), the ride home in which Creighton, in the guise of false authority—the general's uniform—exacts from Red and Sugarbush acknowledgment of his "authority." In this contrast Red emerges as at least Creighton's equal and an attractive potential alternative to the dead-end fallacies of hermeneutics.

Furthermore, in Red the prospect can be imagined that the entire world may be perceived musically. Driven home by a corporal taking orders from the disguised Creighton, Red listens to the engine and is "bemused by its rhythm, which he heard as six-fourths" (53). On his way to fence his stolen diamonds, Red is accompanied in the elevator by a fat man who made "a kind of respiratory music: his overtaxed lungs fought to take air in and fought harder to expel it. Red heard every prodigious breath as it wheezed and snarled through its cycle. The harmonics were a wonder" (78). The instant conversion of phenomenal into aesthetic stimuli marks not only the intensity of Red's musicianship but also a mode of existence that apparently circumvents problems of representation. It is as though Red, the world, and his music were without mediation and had become one.

This impression is strengthened in the description of Red's performance on the night of his quartet's debut (129–32). The notion of jazz as improvisation on an established score is elaborated to the point at which it seems to suggest the possibility of a new ontology, a way of ignoring representation. While he is playing, Red seems to live the paradox that only abstractly bedevils Creighton and NYCRAD. His music seems to express paradox effortlessly, directly, without the mediation of the arbitrary or accidental. This account of Red's original composition, "Blues for the General," summarizes the aims of his aesthetic: "It was an intricate piece with a fugue that he was very proud of; it was an example of the kind of thing he was trying to do. The emotion was tightly locked in the form and there was nothing random about the instrumentation. At its most intense polyphonic moment the full passionate voices were in perfect tension and almost antagonistic, like four entwined dancers struggling to get out of step with one another" (131–32).

There are several points worth noting in this passage. The word "fugue" is a rich pun, one that denotes ennui, depression, or despair as it simultaneously converts these negations into a musical form of originally theological, now secular, praise. The fact that the title, "Blues for the General," contains a dedication recalls the heritage of the fugue's referentiality while it adds a new twist. Although it no longer may be possible for contemporary art to honor divinity—Red has no religion—it may still be possible for art to honor humanity, even to honor, generously, that dangerous, deluded humanity Red saw when he witnessed General Rockelmayer standing, with an erection, over the sleeping Sugarbush, "pointing at her with his old but clearly loaded cannon" (39). From this perspective, Red's music may be profoundly Christian or humanist. It is an art that seeks to transcend the dead repetitions of hermeneutics—the enemy of creativity and art—by subsuming them within a difficult but masterly art of praise. The song's dedicatory title may be applicable to Creighton as well, the man who impersonated the general and is co-opted by the defense function of NYCRAD. Of course, the aesthetics of altruistic affirmation in Red's music fits with the spontaneous generosity of his personality, too.

Music may constitute an alternative to the quagmires of hermeneutics for another reason, because it seems to offer a different response to the notion of the "instrument" or "the instrumental." We have seen that NYCRAD assumes the instrumental view of language; that is, language is an instrument for the representation of objects to subjects. This fallacious assumption is necessary to the conduct of research but doomed to result in misrepresentation. In music, however, the reverse is the case. The "instrument" is not now a means to an end; instead, it combines means and end, or it confounds the distinction between means and end. Unlike words, Red's bass (or any musical instrument) forms directly the expressive meaning it produces; it is as difficult to separate music from instrument from player as it is, in Yeats's familiar figure, to separate dance and body and dancer. (Yeats's figure is invoked in the above passage that describes Red's music.) This rich contrast between the different notions of instrumentality in music and hermeneutics is drawn at the end of the novel, when Sugarbush invites Red to join Creighton, Putnam, and Rockelmayer, who are watching television in the living room:

> He didn't answer. He was remembering his rage. He finished his coffee and the cup rattled in the saucer.
> "Do you?"
> "What's the point? Can any of these guys blow?"
> "Honey, I don't know."
> He was disgusted with her. "None of these guys can play an instrument. So what's the point?" [206]

In Red's defiant reply is the idea that music can challenge and demystify hermeneutic claims to meaning.

Moreover, the passage points to another reason to conceive music as an alternative to hermeneutics: in music is acknowledged the importance of play. Recourse to play, as a response to philosophical dilemmas, has a contemporary provenance extending from Nietzsche to Derrida.[14] In many different guises play is appealed to as an affirmative response to aporia, as a productive, constructive activity that at the very least keeps philosophical questions open and at best may generate new lines of inquiry. With its acknowledgment of a prior score but insistence on improvisation, jazz seems an appropriate musical instantiation of play. In the novel, Red's anticipatory regard for Sugarbush, his tending her fears, seems the existential correlative of his music: their baby will be play incarnate. As Paul Levine points out, their decision to become parents "in the midst of catastrophe proves their commitment to life and provides the novel with a note of muted hope."[15]

There are still other ways in which Red's life seems to act as a counterweight to the novel's otherwise preponderant indeterminacy. In his relation with Sugarbush, Red seems to effect a union between the Dionysian impulses (valorized on occasion even by Nietzsche)[16] and the dialogic or conversational mode (valorized on occasion by writers like Bakhtin and Heidegger).[17] The love of Red and Sugarbush is linked to Red's music. For example, in the first chapter, Red's early morning talk and lovemaking with Sugarbush, following an evening's gig, are narrated in language that emphasizes the rich mutuality, the interdependence, of music, language, and sexuality. The phenomenological unity of Red and his instrument is emphasized in his constant care for it. These patterns of behavior, suggestive of some authenticity in existence prior to or in spite of linguistic dilemmas, are repeated in other scenes, particularly those involving the Redemption Army band.

The intellectual challenge to the text posed by the presence of Red Bloom and Sugarbush must be assessed. If these characters can function to counterbalance or even outweigh this novel's otherwise universal doubt, then a surprising development would ensue. A novel that at first seemed to continue the attack on hermeneutics begun in *Welcome to Hard Times* would become, instead, a novel with a definable, transmittable, hermeneutic meaning capable of paraphrase in the complex of ideas, or similar ones, sketched here. As a means of testing such a possibility, it will help to explore the formal organization of the novel, which includes Red Bloom and Sugarbush, as well as NYCRAD and the giants, among its creatures.

Big as Life consists of a title and four parts, the first three of which are preceded by epigraphs. The title of the novel is a trope (simile) and a cliché, which may function as a commonplace in rhetoric does, to initiate a discourse. At first the phrase "big as life" might seem to refer to the giants, but because they are, after all, enormously *bigger* than life, that reference is made doubtful. Even in common parlance the meaning of the phrase can be puzzling; it can convey a sense of wonder but also irony in the presence of the real, as in the phrase, "There he is, big as life." But in this usage, the phrase becomes a trope, because to be literally true it must refer to nonlife, to something outside of life. Of course, the two abstractions most commonly contrasted with "life" are "art" and "death," but to assert that either is "big as life" is nonsense. This state of uncertainty may be limited by simply reading the title reflexively, as referring to the novel that follows. In this way the title says what may be said of all art, that it is virtually true or apparently real, but in fact neither true nor real. Like *Welcome to Hard Times,* the title *Big as Life* may be read as a sign that calls its referent into question.

Each of the novel's four parts is titled; these titles (three with epigraphs) also function in the same way that the main title does. In fact, the title of Part I is the same as the title of the novel, a fact that calls the referent into question a second time. The practice of giving a work the same title of one of its parts is common in American postmodernism: Vladimir Nabokov uses the technique in *Pale Fire,* as does John Barth in *Lost in the Funhouse,* and Doctorow returns to it in *Loon Lake* and *Lives of the Poets.* The technique has the effect of making the title an instance of the trope synechdoche, which naturally prompts inquiry into the sense in which the part aspires to represent the novel as a whole. In the case of *Big as Life*, the inquiry is puzzling at first because the action of "Big as Life," the first part, is highly inconclusive: the major characters meet after the appearance of the giants, temporarily come together (at the Midtown Towers), then disperse. But then, such waywardness characterizes the novel as a whole, and even in its ending, in which the question of the destruction of the giants is never resolved. Part I ends with Creighton's impersonating the retired General Rockelmayer and reassuring the corporal whose jeep he has commandeered: "Some good will come of all this, Corporal," he said. "Wait and see" (55). This expression of equivocal hope also occurs in the ending when Red and Sugarbush decide to "wait it out" (217); the parallel between part and whole, beginning and end, creates a circular structure that casts doubt on the progress accomplished in the intervening pages. The synechdoche' of Part I thus implies a dead end in reading, which is reminiscent of *Welcome to Hard Times*.

That redundancy is doubled by the epigraph to Part I, which (like all epigraphs?) suggests a dysfunction in the title. The long epigraph to Part I is supposedly an excerpt from a transcript of the Special Senate Emergency Investigation Committee; in it Captain Mickiewicz, a ferry pilot, testifies about his encounter with the "obstruction" in the harbor. On first reading, certain details of the testimony are mysterious ("I found myself hanging on to what I thought was some lines, some ropes"); they arouse the reader's curiosity. The transcript also lends verisimilitude to events through the agency of a sworn eyewitness account on public record. In this way, the transcript functions as a "false document," a literary device Doctorow analyzes in his essay by that title. The initial ambiguities in the testimony (e.g., "this isn't no ship") are clarified soon by the text; the captain's signs find supposed referents. However, no sooner are these "referents" established, in the giants, than the reader understands the initial delusion of reading, of allowing fictional "testimony" to serve as warrant for an ensuing fiction. The process at work is the same alternation of blindness and insight established in *Welcome to Hard Times*: "insight" into the text is possible only at the cost of blindness to its fictivity.

The title and epigraph of Part II function in the same way. The title of Part II repeats the technique of the title of *Welcome to Hard Times*; in a circular way, "Let's All Endure" names both Part II and a sign inside that part, the posters mounted on buses and subways by the Emergency Advertising Council. There is a laconic quality to this phrase, just as there is in "big as life." Such narrative self-mockery is aggravated by the repetition of the phrase (by Red and at the top of each page in this part), which oddly ironizes the question of survival in the novel. It is as if the serious issues raised by the text were, from some other vantage point, susceptible to ridicule. The epigraph under the title of Part II announces NYCRAD's research and defense functions; the juxtaposition has the effect of equating NYCRAD's hermeneutics with the Emergency Advertising Council's exhortation to endure. Perhaps one implication is that while for most people the delusions of hermeneutics are considered necessary for survival, that assumption is not necessarily shared by the novel's narrator.

The title and epigraph of Part III pick up this implication by equating another NYCRAD document—reassurance regarding the sound emitted by the male—with "the benediction," a word used in several different contexts in the novel.[18] The most prominent use is as NYCRAD's term for the male's first gesture, and this act of naming is only the first of many ungrounded assumptions made by NYCRAD. Of course NYCRAD uses the term ironically, just as it uses "Tarzan and Jane," but the giant's gesture remains inexplicable to the end. On the other hand, to the religious pilgrims led by General Rockelmayer, "benediction" may be the correct interpretation after all. For both secular and religious hermeneutics, the identification of signs is considered absolutely fundamental to survival. Thus the juxtaposition of title and epigraph equates the delusions of reassurance, whether offered by religion or by NYCRAD. That the novel does not necessarily share these delusions is implied in the fact that "the benediction" also names the text of Part III; that is, the narration of the intensifying, converging delusions of NYCRAD and religion may itself be a "benediction," or words positioned near the end of a discourse. That these words are surely not blessings adds to the tone of narrative self-mockery already evident at the beginning of Part II.

Part IV has no epigraph, only the title "Practical Systems, Destruction." The absence of an epigraph may imply that the government and NYCRAD—the sources of the earlier epigraphs—have vanished after the predicted attack on the giants. On the other hand, this "interpretation of an absence" is immediately self-canceling, like the many moments of oscillating blindness and insight in the novel. The title's reference to NYCRAD's defense plans may imply an inevitability of destruction inherent in hermeneutics, but once again, even this interpretation is stalled by the novel's open ending. If the self-reflexive character of the first three part titles is taken as context, then "Practical Systems, Destruction" may refer to the novel's process of self-destruction, its anonymous narrator's obliteration of character, language, and plot in the white space following the end of the text, a form of terminal self-mockery. But the movement of the novel toward its end has so deeply shaken interpretive activity that even a final stance of self-mockery seems too stable and finite a description of its endeavor. The novel's end, instead, is radical instability, effected by the exit of hermeneutics (in the characters of Putnam, Creighton, and Rockelmayer) and the lingering of Red and Sugarbush. Their challenge to the novel's dead end must be evaluated.

The apparent independence of Red and Sugarbush from the hermeneutic circle never frees them from the burdens of discourse; immediately after Putnam, Creighton, and Rockelmayer leave, Red picks up the telephone to call the members of his quartet. Nobody answers. His final conversation with Sugarbush is, once more, both literal and figurative intercourse, but it provides no answer to the intellectual collapse they witness but never comprehend. As in Blue's speculation about reconstruction at the end of *Welcome to Hard Times*, the issue of Red's new start seems to be one of both hope and despair, but it is also one of necessity, as this sentence makes clear: "There was nothing to do but start over again" (218). In other words, repetition—of the sort noted throughout the reading of *Big as Life*—is finally experienced as unavoidable. From this perspective, the novel's last scene integrates the challenge Red and Sugarbush posted to it within the larger circle of repetitions of construction/destruction/construction. The novel's ending finds Red suspended between the moments of this cycle. He hopes for a new bass to replace his old one. As soon as one instrument of created illusion is destroyed, another must be envisioned. As soon as one novel ends, in a "practical system of destruction," another must soon "start again" in the eternal return. In this dead end, Red offers no metaphysical alternative to this process; on the contrary, he becomes part of its infinite continuation.

Chapter 3

"The Songs of Billy Bathgate"
The Writer as Orphan, Killer, Performer

"The Songs of Billy Bathgate" consists of seven prose pieces narrated by Billy Bathgate, a popular singer in the folk-rock countercultural tradition of the late sixties. Most of the prose pieces also contain rhythmic or rhymed passages. Each piece's title is followed by a parenthetical numerical notation, like those that follow the titles of popular songs and express their duration in minutes and seconds: for example, the first piece is titled "The Orphans' Home (3:12)." The seven pieces mix naturalistic narration, interior monologue, lyrical passages, and visionary description. They trace Billy's life from childhood to artistic maturity and fame.

Billy grows up at the Hebrew Home for Orphans in the Bronx. His career as a musician begins in earnest only after a long period of wandering and apprenticeship; for example, during his "ethnic period," when he lives in Greenwich Village, he seeks out the influence of a renowned country singer, John Malcolm, in east Tennessee. Billy believes that he finally comes into his own as an artist when he starts singing his own songs, although he also thinks the public misinterprets them. At a concert, Billy watches as one of his songs is sung by Lovegirl, an already established star; the enormous success of her performance helps make Billy a star, too, and brings him together romantically with Lovegirl. Their love is consuming, but Billy senses their separateness. They make only one record together, which is never released. Once, in London, Lovegirl asks Billy to take her to her home in Columbus, Ohio. When the arrive there, Billy meets Carrie Mae Wilson, a black woman who had taken care of Lovegirl since childhood.

Lovegirl and Carrie Mae walk together on a beach in South Carolina, but they are stopped by an armed, racist cattleman and a sheriff. After news of the incident spreads, a civil rights march is organized. Billy refuses to attend the march, which later turns into a riot. He imagines meeting Lovegirl on the beach and that she whispers to him words he writes for her in his mind. Then, in this vision, Billy signals for a cattleman to shoot Lovegirl, who dies.

In Billy's last, most recent song he imagines walking with W. C. Fields, who guides him through a throng of humanity. The scene resembles a dream of apocalypse. Billy recognizes Fields and addresses him. Fields acknowledges that Billy "knows what the game is" and gives him his crooked cue-stick. In the analysis that follows, this short collection is considered first as a whole and next piece-by-piece.

It is obvious from the foregoing that "The Songs of Billy Bathgate" continues many of the concerns of Doctorow's first two works. It addresses itself directly to the question of the persistent misinterpretation of the artist's work. It explores the relation between artistic representation and death. It tells of the artist's complicity in violence, even apocalypse. It initiates three figures for the writer which are important in the study of Doctorow's later works: the orphan, the killer, the clown. Most prominently, it takes up again the subject broached by the love of Red Bloom and Sugarbush: whether a love-relation conceived on a "musical" model can be an authentic alternative to a world given over to misrepresentation. The Billy of this experimental collection is an angry, disillusioned Red Bloom, railing against critics, but in the name of an art he himself suspects is corrupt. As if continuing the story of Red Bloom and Sugarbush, "The Songs of Billy Bathgate" finally acknowledges that even the most intimate, mutual communion cannot serve as a safe haven from interpretation.

Once again, interpretation is misrepresentation, an equation that begins with the titles of the collection and of individual pieces; they seem to imply that the collection's seven separately printed entities are "The Songs of Billy Bathgate." This impression is strengthened by the time notations following individual titles, but at the same time, there is also reason to believe that the individual prose pieces are not the songs. Rhymed or rhythmic passages, sometimes introduced as songs within or at the end of the pieces, suggest that the songs are parts of each piece, not the piece in its entirety. The following, which concludes the first piece, "The Orphans' Home," is typical: "Agon danced a lively tune Misero played the violin Such performances are given To benefit the orphans' home Children who lack a daddio Whose mommas left you on the doorstep Let's have a big hand for Agon And the violin of Misero" (56).

Such passages imply that Billy's "songs" are distinguishable from his "prose." On the other hand, the distinction is often created only by blank space and remote or forced rhymes (tune/violin/given/home; daddio, Misero). Moreover, in one case, "She's Too Good for Me (2:04)," even these markers disappear, so in the end there is no way to know whether it is song or prose. As in *Big as Life*, the device of synechdochal titling is encountered, through which the title's referent becomes undecidable; the songs of Billy Bathgate are wholes and parts, and the seven entities in the collection, like free verse, undermine traditional distinctions between prose and poetry, showing them to be arbitrary. (Doctorow undermines these distinctions again in *The Book of Daniel* and *Loon Lake;* generic distinctions among prose works are also undermined in *Lives of the Poets*.) Naming the seven entities prose or poetry, "songs" or "pieces"—and reading them requires *some* designation—is already to err.

This problem of impossible naming continues the concerns of *Welcome to Hard Times* and *Big as Life*. In "The Songs of Billy Bathgate," the problem is repeated within the short pieces as each depicts struggles to evade it. Billy adopts various postures and strategies in the hope of evading the doom of interpretation: on different occasions he protests his sincerity; he withholds his song; he believes in love; he dreams of Eden; he would silence his reader. Each effort ends in new contradiction. The pieces halt. They begin, but break off at the unanswerable.

The narration of the collection as a whole forms a kind of circle. In the first and last pieces, Billy writes of himself in the third person: as "a boy" growing up in the Bronx (55) and as "the singer" guided by W. C. Fields (69). In the intervening five pieces Billy speaks of himself only in the first person. This split point of view, which will recur in *The Book of Daniel* and *Loon Lake*, illustrates the "death of the author," as described by Roland Barthes.[1] Barthes's famous argument is radically extended in de Man's concept of irony; as soon as the writer writes, a fictional persona is created, belief in whose existence now jeopardizes the previously secure, autonomous presence of "the author."[2] In creating Billy Bathgate, E. L. Doctorow's presence as author is extinguished by Billy Bathgate's immediate capacity to do the same thing, to imagine himself as other in a third-person narration. Of course, the same process was at work in *Welcome to Hard Times*. Like Blue recreating himself in the past, Billy Bathgate must exchange "autonomous" existence for a fictional identity as soon as he begins to write of himself. Billy's assumption of a fictional identity is made plain in the third-person beginning and ending, but of course it is always latent in the fictional "I" that narrates the intervening songs as well.

In "The Orphan's Home (3:12)," this permanent sacrifice of autonomy and authenticity effected by writing is the condition Billy describes in his figure, "an orphan of the mind": "But you don't notice what a place of rolling hills it is unless you are old and hanging between your shopping bag and your cane; or unless you are an orphan. And I am talking about an orphan of my mind who takes these trips regularly, feeling every hill to its height and every valley its depth; and who hopes to find a certain street in the valley of the Third Avenue El" (54).

This passage exemplifies the impasse of representation in Doctorow. Writing, or the imagination of any plenitude or fullness, is orphan-making, because it can be effected only with the loss of the parent/author. This Billy is a literal orphan, but others of Doctorow's narrators are often "metaphoric orphans": Daniel, in *The Book of*

Daniel, orphaned by his parents' execution; the little boy whose father drowns at the end of *Ragtime;* Joe Korzeniowski, in *Loon Lake,* who escapes the "hateful presences" of his parents; the Billy Bathgate of *Billy Bathgate,* whose father left his mother. It is as if the cost of narration is admission of an orphaned status, a permanent separation from the real.

From this perspective, the inaugural story, "The Orphans' Home," describes the writer's starting point or donnée. Of course, a particular orphanage, the Hebrew Home for Orphans, is mentioned as Billy's childhood home. However, the metaphoric sense of "orphans' home" is evident at the end of this song. There, Billy protests against interpretations of his songs which attempt to find referential messages; as he does so, he states his real subject in words that solicit an other-than-autobiographical construction: "Now three things make up my songs, the words, the music, and the attitude. And of these the least understood is the attitude. I mean in this song some critics think I am talking about Life or America or the Futility of Orgasm or some goddamn thing, but I am not, I am talking about the place where I grew up, the orphans' home" (56).

Billy mentioned the actual Hebrew Home only once amid long descriptions of life on the street, so his statement—"I am talking about the place where I grew up, the orphans' home"—may be taken metaphorically. The lower-case "orphans' home" is precise because it establishes Billy's figure, the condition of being "an orphan of the mind." It is the place in which writing or composition—whether of prose or songs—begins.

Immediately after Billy manifests the self-annihilating property of writing, the seemingly nonsensical "real song" begins and mocks his enterprise: "Agon danced a lively tune   Misero played the violin   Such performances are given   To benefit the orphans' home" (56). If writing "orphans" the writer, then its only sure referent and beneficiary is itself. This is writing wholly cut off from the human. The emptiness of the song's "justification" may account for its mockery. At this point, "The Orphans' Home" ends.

Billy describes his musical apprenticeship, in "Short Order Cook (2:35)," including his visit to John Malcolm in east Tennessee. His original thesis—that to "make it" artistically means not listening to advice from others (56)—is borne out when he concludes, of Malcolm's music, that "the only music I had heard that day on that farm was music I didn't have to leave MacDougal to hear" (57). But the piece concludes in a reversal, as Billy suddenly challenges the whole notion of "making it": he compares the artist who has achieved popular success with a short-order cook, the producer of "fast art," who can "serve it up" to a public longing for sustenance from art for consolation. The pun "making it" equates popular success with fabrication. So this song, in Miller's term, "varnishes"; it undoes its own first assertion.

Billy's challenge to the idea of "making it" is consistent with the values of the figure of the author-as-orphan: the cook, like the writer, never appears in his work. In Billy's song the cook is known only "as the waitress calls to him the orders she gets" (58), a fictional presence conferred on absence by discourse. The waitress's orders, expressed as tropes, become "increasingly difficult to fill" (58).

Should these be interpreted as the demands made of contemporary writers to surpass prior achievements for a critical audience ravenous for the new? Autobiographical critics of Doctorow might read the passage as a lament born of Doctorow's sour experience with *Big as Life*, on the heels of his much more acclaimed novel, *Welcome to Hard Times*. In the song, however, the increasing difficulty of the orders is not a function of the desire to please an ever more exacting public or the critics; instead, it is a function of the figural nature of the orders themselves:

> From something simple like Draw one through a ring, which is coffee and a donut, or Gimme the earth before Columbus, which is a waffle; to Paint the stripes and cut the grass and satellite some succotash, which is the spaghetti special but instead of the tossed salad that goes with it substitute a vegetable. Till finally a man comes into the diner and asks for God, he orders God, and the waitress calls over the counter to the short-order cook: White on rye and hold the bread Sorry mister, the cook is dead. [58]

The passage implies that the cook can produce, as the writer can write and the reader read, only as long as an agreed-upon convention is observed, as long as natural referents for metaphors are accepted, as long as some representational assumption exists of a necessary relation between signifier and signified. The request for "God" from the cook exposes this arbitrary convention. The request for "God," as for signified meaning from art, is communicable not in "translatable metaphor," but only in unanswerable paradox: "White on rye and hold the bread." The ensuing "actual" death of the cook only acknowledges his prior exclusion from the song, Billy's from the piece, and Doctorow's from the collection. Finally, it suggests the ultimate impossibility of "making it," of art's providing true signification for those who demand it. On this note the second piece ends.

Billy protests against the popular reception of his first two songs in "She's Too Good for Me (2:04)". He first complains that it is only fame that has made people misinterpret his work; for example, the assumption that the pronoun "she" of this song's title must refer to Lovegirl, when in fact it refers to an unidentified girl he made love to on a California beach. With this gesture Billy tries to reassert sovereignty over the texts that have orphaned him. His complaint is against "the disease of fame, gigantism, the crude enlargement of every single feature including one's own words" (58). He claims mass communication always falsifies and insists he can represent truly. When he is too depressed by misinterpretation, Billy writes songs "just for myself, because there is no question then that the person who hears them will know what their truth is"; he also assures his reader, "It's all lies unless it's face to face" (59). In these assertions of authentic, true understanding—by a person alone, by two persons together—Billy restates the hopes for integrity and, perhaps, for dialogism expressed earlier in Blue's commitment to writing and in the love of Red Bloom and Sugarbush.

The problem with Billy's appeal to simple sincerity is all too obvious. It is expressed in this prose piece, in this public, printed medium of mass distribution. The reader thus encounters a specimen of the paradox of the Cretan liar; Billy's statement that true representation is impossible in mass media is made in the mass media, as are his claims for self-communion or dialogue.

There are other notable fallacies in Billy's protest. Rebuking those who call his supposedly authentic singing to himself prayer, Billy cries, "And for Christ's sake don't turn that on me and call it praying. Relent in your categories. Categories are public conveniences. Remember that oh you who buy the records." Billy does not notice that his disavowal of prayer invokes a deity, and surely Billy contradicts his own condemnation of "categories" only a few sentences later, when he introduces his song: "The she is not Lovegirl. And by her moral goodness, her virtue, I mean her body. This is a sex song" (59). Of course, here Billy himself categorizes, by naming his song's genre. His final fallacy is his insistence on the "true" referents of its words. What he does not see is that the artist, extinguished from his work, is no more able to fix its signification than the reader. Once the work leaves the writer's hands, he himself becomes only another reader.

At this level, the song's self-undoing is hardly subtle, but there is, nevertheless, one further "varnishing" in his defense of sincerity, namely, his use of the figure of "gigantism" for misinterpretation born of fame. Now if fame has the effect of making misinterpretation patent through "the crude enlargement of every single feature including one's words," then fame only makes explicit what was already implicit—in miniature, as it were—in the quotidian discourse of the unfamous. In this light, fame does not cause misinterpretation; on the contrary, fame only spotlights what might otherwise escape notice in everyday "idle talk." As in "Short Order Cook (2:35)," the idea of "making it" redounds against the artist; once a song is uttered, it can never interpret itself. Notice that Billy *introduces* his "sex song," but he may also withhold it, since no rhyme, rhythm, or blank space mark the "lyrical prose" that follows. Withholding the song would be a natural response to the dilemma Billy finds himself in. But sadly, it offers no solution. Even if Billy withholds his song, that silence and his final words—now prose, not song—cannot escape being read.

"She's Too Good for Me (2:04)" implied a necessary "fall" into interpretation and that idea continues in "Song to the Leaders of the World (3:26)." Billy first describes his discovery of an authentic voice: "I stopped singing like other people after I stopped singing other people's songs" (59), but that supposed autonomy conceals a ruse: "when I began to sing my own songs I thought that since they were my own songs no one else could sing them" (59). Billy goes on to describe a concert in which Lovegirl sang his vaguely apocalyptic, warning song in a new way, not with Billy's bitterness but with a cappella purity, like a "harrowing sermon" (60). Lovegirl's electrifying rendition of the song hastens Billy's fame and brings the two singers together; it also evokes an acknowledgement from John Malcolm—Billy's mentor-predecessor—of the power of their music. The scene is worth examining as the moment the artist "makes it," the main subject of Billy's first three songs.

At the concert Lovegirl's "reading" of Billy's song incites him to outdo her and himself as well; their two songs seem true "performatives," words that like baptism create and constitute new selves, but Billy's account of this moment's joyous flash of insight includes retrospective knowledge of its blindness: "the disquiet of her voice, and her mystery, were still in that park, and so I had to take her, make them forget her, and I moved into a realm of giving where I had never been before, and I gave, I mean to say I gave so good that in that long big-time night of work only two things happened, Lovegirl and Billy Bathgate. I would not learn to resent her feat for a long long time. You stand in the blinding light and the approval splits your eardrums and you are made blind and deaf by your own glory" (60).

The moment of "making it" in art is a "blinding light"—a de Manian oxymoron. That this blinding light seems to confer a self and to ratify love is the essence of its illusion, which can only be exposed belatedly, in retrospect. In fact, Billy the writer *does* come to resent Lovegirl the reader, in the same way authors might come to resent interpreters who see new dimensions in their works; interpretation, which is inevitable, orphans writing and kills authors by invalidating their claims to sovereignty over their texts. In this way "Song to the Leaders of the World (3:26)" reiterates the paradox of the first three pieces.

"Even and Odd in the Garden of Adding (5:15)," the longest piece in the collection, narrates the breakup of Billy and Lovegirl, the exposure of the fissure hidden in the oneness they sought. This gradual revelation appears on four occasions: the day he refused to accompany Lovegirl on a civil rights march; the day he joined Lovegirl at her home in Columbus, Ohio; the day on which he and Lovegirl sang together on the same record; the days on which Lovegirl joined Billy in a retreat to his "hideaway" from the world. Billy narrates the events in this reverse chronological order. It is of interest that this flashback technique accompanies Billy's "enlightenment." The implication is that once recognized, disillusion may have been "always, already" inherent in previous moments; such moments comprise Nietzsche's "eternal return." Indeed, the earliest event, their "hideaway" bliss memorialized in the title song, indicates that even their days of greatest intimacy hid delusions.

Billy celebrates and satirizes those moments in the song that ends the piece: "And let us make up the names of grasses we found and bushes and berries. And love each other's face in the different lights of morning and afternoon. And eat crackers and canned fruit and go to bed early. And it was Even and Odd in the Garden of Adding And we ate all the fruit we could find From apples persimmons peaches and plums To the sour green watermelon rind" (65). Of course, Billy's hideaway evokes and disavows Eden; in his hoped-for bower, the natural and artificial, the sweet and sour, are inextricably blended.

The "Garden of Adding" also develops the metaphor of "adding" that Billy introduced at the beginning of the piece, where he reflected on the irony that whatever the famous do "adds" to their stature. Billy used the example of famous singers, like himself and Lovegirl, performing for free or for "worthy" causes, while knowing all along that doing so enhanced their market value. (Such an irony recalls the undecidability of selfless/selfish motivation in *Welcome to Hard Times*.) Billy concludes, "Everything adds on, even what you do to diminish yourself" (61). By using this metaphor to describe his hideaway, Billy concedes that the inevitability of misinterpretation also exists even in his most private moments. For artists it is impossible not to add, to generate new misunderstanding with every act.

Billy's duet with Lovegirl reveals the true separateness that their passion concealed. Together they record "The Single-Bullet-Theory Blues," but the effort falters: "we sang many takes, and tried many ways, and finally stood at the same mike and held hands and closed our eyes and sang, as if closeness would make our voices match. But they didn't" (64). It is as if the simple fact of human separateness makes true expression, the matching of voices, impossible. Billy recognizes the point in Columbus when he listens to the sound of singing and identifies the voice first as Lovegirl's, next as a record, and finally as Lovegirl singing along with a record. The series of misidentifications—a kind of oral palimpsest—points to the arbitrary nature of the attribution of a unitary "self" behind a voice. Finally, when Billy refuses to go with Lovegirl on a civil rights march, she perceives their profound differences, for the first time. In each of these events, an illusion of presence or unity "varnishes" its later undoing. Lovegirl's departure for the march precipitates Billy's final reaction to this eternal reiteration of the same thing—the despair of his last two songs.

In "Billy's Dream of a Dead Friend (3:40)," Billy imagines ordering the killing of Lovegirl in the aftermath of the civil rights march and riot. Billy was not present at the riot, and from his account, the question as to whether Lovegirl was "actually" shot by a carbine-wielding cattleman is not answerable. It may be that Billy's dream, or imaginative construction of her death, is only his symbolic means of expressing his responsibility for the end of their love. In any case, Billy says that his raised-hand signal fells Lovegirl. The piece concludes with Billy's worried, ambivalent paean to her voice, but his plangent elegy cannot mitigate the shock of the figure of the artist as killer.

In Billy's account of Lovegirl's death, the first analogy is apparent between the pursuit of art and a figure reminiscent of Robert Graves's white goddess.[3] Lovegirl is the first in this series of women in Doctorow's texts who are variously compared to Aphrodite (Venus) or Artemis (Diana): Evelyn Nesbit, Clara Lukacs, Drew Preston. The seeming impossibility of loving these fatal women correlates with the futility of the artist's endeavor to possess truth: "What I see is myself walking up to Lovegirl who faces the ocean like Venus about to go back into the sea, and I gently touch her shoulder and she turns and smiles at me her lovely smile of recognition and whispers the words of a song I write for her in our minds: What do you believe, Billy Tell me what you believe, Billy And I raise my hand, which is the signal for the carbine bullet to slam into her throat" (68).

This is the climax, the concluding moment in the struggle that has marked both Billy's artistic career and Lovegirl's presence as one of its interpreters. Although Lovegirl plays the part of the reader whose necessary presence orphans the writer, she also embodies the mirage of communion, of understanding, of the matching of voices. In this climax, when these illusions seem fully revealed, Billy's song can express only the sorrowful emptiness of belief itself: "What do you believe, Billy Tell me what you believe." These words may seem like inquiries or requests, but they are not. They do not endorse nihilism, negation, or any "theme." Instead they are words that acknowledge unanswerability: telling, or representing, contradicts believing. The fact that Billy "answers" only by trying to silence them suggests their residual, ultimate character. But because Billy is at the same time the author of "Billy's Dream of a Dead Friend (3:40)," his song sung through Lovegirl and his response comprise yet another act of self-undoing in language. In the death of Lovegirl, Billy seems to come as close as possible to rendering in language the incapacity he has been led to understand about his art.

Even "Billy's Dream of a Dead Friend (3:40)," which seems to state so well the residual or ultimate character of an aporia, is itself a mirage. It cannot, after all, "summarize" or encapsulate a truth, even a truth of incapacity. Therefore Billy's collection continues, first with his elegy and finally with one more song. These codas reject the assumption that in a literary "climax" may lie some final terminus for the infinite unfolding of interpretation. Billy's practice here is consistent with Blue's acknowledgement of future interpretations, in *Welcome to Hard Times,* and with the redundant ending of *Big as Life,* and so it is fitting that Billy's last song plays with the notions of ending and apocalypse.

Billy imagines, in "The Ballad of W. C. Fields (2:20)," that W. C. Fields is his guide to a modern "underworld," perhaps as Virgil had guided Dante—Virgil's walking staff becoming Fields's crooked cue-stick. At the outset Billy, safe by a window in his house, resists

Fields's journey, but finally he is shown a vision of "the bubbling sulfur pits of intentions, and the slake mountains of ideals, and great plains of grey ash as far as he can see, the ashes of innocence creased by rivers of blood. And every man he sees is blind and running around in circles and no sound from the tapping of his cane to tell him where he's going" (69).

This scene of universal blindness accords well with the inescapable human delusion traced in Billy's relation with Lovegirl; however, Fields also shows Billy an "aged couple, a beautiful fair girl and boy in their youth who have grown old together" (69). After a lifetime of mutual love, they sit together oblivious to the misery around them. This image mocks Billy a final time by showing him the possibility of the very love his hopelessness led him to destroy; after all, if there were no truth even in his despair over the truth, then loving the white goddess may be possible after all. These two visions, of blindness and insight, are merely juxtaposed without comment. Then Billy sings a song to Fields about his wish to be taken seriously one day. Fields, a vaguely menacing, Dionysian clown-saint, pours two drinks and offers "my crooked cue-stick, Billy boy   Cause you know what the game is" (69). The passing of the wand of the magus may suggest traditional and grandiose versions of literary succession, as from Virgil to Dante, but the modern invitation, to accept the crooked cue-stick, beckons Billy toward art conceived as a fraudulent game of misrepresentation, knowingly played by clowns. This figure for the artist is the first in a series, which is elaborated in the clown-acrobat of "False Documents" and in *World's Fair;* resonances of the figure are present in Houdini in *Ragtime* and in Billy, the juggler, in *Billy Bathgate*.

To Field's offer of the cue-stick, Billy remains silent, as if in reluctance to acquiesce in the world of fraudulence it portends. But of course, Billy wrote the song, "The Ballad of W. C. Fields."

CHAPTER 4

Ellipses and Death in *The Book of Daniel*

Narratives of emotionally charged events of American history now comprise a distinct literary genre, one that includes such diverse works as William Styron's *The Confessions of Nat Turner,* Gore Vidal's *Burr,* Norman Mailer's *The Armies of the Night,* and Truman Capote's *In Cold Blood;* the category "nonfiction novel" has evoked extensive, although inconclusive, critical response.[1] *The Book of Daniel* is Doctorow's fictional adaptation of the Rosenberg case, written by Daniel Isaacson, whose parents are executed after being convicted for passing secrets of the atomic bomb to agents of the Soviet Union. Daniel writes his account in both the first and third persons; he does so at the Columbia University Library while he is supposed to be writing a doctoral dissertation. His narrative spans the period from the late thirties, when his parents met, until the student riots at Columbia in 1968. Events are not presented in order—Daniel flaunts his indifference to strict chronology[2]—but the main action includes scenes from his (and his sister Susan's) childhood; their reaction to their parents' arrest; their life with foster parents; the execution of their parents; Daniel's estrangement from Susan, owing to her more activist commitment to their parents' radicalism; Daniel's marriage and his savagery toward his wife, Phyllis, and their son, Paul; Daniel's effort to learn the truth of his parents' innocence or guilt, undertaken during the antiwar movement of the late sixties. Daniel's quest is inconclusive, and the suicidal Susan finally dies in an institution for the insane.

Paul Levine's apt observation that "[n]othing in Doctorow's earlier work quite prepares us for the extraordinary achievement of *The Book of Daniel*"[3] is born out by the great number of essays it inspired; among the eight novels so far in Doctorow's oeuvre, *Daniel* still rivals *Ragtime* in generating critical commentary.[4] The most controversial issue is disagreement as to whether the novel finally "endorses" Daniel-as-artist and the process of narrative in general. The division of opinion on this subject bears out the claim of this study that the tendency of hermeneutic criticism to evaluate endings—in the quest for an "author's view" or "novel's view"—ends in contradiction.

For example, Geoffrey Galt Harpham believes that the end of Daniel's text, however cruel, confers consolation.[5] Susan E. Lorsch argues that as *Kunstlerroman* the novel finally valorizes Daniel's efforts to find in art a means of straddling the anguished oppositions of his life.[6] Sam B. Girgus also advocates this view, arguing that for Daniel "the book functions therapeutically."[7] John Stark agrees, concluding that "articulating emotions and ideas in a book brings them under control."[8] Other readers doubt the efficacy of Daniel's narration. In a Lacanian reading of the novel, Robert Forrey sees the narration's nonsequential structure as a function of the "disintegration of the ego;" he suggests that Daniel may be mad, like certain narrators in works of Edgar Allan Poe.[9] Barbara Cooper also questions whether Daniel's narrative should be valorized: "To the end, Daniel's book is a random jumble of data and brief insights that mirror the formlessness of his memories."[10] Barbara Estrin believes Daniel's work sacrifices his integrity: "The completion of the work becomes, like the Ph.D. thesis it mocks, merely a meal ticket purchased towards a minimal subsistence."[11] This debate resembles the earlier one over the ending of *Welcome to Hard Times;* in both, the silent assumption is that an author's view is derivable from the study of endings.

The stalemated critical debate over the message of Daniel's text obviously raises the general issue of hermeneutics, which is also the novel's subject. As in *Big as Life*, hermeneutics is treated in terms of history, but unlike *Big as Life*, in which the historian, Creighton, is observed from the outside, *The Book of Daniel* presents a work of history as it is being written. The professorial, ascetic, middle-aged Wallace Creighton is replaced by Daniel Isaacson, the virile, impulsive graduate student. It is as if the issues raised by Creighton-as-historian were being examined again, now in the light of the Dionysian, dialogical values tested by Red Bloom and Billy Bathgate. Perhaps Daniel's voice—his blend of Billy's anger and Red Bloom's eros—is the "new" that Doctorow tests here, the alternative to the acceptance of repetition. As historian, Daniel makes a collage from fragments of his agonized family life and the materials of "objective" history. The two sources of his text, as well as his free improvisation on them—at one point he calls a "true history" a "raga"[12]—suggest that Daniel may reenact Red's and Billy's celebrations of play as a hoped-for alternative to deathly hermeneutics. Can Daniel's furious, engaged, playful narration provide a vindication for writing that escaped the apparently universal subversion of it in preceding Doctorow texts? The biblical Daniel is saved because he refused to worship the golden images of Nebuchadnezzar, as the novel reminds the reader. Like him, Daniel disdains the mere signifiers that haunt his life and the fate of his parents: his Yahweh is the signified truth, not the image, and his narrative records his effort to find it.

But despite all of Daniel's passion, his engagement, and his commitment, the failures of articulation are finally as inescapable for him as they were for Billy Bathgate, Wallace Creighton, Red Bloom, and Blue. His hopes collapse as he writes, a process especially evident in tropes like ellipses.[13] One of the novel's most disturbing scenes demonstrates this.

This moment occurs when Daniel is about to shove his car's hot cigarette lighter into the rectum of his wife Phyllis (69–72), but the actual depravity is not narrated. Instead, the scene is omitted; it becomes an ellipsis, a literary strategy deliberately adopted by the narrating Daniel. He compares his omission with the notorious eyeball-slicing scene in Buñuel and Dali's *Andalusian Dog* in order to argue that when the grotesque is left to the imagination, the effect is "worse than telling what happened" (72).

Problematically, Daniel lets his ellipsis stand, and the reader never learns whether his threatened assault on his wife actually occurs. One explanation may be that the narrating Daniel sadistically subjects the reader to what he believes to be the greater pain of the "wordless" conjuring of an image. On the other hand, the process by which an absent image becomes immanent is exactly the same in ellipsis as it is with any other trope: the silence, gap, or emptiness filled up is only ostensibly more arbitrary than words, which also, necessarily, conjure character and event. This homology between ellipsis and normal verbal evocation is evident when the cigarette-lighter scene is compared with its structural complement—that other, fully narrated application of electrical heat, the execution of the Isaacsons. In that supposedly climactic scene (311–15), the sensory details of smoke, urine, and burning flesh are "explicit," but the image conjured is no sharper, no more authentic or representative than that conjured by the ellipsis in the case of the threatened assault on Phyllis. This paradox—that equally plausible signifieds can be generated in the act of reading as easily from nothing as from something—shapes Daniel's dilemma. For in order to ascertain his parents' guilt or innocence or in order to find something commensurate with his wrath, Daniel must first assume the existence of referents that his writing will deny. So despite his passion, Daniel's empirical and narrational quests may be foredoomed to contradiction. In fact this suspicion is raised in the novel's first paragraph: "The day was hot and overcast with the threat of rain, and the early morning traffic was wondering—I mean the early morning traffic was light, but not many drivers could pass them without wondering who they were and where they were going" (13).

In this passage the narrating Daniel interrupts to correct a seeming error; he replaces an obvious trope ("traffic wondering," a personification) with "more explicit" prose. This correction calls attention to the two representations of the drivers; however, the image is no more "real" without the trope. The hermeneutic aids of correction, editing, rewriting—the business of the narrating Daniel—fail to bring the truth nearer. Daniel's unsuccessful struggle to make his book articulate a moral outrage that corresponds to events is evident in the rhetoricity and the tropes, especially ellipses, that permeate both his narration and his appropriation of other texts.

Because ellipsis implies the existence of an emptiness "filled in" by the reader's verbal constructions, it is an appropriate trope for the narrating Daniel, the writer-as-orphan on a quest to fill the legal, parental, and moral voids left by the executions of his parents, to recover the truth as signifying presence. The Isaacsons' crime involved fraudulent manipulation of documents; in his narrative Daniel repeats the crime.

To begin with, Daniel is moved by the detective motive of determining guilt or innocence, a quest that the act of narration, inherently figurative, undermines. Note Daniel's pun as he approaches Linda Mindish's door: "I rang the bell, the novel as private I" (285). His empirical quest ends in nothingness when the Isaacsons' senile accuser, Mindish, cannot establish the reliability of his own account of events—a debility from which Daniel himself suffers. In any case, Daniel's speculation on moral guilt or innocence soon transcends the empirical ambiguities he discovers in the trial history, documentary evidence, and personal recollections. The Isaacsons' crime is a void that is filled in, automatically, with one or more theories generated by verbal constructs, and Daniel remains unenlightened after his review of six books that make different cases for and against his parents' conviction and sentence (243). Susan E. Lorsch correctly observes: "Though the catalyst for the hero's quest may be his need to know the truth of his parents' innocence or guilt, the quest transcends such concerns, rendering them finally irrelevant."[14] In the light of the cold war and the world history of torture and treason discussed in Daniel's digressions, the issue of the Isaacsons' guilt moves from a legal to a philosophical plane. Can the meaning of any act—the Isaacsons' crime, Susan's suicide, antiwar protest—be known? The novel answers this more general question with a mystery, an emptiness, a silence. Daniel's approaches to this enigma are verbal and intellectual, the effort to make the silence speak, though everywhere he finds his effort vitiated.

In its resistance to unequivocal representation, the Isaacsons' crime resembles the mystery of death, which here, as in *Welcome to Hard Times,* is depicted in Heidegger's sense of *Sein-zum-Tode,* the insertion of an emptiness into being which undermines all representation of it.[15] The novel seems to build to the parents' deaths. Daniel precedes his account of the execution with a mock boast to the reader of his power of representation: "I suppose you think I can't do the electrocution. I know there is a you. There has always been a you. YOU: I will show you that I can do the electrocution" (312).

But after the detailed description of his father's electrocution, Daniel writes: "When the current was turned off my father's rigid body suddenly slumped in the chair, and it perhaps occurred to the witnesses that what they had taken for the shuddering spasming movements of his life for God knows how many seconds was instead a portrait of electric current, normally invisible, moving through a field of resistance" (314).

Death is unrepresentable, undecidable. The scene that witnesses "had taken" in one sense may be, instead, "a portrait" of something else. What was signified here? The "spasming movements of his life" or "a portrait of electric current"? Both? What is the "original" of such a portrait? Does Daniel's prose not paint a second portrait? These questions, prompted by the visual spectacle of death, remain undecidable; in fact, their very existence, undermining representation-in-death, is created by the process of narration. Notice that Daniel writes that "it perhaps occurred to the witnesses" to wonder. So the doubt he raises is itself put in question, and at the end of Daniel's (vaunted? ironic?) effort to shape a representative scene of death, only the undecidable remains.

The conflation of the Isaacsons' funeral with Susan's, in the second ending of the novel, also illustrates death as such an inarticulable emptiness. Daniel's fantasy of running around the cemetery, hiring and corralling shamuses to chant prayers he cannot understand, seems an implicit acknowledgment of narrative breakdown and the futility of representing death. His sad reflection, "My sister is dead. She died of a failure of analysis" (317), is thus appropriate. The failure of analysis and narrative to render death is only a prominent instance of its more general dysfunction, and the second ending concedes this failure. The fact that even this seemingly most "accurate" ending is, after all, but one of three—it is followed by the "new rhetoric" of 1960s protest—attests to the severity of the dysfunction, since even the privilege of a Heideggerian depiction of death is refused in favor of a presumably open-ended series of possible endings, a signifying chain of interminable rhetorical substitutions for a nothingness. It is hard to think of an ending that more dramatically trashes the idea of meaning in an ending.

The breakdowns in meaning signaled by the deaths of Daniel's parents and sister recur in other ellipses and in figuration, which misrepresent both his own motives and the sources he relies on. For example, there is the "shameful" letter Daniel wrote to Robert Lewin but suppressed (170). Its contents are wholly suppressed. It may be conjectured from Lewin's reply that Daniel feared Artie Sternlicht might seek to persuade Susan to turn over to him her half of the trust fund; such a reaction would be consistent with Daniel's ambivalence toward his sister's radical activism. Thus Daniel acquiesces in the omission of a letter that might disclose his self-interest. The resulting ellipsis creates a void that undermines the integrity of his narration, since it permits these mutually exclusive interpretations: that Daniel is concerned for Susan or for himself. The effect of ellipses is to create an undecidability in Daniel's narrative motivation similar to those inadvertently disclosed by the disingenuous Blue of *Welcome to Hard Times* and Billy Bathgate of the "Garden of Adding."[16]

The narrating Daniel commits a second guilty act of suppression, which further calls in question the decidability of his motivation, in an editorial ellipsis, conspicuously misplaced, from the Constitution's definition of treason:

> Treason was defined as an action rather than thought or speech. "Treason again[st] the U. S. shall consist only in levying war against them, or in adhering to their Enemies, giving them Aid and Comfort. . . . No [P]erson shall be convicted of [T]reason unless on the [T]estimony of two [W]itnesses to the same [o]vert Act, or on Confession in Open Court." This definition, by members of the constitutional convention, intended that T. could not be otherwise defined short of constitutional amendment. (183)

The letters bracketed above make Daniel's transcription conform to the original. Daniel's errors in spelling and capitalization may betoken haste, but the ellipsis is clearly inaccurate: there are no words in Article III, Section 3, between "Comfort" and "No." Daniel's misplaced ellipsis calls attention to itself; his more damning omission is the remainder of the section, which follows his excerpt: "The Congress shall have Power to declare the Punishment of Treason, but no Attainder of Treason shall work Corruption of Blood, or Forfeiture except during the Life of the Person attainted." Daniel's true, guilty ellipsis conceals that section of the Constitution which prohibits forfeiture by heirs, a feature that he himself noted, earlier, as a source of abuse under English law. Of course, Daniel owes his present freedom (to pursue graduate studies, for example, or to travel to California) to the existence of the Isaacson Trust Fund; therefore, he profits from the section of the Constitution he omits. As in the suppression of the "shameful" letter to Lewin, what Daniel leaves out of his text might have called it into question.

Of course, undecidability in motivation extends to all characters, not just to Daniel. Daniel's analyses of the FBI's arrest of his parents, of the trial, and of the execution indicate that mainstream America, too, is hopelessly mired in the contradictions of patriotism. His analyses of Susan's activism, the Lewins' liberalism, and Artie Sternlicht's radicalism depict the contradictions of the political left. Only his own contradictions, the aporia of writing, remain hidden from him.

For example, Daniel does not see that his omissions from the Old Testament Book of Daniel create a radical reinterpretation of it. Of the biblical Daniel's dream, Daniel asserts: "One night he suffers his own dream, a weird and awesome vision of composite beasts and seas and heavens and fire and storms and an Ancient on a throne, and ironically he doesn't know what it means: 'I, Daniel, was grieved in my spirit in the midst of my body, and the vision of my head troubled me. . . . My cogitations much troubled me: but I kept the matter in my heart'" (22).

Daniel quotes from the Book of Daniel 7:15 and 7:28 and thus omits the entire explanation of the meaning of the dream that is delivered to the prophet as it takes place. This misrepresentation is flagrant. Surely the biblical Daniel, confident in the *archē* or origin of his faith, "knows what it means" to a degree that the modern Daniel, anguished by the burden of narration, cannot acknowledge; ellipsis calls attention to Daniel's misinterpretation. Such blithe, outright distortion suggests that the process of selection inherent in narration may function only at the cost of misrepresentation. Daniel later cites the biblical text again and links his agony with that of his predecessor: "The Isaacson Foundation. IS IT SO TERRIBLE NOT TO KEEP THE MATTER IN MY HEART, TO GET THE MATTER OUT OF MY HEART, TO EMPTY MY HEART OF THE MATTER? WHAT IS THE MATTER WITH MY HEART?" (27). Daniel's design may be to borrow the prophet's prestige, but the capitalized sentences contrast sharply his passionate narration with his predecessor's calm resolve. Although their sense seems to solicit sympathy for Daniel's narrative plight, the opposite results; the sentences' elaborate artifice dilutes their ostensible outrage. As in other instances of "capitalized outrage," the added emphasis becomes self-canceling.

Even without the hyperbole of capitalization, the passage would show that even the most vehement statements of moral agony cannot escape troping: the first question's parallelism is rendered contradictory because of the ambiguity of whether its clauses are governed by the word "not." The first two clauses form epistrophe (repetition of the same word or phrase at the end of successive clauses): "Is it so terrible not to keep the matter in my heart, to get the matter out of my heart." This scheme is followed by an example of antimetabole (the repetition of words, in successive clauses, in reverse grammatical order): "to empty my heart of the matter? What is the matter with my heart?" The repetition emphasizes the pun on the word "matter" (both subject and problem). Thus Daniel's outrage over his narrative predicament—again associated with his inevitably compromised relation with the Isaacson Trust Fund—cannot find expression without a rhetoricity that dogs his attempt to escape it and without misrepresentation of the sources that are his models.

Daniel's figures, especially ellipses, disclose the undecidability of motivation and the distortions inherent in citation, but these impediments to representation arise, in turn, from the sequential, iterative nature of language, a constraint Daniel soon comes to despise. In a memorable passage precipitated by his recollection of a visit to his parents in jail, Daniel rails against the "monstrousness" of sequence. He seems to see that the mere fact of diachronic existence subverts his narrative attempt to fix a presence—truth, beauty, love—in language:

> What is most monstrous is sequence. When we are there, why do we withdraw only in order to return? Is there nothing good enough to transfix us? If she is truly worth fucking, why do I have to fuck her again? If the flower is beautiful why does my baby son not look at it forever? Paul plucks the flower and runs on, the flower dangling from his shoelace. Paul begins to hold, holds, ends hold of the flower against the sky, against his eye to the sky. I engorge with my mushroom head the mouth of the womb of Paul's mother. When we come; why do we not come forever? The monstrous reader who goes on from one word to the next. The monstrous writer who places one word after another. The monstrous musician. [262]

The temporal condition of reading and writing is here aligned with the intuition of the impossibility of finally fixing a present truth. Daniel seems to understand that the pathos of his visit to his mother loses all significance merely by virtue of its sequential place in narrative; it becomes just one more scene among many in a repetitive succession, none of which has the power to compel assent.

Of course, the import of Daniel's rage runs even deeper, for in the sequential nature of language, he also intuits the necessity for return, that "burdensome" Nietzschean thought that marked the suffering of Blue, the conclusions to *Big as Life,* and "The Songs of Billy Bathgate." To write, for Daniel, is to be condemned to return and to repeat; repetition permeates his narrative. Daniel's three endings undermine the nature of endings and suggest instead that history is an open-ended series of repeated events. Certainly repetition is the lesson of Daniel's analysis of his parents' crime; he comes to see it as one instance, among many, of civil disobedience. The execution is a minor manifestation of the tautology of "state sovereignty" in history. The New Left of the sixties, especially Artie Sternlicht, is a reminder of the "eternal return" of protest. Even the title of Sternlicht's mural acknowledges repetition: "EVERYTHING THAT CAME BEFORE IS ALL THE SAME" (151). (Of course, for Sternlicht the title voices his hope for a first, "genuine" revolution; but for the reader—who is mindful, with Daniel, of the sweep of history and the quixotic gestures of the New Left—the title reinforces the impression of the unavoidable repetition of history.) Susan's message to Daniel also finds redundancy in the political process: "THEY'RE STILL FUCKING US. She didn't mean Paul and Rochelle. That's what I would have meant. What she meant was first everyone else and now the Left. And if they can't make it with them who else is there? YOU GET THE PICTURE. GOODBYE DANIEL" (169).

To Daniel, the anonymous "they," linking both the establishment and the New Left, continually reinflicts suffering. Even the message itself is repeated. Susan first whispers it to Daniel after her suicide attempt (19); he later jots down the remark as a topic to be further explored (26); it reappears in a taunt to the reader delivered in a black dialect (33); and Daniel recalls the message when Sternlicht "gives him the picture" (the poster of their parents [169]). Repetition is the organizing device of the sinister poem that interrupts Daniel's narrative, equating the incantatory "om" of peace with the "ohm" of his parents' electrocution:

> om om om omm omm omm om om ommmmmm
> ohm ohmm ohm ohm ohm ohhmm ohm ohmmmmm
> what is it that you can't see but you can feel
> what is it that you can't taste and can't smell and can't touch but can feel
> ohm ohm ohm ohm ohm . . . [242]

The intrusion of this "poem" and others in Daniel's text functions in the same manner as the "songs" in "The Songs of Billy Bathgate," erasing the distinction between prose and poetry and emphasizing, instead, language as the repetition of the arbitrary. It is as if the text at any moment were capable of collapsing the momentous distinctions it seeks to sustain (innocent and guilty; om and ohm) into repeated nonsense sounds.

The menacing hegemony of repetition shadows Daniel's writing. Though his breaks in ordinary chronology may protest the "monstrousness of sequence," such protests only reveal repetition more clearly. For example, Daniel's rush to comfort Susan after her suicide attempt (13–25) is followed by his memory of wiping away a mote from her eye when as children they were led by Ascher to a political rally (27–33). The arrest of Paul and Rochelle Isaacson (124–43) is followed by Daniel's visit to Artie Sternlicht (145–55), who announces, in yippie fashion, the arrest of everyone on his block. Daniel's visit to his parents in jail (254–66) is followed by his own imprisonment after the antiwar demonstration at the Pentagon (267–74). So despite Daniel's efforts to escape diachrony, these and other juxtapositions make history appear redundant.

The fractured chronology also discloses the arbitrary character of reading. Action in the narrative present takes place between Memorial Day, 1967, and the following winter. Daniel interrupts this sequence to present flashbacks to his childhood, to his parents' arrest, trial, and execution. These flashbacks are themselves presented out of sequence, so that the reader must, as with Faulkner, reconstruct a chronology to identify characters and establish causality. (*The Book of Daniel* is the first of Doctorow's texts to employ this device; it recurs in more subtle forms in *Loon Lake, World's Fair,* and *Lives of the Poets.*) The result of this reconstruction is a disappointment, however: although Daniel seems scrupulous about dates and times, in the end his chronology is incoherent, mistaken.[17] Having troubled to reconstruct chronology, then, the credulous reader is gulled. (This is an "insight" that would occur anyway, only later, had the chronology been "true.") Some assumption as to sequence is necessary to inferences, to the act of reading, but at the same time, diachrony deludes.

The novel's chronology engenders this two-stage process of "blindness and insight." The reader must ignore narrative discrepancies and redundancies in order to get on with the task of reading; in this way the arbitrary character of reading may be suppressed, but only temporarily. Then again, the necessity for blindness has been apparent from the start, even in the novel's form, even in its title.

The novel's formal properties illustrate this two-stage process first in the title, *The Book of Daniel,* whose pun (made possible by the double genitive) broaches the question of autobiographical authorship at the outset: Is Daniel the author, the autonomous originator of his book? Or is the book—a function of language—the true creator of Daniel? Paul de Man describes the ruse of autobiographical writing:

"[T]he author declares himself to be the subject of his own understanding, but this merely makes explicit the wider claim to authorship that takes place whenever a text is stated to be *by* someone and assumed to be understandable to the extent that this is the case. Which amounts to saying that any book with a readable title page is, to some extent, autobiographical."[18]

Just as Billy Bathgate saw "the orphan's home" as the true subject of his song, so Daniel's writing begins, in its title, with equivocation as to his mastery of himself, his proprietorship of the text. Of course, this effect of the pun is sustained by its allusion to a biblical book that some consider apodictic; questions must now arise as to both texts' claims of truth. The modern Daniel's authorial autonomy may be subverted if his text is part of an "infinite reiteration." Of course, the title's pun and allusion center these doubts upon Daniel, thereby—though only momentarily—exempting both the biblical Daniel and Doctorow from their insinuation. Insight into the destabilization of the author Daniel requires temporary blindness to the operation of the same process in the conception of any other author, including the unknown writer of the biblical Book of Daniel or Doctorow.

This two-stage process is also elicited by other formal properties. For example, the novel's three epigraphs establish a homology among the Old Testament Daniel, Walt Whitman, and Allen Ginsberg: the passages concern state power and its enforcement of "correct" interpretation; however, the role of art in this predicament is neither benign nor enlightening. In the Old Testament text, the instruments of art (the sound of the cornet, flute, harp) collude with the regime in announcing the subjugation of Nebuchadnezzar's people to golden images (a coercion that the biblical Daniel, only by virtue of his faith, successfully resists). In Whitman's text, the strong music of poetry commemorates, neutrally, both the official victors and the defeated; it refuses to privilege either prevailing public belief or private martyrdom. In Ginsberg's text, the speaker has yielded so much to the state that he is left with only self-loathing, rhetorical questions, obscene curses. None of the passages imply that art can distinguish "true" interpretation from the presumed lies of the state. On the contrary, these sober quotes confess art's helplessness in the face of the day's dominant delusions. The fact that art is equally futile in Old Testament, canonical, and "noncanonical" literature shakes the legitimation of canons. It also discovers among the passages an "eternal reiteration of the same," hinting that new creative texts, like the one about to begin, may simply be redundant.

Of course, the hypothesis—of "something in common" among the three quotes—is itself an inference, derived from the assumption that an autonomous author selected the passages as prelude and heuristic of *The Book of Daniel*. The hypothesis of the dysfunction of art, therefore, was made possible only by a prior blindness to the question of the provenance of the quotations, which arises in the question of whether the modern Daniel or "Doctorow" adduced them and what relation they bear to the text that follows. The novel gives no help; therefore the epigraphs remain "inside and outside" the text, blurring the distinction between the orphaned Doctorow and Daniel.

But whoever cited the quotations used ellipsis in the excerpt from Allen Ginsberg. The complete passage reads as follows:

> America I've given you all and now I'm nothing.
> [America two dollars and twentyseven cents January 17, 1956.]
> I can't stand my own mind.
> America when will we end the human war?
> Go fuck yourself with your atomic bomb.

Reference to a specific date in the 1950s might have created new problems of chronology in the novel to come, which spans that decade, but because such problems would differ between Doctorow or Daniel, the question of authorship—here literally the question of selector—is raised again. Like most of "America," Ginsberg's second line is self-mocking: if the "all" of line 1 is, ironically, only $2.27, then the passage's already involuted patriotism is snarled again. Whether it was elided by Doctorow or Daniel, line 2 might have subverted with comedy the outrage against America. So this ellipsis foreshadows the ultimate undecidability of Daniel's savage indignation. In addition, the elided line might have tempered the depressing collective effect of the epigraphs, that art cannot demystify, with some modest expression of irresponsibility or play. This, of course, seems one of Daniel's attractive traits. So the ellipsis questions the validity of play before the text begins; it signals undecidability by alerting the reader to a possibility and its cancellation.

The titles of the novel's four books point to new signifiers, that are consistent with the tradition established in *Welcome to Hard Times* and *Big as Life*. Three titles are "proper nouns" that aspire to fix the diachronic time Daniel despises (Memorial day, Halloween, and Christmas); the fourth (Starfish) was originally such a word—it named the thirteenth sign of the Zodiac—until becoming "lost" over the course of history (266–67). The capacity of Starfish to undermine the other "proper noun" dates may already be apparent. That these signs function ironically in the plot is evident from the fact that Memorial Day is the occasion of Susan's suicide attempt, which was prompted in protest against the state. Halloween is the occasion on which the frightened children first return to their house, emptied after their parents' arrest; the skeletons they are given may foreshadow their parents' executions (194–95). Early in the novel, Christmas is ironized because it is celebrated in the wholly assimilated Lewin household and because it marks Daniel's bitter estrangement from Susan (90–95). Later, in the book that bears its name, Christmas is the holiday during which Daniel's uncomprehending talk with Mindish takes place at Disneyland. Starfish denotes Susan's suicidal silence, and the "lost sign" Starfish testifies to the futility of both Daniel's quest (a matter of signs) and Susan's nihilistic alternative (silence and death). So the four book titles in *The Book of Daniel* convey delayed warnings against all signification, just as the main title does.

Within each book, the text is further subdivided, at first by introductory words in boldface. The three books titled after holidays begin with additional temporal markers, connected syntactically to the text. Starfish begins differently, with the boldface sentence "Elected silence sing to me," a quotation from Gerard Manley Hopkins which is disconnected from the text and is surely allusive to Susan.[19] As with the epigraphs, the identity of the citer of this quotation is uncertain, so authorial undecidability spreads further into the text. Of course the voluble Daniel never elected silence; if he is the citer, the quotation is surely disingenuous. On the other hand, perhaps Daniel cites the line "in the voice of Susan" (as, arguably, he speaks earlier in an aggressively defiant black dialect [33]); if so, his parallel between his sister's alienated withdrawal and the tradition of Roman Catholic asceticism, the subject of the Hopkins poem, mocks Susan's Jewish heritage and suffering. So many articulations undo: this one converts Hopkins's hushed hope into a sarcastic statement of futility.

The main subdivisions within each book are the capitalized subtitles, "more or less certainly" the work of Daniel, although even here a residual ambiguity remains. Taken as Daniel's work, many of the ironic subtitles darken his self-mockery: "AN INTERESTING PHENOMENON (33), BINTEL BRIEF (76), SEVERAL EXPLANATIONS (81), DIDN'T MY LORD DELIVER DANIEL?—Paul Robeson" (143).[20] The relation between the subtitles (which only appear to divide the text coherently) and the text itself is never stable. One example (ALONE IN THE COLD WAR—with Fanny and Zooey [177]) indicts its maker on two counts. First, its implicit comparisons of Daniel/Zooey and Phyllis/Franny mock the integrity of the brother-sister alliance by construing it as a literary expression, one frequently accused of bathos. Second, the subtitle connects with an earlier allusion to Salinger, catching Daniel's writing in an intertextual web: "Let's see, what other David Copperfield kind of crap. So the Trustees of Ohio State were right in 1956 when they canned the English instructor for assigning *Catcher in the Rye* to his freshman class. They knew there was no qualitative difference between the kid who thinks its funny to fart in chapel, and Che Guevara. They knew then Holden Caulfield would found SDS" (108).

Daniel's literary-political analysis is arguably consistent with his left-wing upbringing; his self-mockery is also in character. But the important point is that, even while indicting his own narration, Daniel cannot escape literary language; contempt for "David Copperfield kind of crap" is Holden Caulfield's opening gesture in *Catcher in the Rye*. Daniel's political analysis is neutralized by the intertextual dimension that defines it ahead of time. In this way, Daniel and Susan become Holden and Phoebe, or Zooey and Franny, even as Daniel's narration struggles to define them as political victims rather than spiritual pilgrims.

The subversion of narration achieved by the subtitles is redoubled if, at second reading, they are taken as Doctorow's work, in which case they attack the text *The Book of Daniel* in the same way the epigraphs did. Internal evidence cannot resolve the ambiguity of authorship. Daniel never comments on the function of the subtitles, but even an explicit reaction could not remove a doubt raised by typography. The undecidable issue of authorship never disappears; it intrudes—through the title, epigraphs, book titles, subtitles, and allusions—into the heart of the novel. Like Blue's and Billy's, Daniel's book is an illusion conferred by intertextual stutter. These unrelenting hard times worsen in the novel's last words.

This novel's eternal return, or infinite reiteration of the same thing, occurs in its final passage, a last reminder of the intertextuality of *The Book of Daniel*, of its dependence on its Old Testament model. Daniel's previous allusions to his predecessor-text elide the theological "signified" of Hebrew prophecy, but in the quote that ends the novel, the issue of Daniel's misappropriation of the biblical Daniel's text arises again, in the seeming convergence of the modern and biblical Daniels. The convergence is "seeming," of course, because the question—"Who quoted the biblical text?"—remains. The ambiguity occurs because Daniel's text promised "THREE ENDINGS" (315), and three distinct, plausible, numbered endings do follow; each continues, albeit in contradictory ways, the narrative lines established previously. The quotation from the biblical Book of Daniel follows the third ending, however, and it is written in italics; moreover, it follows the passage "DANIEL'S BOOK," the mock-endorsement of his dissertation, which, ordinarily, would itself be considered separately, maybe as a fourth ending. So the excerpt from the Bible *is and is not part of the ending*. The passage does appear separable from the promised three endings, but the quotation *is* the ending in that it "ends" the novel, *The Book of Daniel*.

As noted earlier, Daniel's first three endings confess the inability of narrative to represent death truly, even to represent death in the Heideggerian theme of *Sein-zum-Tode*. In this way the ending of *The Book of Daniel* mocks endings and implies that an open-ended series of scenes could be attached to any novel that repeatedly misrepresents. The ambiguous or paradoxical ending also calls in question the hermeneutic efforts of establishing meaning through reflection on an ending as the repository of the author's final, achieved signification. On its last page, the novel implies that a passage from the biblical Daniel would be just as adequate, thereby embodying the "eternal return" and relinquishing the fiction that "Daniel's point of view" is the privileged destination of the reader's quest.

Because the provenance of the biblical passage in the novel cannot be decided, the issue of ultimate authorship—"Doctorow's point of view"—also remains unresolved. Of course, this undecidability was "always, already" in the text; according to secular scholars, the "original" prophet Daniel may be nonexistent, and the original book therefore fictive. Moreover, the original chronicler or "author" of Daniel is, for such scholars, also unknown. On the other hand, for Jews the original author's account invokes a sure theological presence in Daniel's prophecies, and with analogous conviction, Christians may believe the original author to be the Deity. Therefore the question of the authorship of the ending becomes a *mise-en-abyme*: the hermeneutic endeavor is estopped because any interpretation of the passage presupposes a certain authorship that will determine its content, even before its application to Doctorow's novel.

In fact the only indications that this passage belongs in the novel at all—to be attributed perhaps to Daniel, perhaps to Doctorow,—are three final ellipses, the last suppressions. The novel's conflicted residue prompts this speculation: maybe the existence of an author is inferable only by an absence in a text; in other words, the author becomes the last of the many illusory signifieds of ellipses. The excerpt is from Daniel 12:1-4, 9, and the two ellipses included are innocuous. However, they divert attention from an egregious omission, not marked at all, which is indicated here in square brackets: "And many of them that sleep in the dust of the earth shall awake, [some to everlasting life] some to everlasting contempt" (319).

The anonymous quoter suppresses the most famous passage in Daniel, unique in the Old Testament and traditionally valorized by Christian interpreters. At a stroke, through an unmarked ellipsis, the Bible is reinterpreted and the afterlife—some respite from the eternal reiteration of the same?—is denied. This excision again exemplifies the interpretive implications of the selectivity necessary to writing and language. The modern Daniel's apocalyptic jeremiad against contemporary America cannot result in unequivocal interpretation. In fact, the opposite is true; all of Daniel's efforts to establish intellectual dominion over his text and those of others, known or unknown, succeed only in calling attention to their failure, their suppressions, their elisions. In this context, the very last line of the quotation may crystallize this irrevocably double gesture of all language, prophecy included: "Go thy way Daniel: for the words are closed up and sealed till the time of the end" (319). Language and prophecy remain "closed up and sealed" in the sense that their efficacy—their ability to represent or to name truths—remains impossible to assess "till the time of the end," or as long as time, sequence, and selection govern discourse.

This chapter does not end with the ending. Tracing Daniel's tropes, especially ellipses, brings the reader at every turn to the dysfunction of the text of *The Book of Daniel*. Whether as an event "left to the imagination" or as a sign of guilty excision, ellipsis testifies to the inherent selectivity of language and promises the existence of more "outside itself"; but on closer inspection, the authenticity of that "more" is undermined. Daniel seems to acknowledge this fact in his paean to "the master-subversive Poe, who wore a hole into the parchment and let the darkness pour through" (193). Daniel's figure implies that the subversion wrought by the author of "The Purloined Letter" exposed flaws in the Constitution, perhaps in its confident assertion of inalienable rights or natural laws. But the ellipses in *The Book of Daniel* suggest that such erosion may be already inherent in any text, not simply in the "dark" works of Poe. Despite Daniel's passion for the truth, his ellipses, which persist even in the open-ended mock conclusion, mark a narration conceived as only the oscillation of inclusion and omission, sound and silence, presence and absence.

CHAPTER 5

Illusions of Demystification in *Ragtime*

Ragtime recounts and intertwines three main stories: of an upper middle-class family identified only as Father, Mother, Mother's Younger Brother, and the little boy; of Tateh, a Jewish Latvian immigrant; and of Coalhouse Walker, a black pianist. The unnamed family is outwardly happy and prosperous, but over the course of the novel the three adults become estranged. Tateh begins as an impoverished socialist but becomes an entrepreneur and successful film-maker. Coalhouse Walker is humiliated by Irish firemen; when his fiance dies as an indirect result of Walker's search for justice, he and a few confederates avenge themselves in acts of violence that eventually lead to his death. In addition to these three connected plots, the novel contains a number of characters and incidents from the years 1906 to 1914, the chief temporal setting.

Ragtime is the first of a series of works in which Doctorow experiments with narration; more specifically, in this novel, *Loon Lake, Lives of the Poets,* and *World's Fair,* the principal narrator cannot finally be determined, either as "omniscient" or as an identifiable character. By detaching discourse from any ultimately determinable source, this series of experiments may attest to the severity of previously explored narrative predicaments; it shows in new ways the delusion of the self as the autonomous manipulator of language; it shows the writer orphaned by writing. At the same time, these narrational innovations explore alternatives to the specter of eternal return. Of course, from the existence of experiment, no sure motive and no sure author can be deduced; indeed such an impossibility becomes a subject of these later works, perhaps because *Ragtime*'s experimental quest for alternatives is in the end disappointed.

The undecidability of the narrator of *Ragtime* is the result of the generic names assigned to the primary family: Father, Mother, Mother's Younger Brother, and the little boy. The first three names appear to imply that the narrator is the little boy, the only child in the family. However, throughout the novel the little boy is referred to in the third, not the first person, as though he is not the narrator. The anonymous narrative voice of *Ragtime* appears to be the voice of an American writing in about the year 1975,[1] a person familiar with American cultural history and one who is given to both irony and rhetorical flourish.[2] With one exception, this narrative voice refers to itself as the editorial "we" when generalizing about history ("This was the time in our history"). The exception to this practice occurs near the end of the novel, when Father's death at sea, in the sinking of the *Lusitania,* is recounted: "Poor father, I see his final exploration. He arrives at the new place, his hair risen in astonishment, his mouth and eyes dumb. His toe scuffs a soft storm of sand, he kneels and his arms spread in pantomimic celebration, the immigrant, as in every moment of his life, arriving eternally on the shore of his Self" (368).

Some critics conclude, on the basis of this passage, that the narrator is the little boy grown up.[3] This inference can be supported by other internal evidence; for example, the narrator's knowledge of a visit from Houdini comes from "the family archives" (366). The full implications of this inference will be analyzed later; for now it is important to emphasize that the identification remains only inference: nowhere is the "I" explicitly identified as the little boy. Because the reader acquiesces to the convention of an anonymous narrator telling a story about characters known as Father, Mother, Mother's Younger Brother, and the little boy, the introduction of "I" instead of "we" does not remove the mystery. As other critics have maintained, the exceptional use of "I" can still refer to an anonymous narrator who names only an object of his narrative, not necessarily a relative.[4]

The ambiguity does not end there, for a third possibility is that the narrator is the little girl, Tateh's daughter Sha. Since the Yiddish words for father and mother are Tateh and Mameh, she occupies a position in the narrative equivalent to that of the little boy. If Sha is the narrator, then the scene in which she and Jung mutually experience a moment of recognition or telepathy (43) makes more comprehensible the narrator's otherwise inexplicable condemnation of Freud (39). Also, if Sha is the narrator, then the vivid detail in her recollection of a chance meeting with the little boy (104) becomes more comprehensible. There is yet a fourth possibility, that the editorial "we" refers to both Sha and the little boy speaking together. At the end of the novel, in Atlantic City, the two children are depicted as ideal, telepathic playmates, in the spirit of Goethe's "elective affinities" or Shelley's complementary lovers.[5] Although this possibility cannot be dismissed, it obviously creates new problems in examining the exceptional use of "I."

Geoffrey Galt Harpham captures the radical quality of Doctorow's experiment when he refers to "the unplaceability of [the novel's] narrative voice."[6] In fact, the narrational uncertainty is an enigma that forces the reader to concentrate on the issue of pronoun references. The identity of the narrator can be decided only by the conferral of equivocal referents to the pronouns "I" and "we," linguistic shifters without inherent meaning. Four different interpretations of the novel can flow from the four different identifications of the narrator; at the same time, each ends in contradiction, for to adopt one is to exclude others equally plausible: male pronouns exclude the female; singular pronouns exclude the plural; the three specific attributions (the boy, the girl, both) exclude the anonymous narrator; and vice versa in each case. This wholesale indeterminacy, which mandates error in interpretation, forces the reader to entertain the possibility that the whole concept of a narrator may be only the fabrication of novels.

In order to read the novel, however, ultimate uncertainty cannot be tolerated; some attribution of a source to the words must be made. One act of naming that respects the enigma is to consider the narrator "double," that is, *simultaneously* two different entities, a specific attribution and a separate, anonymous voice. In fact, such a practice could find some support in the novel's many images of duplication, especially in this description of the little boy's gazing at himself in the mirror: "He would gaze at himself until there were two selves facing one another, neither of which could claim to be the real one" (134). If no determinable source for this sentence (or for others in *Ragtime*) can be settled upon, then it embodies the very doubleness it describes. It suggests that an integral Cartesian self is not the originator of discourse but that, instead, a story can be told by *two equally unreal entities*. In this way, the novel's two unreal sources seem to demystify the illusion of a single consciousness as narrator.

Nevertheless, the demystification is only *seeming*, since in any practical reading it is next to impossible to posit unreal, plural sources. In the next few paragraphs, the awkward "narrator(s)" and "they" are used to refer to the narrative voice. (It is understood that this procedure is already in error. In this state of indeterminacy, to name at all is already to err; any "insight" afforded by the problem of the novel's narrator(s) is made possible, after all, only by a prior blindness.) The reader is falsely demystified in the attempt to interpret characters as well as narrator(s), but that delusion is anticipated in the narrator(s). For example, the very first pages of the novel try to represent the ragtime era: "Everyone wore white in summer. Tennis racquets were hefty and the racquet faces elliptical. There was a lot of sexual fainting. There were no Negroes. There were no immigrants" (4).

After one page of further description, centering on the murder of Stanford White by Harry K. Thaw, the narrator(s) write: "Evelyn fainted. She had been a well-known artist's model at the age of fifteen. Her underclothes were white. Her husband habitually whipped her. She happened once to meet Emma Goldman, the revolutionary. Goldman lashed her with her tongue. Apparently there *were* Negroes. There *were* immigrants" (5).

The narrator(s) now speak from the vantage point of a completed narration, from knowledge supposedly derived from the tale, because they refer to the meeting between Evelyn and Emma, which has not yet been narrated. At the same time, the futility of their own "learning process" is obvious in the irony and self-mockery that accompanies their supposed demystification. Paul de Man's two-stage process is evident here: first, the reader believes in a demystification; next, that demystification is perceived as only a construct. What will be the value of narrating (or reading) *Ragtime* if the illusions it depicts can be destroyed only by new illusions?

In fact the narrator(s)—whether anonymous or specific—never learn; illusions persist until the end. Consider first the case of the anonymous narrator, whose continuing blindness is brought home to the reader on the last page, in the description of the origin and nature of Tateh's new films. Tateh gets his idea for the films one day while watching the three children (his daughter, his stepson, and Coalhouse Walker III) playing together in his California backyard. The narrator(s) endorse the films' sentimental depiction of a "society of ragamuffins, like all of us, a gang, getting into trouble and getting out again." (369). Of course, the "vision" of these new films is a gross misrepresentation of the bulk of the action of *Ragtime,* which tells of violent, incurable racial and ethnic conflict, but the narrator(s) identify themselves with the gang of ragamuffins, thereby accepting Tateh's Pollyannaish vision and revealing a blindness to the events of their own completed narration.

Now suppose the narrators are identified specifically, that is, as the boy, the girl, or both. In this alternative, either or both specific narrators, in their California backyard, serve as the very model for the cinematic misrepresentation that Tateh, in ignorance, perpetuates. There is no retrospective denunciation of this irony. If error is generated and perpetuated in this way, then narrating is misrepresenting, learning is illusory, and the circularity of error is inescapable.

Illusory demystifications also afflict the major characters in the three principal plots. Within the New Rochelle family, Father is at first depicted as the embodiment of the unexamined pieties of his day, benign capitalism and patriotism, which—as we seem to learn—mask exploitation, racism, and sexism. He is a manufacturer of the signifier of these illusions, the American flag, which draws credulous immigrants in ships to New York Harbor (16). Over the course of the novel, Father undergoes two seeming transformations. The first occurs during his trip to the Pole with Peary, when his adultery with an Esquimo woman appears to teach him a new knowledge of female sexuality, but despite this knowledge, he quickly becomes emotionally and sexually estranged from Mother. A second false lesson grows out of his contact with Coalhouse Walker, which seems to teach him American racism, but despite this knowledge, Father commits himself even more faithfully to the patriotic dimension of his business; eventually his firm supplies the government with advanced munitions. In both cases Father's supposed demystification is only apparent; he remains in thrall to the false values symbolized by the now-discredited flag he manufactures.

Mother also undergoes a seeming demystification. After she is forced to assist in the management of Father's flag-making company, Mother no longer holds the world of business in awe. As critics have noted, Mother seems to become, simply through practical experience, a working example of the abstract doctrines of women's liberation espoused by Emma Goldman,[7] but this supposed learning process does not lead to her independence and autonomy. Instead, Mother's liberation from Father's sexism is finally accomplished through her enchantment with another man, another manufacturer of (and believer in) illusions, Tateh. Tateh's new false identity, as Baron Ashkenazy, adds to the sense in which she is again seduced as soon as she flees from Father's demystified values. It is as if one set of illusions can be exposed only when they are exchanged for the new.

Such empty learning is obvious in Mother's Younger Brother, whose life first has meaning for him when he is dazzled by the glitz of Evelyn Nesbit. The memorable scene in which Mother's Younger Brother observes her from a closet (62–71) recalls the story of the intrusion of Actaeon into the bath of Diana, an allusion suggested by other details as well. For this intrusion, Actaeon is punished by being transformed into a stag that is later hounded to death by his own dogs; like him, Mother's Younger Brother becomes a kind of prey, possessed by self-destructive delusions.[8] First the spell of Evelyn herself victimizes him, but he recovers from this mystification with the aid of a new belief system, Emma Goldman's anarchism, which propels him into the causes of Coalhouse Walker and Emiliano Zapata. Mother's Younger Brother believes that in adopting Goldman's anarchism he has demystified the American political system. But the self-contradiction in anarchism is made clear by Goldman's highly organized, very unanarchic way of life: a small but telling example is her habit of having a change of clothes and a book ready in case of imprisonment on short notice. A *purely* "anarchic way of life" may not be possible. In order to help Coalhouse Walker, Mother's Younger Brother and Walker's anarchic confederates must be highly disciplined. As a munitions expert, Mother's Younger Brother has sophisticated technical skills; moreover, this intellectual prowess appears in blueprints later put to use in maintaining American state power—the opposite of anarchy. In any case, Mother's Younger Brother's false belief in his demystification of politics becomes clear in the suicidal final stages of his career when he loses his hearing just before dying in Zapata's cause.

Insofar as the boy may be considered solely as a character, his education follows a familiar literary path of imaginative and sexual awakening which holds forth the prospect of exchanging innocence for reliable knowledge. From his beginnings in a nearly solipsistic absorption in his own small world, the boy becomes aware of the world through examining its detritus—the oil-stained letter from Father, the silhouettes of Evelyn Nesbit discarded by his despondent uncle. He passes through moments of usual childhood belief in the omnipotence of thought. He becomes aware of his mother's sexuality. By the end of the novel, the boy experiences a relationship of ideal intersubjectivity with Tateh's daughter Sha. So outlined, the boy's maturation is an apparent demystification, a movement from innocent illusions, through engagement with the world, to love, and yet this demystification vanishes whenever the reader recalls the possibility that the boy alone narrates the events. When this thought obtrudes, a whole series of new considerations rapidly destroys confidence in his learning. As a sixty-year-old cultural historian, the grown boy endows himself, in retrospect, with preternatural powers concerning the assassination of Archduke Franz Ferdinand (11). He reconstructs his parents' sexual relations with detail bordering on the obsessive or voyeuristic (13, 125, 241–42, 248–49, 289–91); he blandly narrates Tateh's erotic attraction to his mother while his Father sleeps (307). On other occasions he is ironic; by kidnapping young men, he writes, Harry K. Thaw was "beginning to work out his problems" (226). He inserts dogmatic opinions about cultural history (39), makes generalizations about history without supplying evidence (175), and concludes by imagining himself as part of a happy "society of ragamuffins" (369). In short, study of the boy as narrator suggests that he has shed the illusions of youth only to acquire new ones in maturity.[9]

If the experiences of the New Rochelle family suggest deceit in the idea of learning, they are no more its victims than are Tateh or Coalhouse Walker. Some of the illusions have already been noted which change Tateh from a starving Jewish socialist—one who adheres strictly to Hebraic codes governing adultery—into a pseudonymous, seducing director of films that misrepresent his country and his past. Although Tateh sees his progress as a movement away from the mystifications of politics and class conflict, the reader sees that he gains success only by renouncing his heritage and accepting a vision of America that contradicts his own suffering. Tateh does not regress from an earlier, authentic perception to later illusion; on the contrary, nothing in the novel suggests that his treatment of Mameh, his denunciation of Evelyn Nesbit, his flight from the strike of Lawrence, or his work on flip-books represents either progress or regress. Indeed, critics believe that these episodes, too, can be interpreted as symptoms of blindness in Tateh.[10] Thus his life may be regarded as a series of false demystifications, the shift from one illusion to another.

Of all of the major characters, only Coalhouse Walker seems a probable candidate to embody an authentic demystification. The music he plays gives the novel its presiding metaphor and principle of organization; it recalls the nonverbal alternatives to delusion tested in Red Bloom's jazz and Billy Bathgate's songs. Walker's belated courtship of Sarah seems a direct expression of human dignity. His revolt against racial humiliation appears to be designed to demystify, to expose contradictions in the heart of the political and economic systems. His insistence on the particular—his car and Willie Conklin—seems to give the lie to other characters' absorption in theory and fantasy. As long as readers concentrate on the Coalhouse plot by itself, the novel provides a seeming anchor by which to judge the circularity of its other characters' behavior: whatever the excesses of his revolt, it is a response that at least confronts a world that other characters avoid or flee. The novel's movement toward climax proceeds inexorably. The precipitation of an ultimate disclosure is promised in the still tableau of Coalhouse bending over the plunger wired to blow up the Morgan Library, to explode the decadent repository of Western metaphysics. The considerable intellectual recourses of the novel—its critiques of enlightenment, of capitalism, of the melting pot, of America itself—are evidently at stake in the moment of Coalhouse's silent surrender. If the lives of other characters remain mystified, then this moment may bring truth. Such is the expectation wrought.

The story of Walker is drained of this potential for signification, however, the moment the reader sees it intertextually, as the adaptation of Heinrich von Kleist's "Michael Kohlhaas" (1808). Coalhouse now appears not a representation of an authentic mode of existence but of only another representation. As a sign his putative referent—racial or human justice, the dignity of man—is replaced by another sign, Kleist's Michael Kohlhaas. Likewise Sarah now recalls Kohlhaas's wife Lisbeth, Booker T. Washington, Luther, Conklin, Junker von Tronka. Since Kleist's story, in turn, is based on a previous text (a medieval chronicle of incidents in history befalling one Hans Kohlhasen), there is now the prospect of even further regress. As recent studies suggest, interpreting Kleist is no simple matter.[11] The famous "deadpan" narrator of "Michael Kohlhaas" provides a foretaste of this difficulty in his initial remark that Michael Kohlhaas was "one of the most upright and at the same time one of the most terrible men of his day."[12] If Coalhouse is derived from a Michael Kohlhaas who is undecidable from the outset, then contemporary interpretation will only commit once more, in modern trappings, the necessary error of interpretation exposed in the execution of Kohlhaas. Instead of escaping the circularity afflicting other characters' phony learning, Coalhouse Walker, too, becomes a manifestation of Nietzsche's "eternal reiteration of the same thing."

Once this moment of intertextuality occurs, the problem of narration becomes a new morass. Whether Coalhouse's story is being told by an anonymous or nonanonymous narrator, the narration now loses its once-supposed anchor in the real. If the story of Coalhouse/Kohlhaas is told by the boy or the girl grown old, or both, the novel's credibility collapses: earlier suspicions of their illusions are confirmed; they become palpable fiction writers. Even if the Coalhouse/Kohlhaas story is told by an anonymous narrator, its meaning in *Ragtime* now depends on a prior interpretation of Kleist's story; but that story's narrator, like its critical history, warns that secure interpretation may be impossible. Once again, the very moment that insight into *Ragtime* appears to be approachable, blindness is evident. The reader sees in fleeting moments of demystification only phantasm.

Inducing this momentary illusion of learning is one of the exertions of art. In *Ragtime* the perils of that effort are dramatized in Houdini, who has been analyzed as a figure for the artist.[13] Houdini follows in the tradition of the artist-as-performer, which was begun with the image of the clown in "The Songs of Billy Bathgate." In addition, he continues the depiction of the artist as struggling with the representation of death in ways observable in Blue and Daniel. Like his predecessors, he strives to demystify but only spellbinds and, in so doing, shows the limitations of art in the crucial test case of representation, death.

Even before the death of his mother, Houdini's feats are geared to defy mortality. After escaping from sealed milk cans and chains, Houdini asks to be buried alive but finds he cannot escape. Nevertheless he continues to be fascinated by events that seem to defy death; he pays homage to a sandhog who somehow survived an explosion during the construction of a tunnel under the East River. After the death of his mother, Houdini's acts become frightening as he risks death with even greater intensity. Houdini's art raises the Heideggerian issue of the fallacy in representations of death. In this way, Houdini also resembles Blue: death is the end point and origin of their quests. And like Daniel, Houdini feels driven to display his artistry in the composition of a death scene. In retrospect these representational efforts were doomed from the outset. In Houdini's case, it becomes obvious that death cannot be truly represented by artifice (if only because no successful performance could be iterable). Thus, even in his harrowing performances, Houdini can only repeat an artifice that can never "more closely approximate."

This futility also haunts other representations. After his mother dies, Houdini arranges framed photographs of his mother in his New York brownstone "to suggest her continuing presence" (228). He puts a picture of his mother on the very chair in which she posed for it. He hangs a picture of her entering the house inside his door. This futility is not confined to visual representations. A delusion of presence is induced by the music-box songs his mother once loved and "the redolence of her wardrobe" (228). These are pathetic models of misrepresentation.

In this delusion Houdini nevertheless tries both to perfect his own art and to find a "genuine medium" to make the absent present. Even as he persists in this delusion, he works to demystify the artifice of others, his colleagues or competitors in the art of deathly illusionism. Desperate to make contact with his deceased mother, Houdini hires a detective agency to investigate the claims of spiritual mediums; he casts about for some scientific means of reaching his mother. Like his performances, these efforts at enlightenment cannot succeed, because they assume that the absent can be represented. For the reader of Houdini (as of Blue and Daniel), death uncovers the dysfunction of language.

Whatever its dysfunction, there seems to be no alternative to the artifice, whether the illusions of Houdini or such fiction as *Ragtime*, to which they allude. This sense of the absolute necessity for illusion-making and illusion-believing is conveyed by the narrator's comment that today "nearly fifty years since [Houdini's] death, the audience for escapes is even larger" (8). In this famous aside the narrator makes self-canceling statements about illusions; audiences, like readers, are gullible, but the narrator—the fiction-writer of the Coalhouse/Kohlhaas story, for example—is busy writing the "escape." What Miller calls "varnishing"—the authorial assertion of a center that reveals, instead, its own incipient collapse—is once again disclosed. Like Houdini, the narrator demonstrates that both writer and reader, performer and audience, are escape artists. It is as if the attempt to represent must necessarily delude with the false promise of escape, in the face of a necessity.

If escape from delusion is impossible, the events of human history become repetitions, duplications of attempted escapes and failures. This is, again, the "burdensome thought" of Nietzsche's eternal return, which haunted Doctorow's earlier work. In *Ragtime* the eternal return is "the duplicable event," a phrase that links reiteration in history with narration.

The phrase first appears in an account of the ragtime era: "All across the continent merchants pressed the large round keys of their registers. The value of the duplicable event was everywhere perceived. Every town had its ice-cream soda fountain of Belgian marble. Painless Parker the Dentist everywhere offered to remove your toothache. At Highland Park, Michigan, the first Model T automobile built on a moving assembly line lurched down a ramp and came to rest in the grass under a clear sky" (153–54).

The duplicable event is here associated with a seemingly inexorable loss of individuation—a kind of cultural entropy of the sort depicted in the novels of Thomas Pynchon. The imminent homogenization of America will be accompanied by an equivalence of people and of things mandated by Henry Ford's application of the principle to industry: "not only that the parts of the finished product be interchangeable, but that the men who build the products be themselves interchangeable parts" (155). Both passages suggest that behind the apparent diversity of men, of machines, and of environment lie only the monotonous repetitions of history.

Of course, repetition is a structural principle of the plot. Harry K. Thaw has two trials. Evelyn Nesbit bathes Tateh's daughter, Sha; then Emma Goldman, in turn, ministers to Evelyn's body. Theodore Dreiser repeatedly tries to find the perfect alignment in his room. Admiral Peary searches for the precise position of the North Pole. To win back Sarah, Coalhouse repeats his Sunday visits. Tateh cries twice for his daughter and makes numerous silhouettes of Evelyn Nesbit. J. P. Morgan finds evidence of the same doctrine of reincarnation in Rosicrucianism, in Giordano Bruno, in the Hermetica. Scott Joplin rags are heard in New Rochelle and Atlantic City. The first explosion at a fire station is followed by a second. These explosions are framed by the tunnel blast that nearly kills a sandhog and by Younger Brother's detonations in Mexico. Booker T. Washington's mediation is followed by Father's. Coalhouse Walker's ruined Model-T is replaced by a rebuilt one. Tateh's films are made in series, as sequels. This list only begins to suggests the extent of repetition in the novel. The futility and monotony of such repetition suggest that history signifies nothing at all.

This suggestion is supported by the novel's many scenes of imprisonment and false liberation. Houdini's numerous escape attempts result only in the persistence of his delusion that human effort may produce some correct understanding of death. The futility of Houdini's imprisonments and escapes is repeated in the imprisonment and eventual release of Harry K. Thaw, events that purport to distinguish madness from sanity but obviously do not. Like the incarceration of Susan in *The Book of Daniel,* the institutional distinction between madness and sanity in *Ragtime* is shown to be fictional. The saddest example of phony freedom is the experience of immigrants, who are first "arranged on benches in waiting pens" (17) after landing in New York. The presumed further liberation of the immigrant can be tracked in Tateh; the novel's imagery suggests that Tateh's life in New York is also a kind of prison from which he makes several escapes—first to Lawrence, Massachusetts, then to Philadelphia, Atlantic City, and California.[14] However, each of his attempts at human or spiritual liberation lands him in a new mirage world: the "Hollywood ending" of *Ragtime* repeats the Disneyland climax of *The Book of Daniel* and anticipates the dream pavilions of *World's Fair.* In *Ragtime* the duplicable event means the movement from one imprisoning illusion to another. Each promise of demystification turns out to be false, a model of misrepresentation.

A similar effect is created by the many empty coincidences in the novel. Readers agree that the novel teems with them. For example, Tateh got his start on a career in film-making by designing flip-books for the Franklin Novelty Company in Philadelphia. The same company manufactured a cheap pamphlet that taught Henry Ford the doctrine of reincarnation. Stanford White planned the home of Mrs. Stuyvestant Fish, who hired Houdini to entertain guests at her party; White's assistant, Charles McKim, designed the Morgan Library. In Egypt, J. P. Morgan sees the same New York Giants baseball team that Father took the little boy to see at the home ballpark. Such intersections of independent plot lines seem portentous, but in the end they reveal nothing. Equally teasing are the accounts of Freud's visit to America to lecture at Clark University in Worcester, Massachusetts, and of Theodore Dreiser's artistic depression following the publication of *Sister Carrie*. Such coincidences seem to invite interpretation; indeed, critical discourse about the novel, including the one now in progress, has been drawn to them as loci of meaning, but Arthur Saltzman aptly summarizes the mystifying effect of this lure: "If we are gratified by the connections our narrator makes for us . . . we are still disheartened by how seemingly fruitless those connections are."[15] By themselves, coincidences express nothing other than their existence; the impulse to make them represent creates new error.

This de Manian delusion in reading is underscored by a second reference to the duplicable event, one that further links the repetitions and coincidences of history to narration. It occurs as the boy perceives the "instability of both things and people" (133). In a kind of radical solipsism, he acknowledges no permanent reality separate from his own perception. The movies and his grandfather's stories are images of an importance equal to his hairbrush or his window, which seem to conform to his will. He listens to the Victrola and plays "the same record over and over, whatever it happened to be, as if to test the endurance of a duplicated event" (133). In this passage the boy—one of the putative narrators—occupies himself in a *double* repetition: the recorded song is of course a "duplication," and the repeated playing duplicates it. Whatever the narrator's identity, narration and reading may resemble the repeated playing of the recorded song; both are double duplications that have the effect of testing art's "endurance." The open-ended "playing" of the song is like the potentially infinite, repetitive sequence of reading and interpretation. Only in this logical necessity can it be said that the duplicated event of art endures.

The novel seems to endorse the boy's version of the eternal return, as meaningless redundancy, especially when that idea is contrasted with more obviously mystified versions, such as J. P. Morgan's belief in reincarnation. According to Morgan's doctrine, divinely inspired leaders reappear throughout history to lead people and to inaugurate new epochs. In a secret room in his Library, Morgan propounds this theory to Henry Ford. He finds evidence for it in Rosicrucianism, Giordano Bruno, and the Hermetica. The first such leaders, Morgan confides, were the Egyptian pharaohs. In the belief that he and Ford are modern avatars of those demigods, Morgan invites the industrialist to accompany him on a trip to the Pyramids. In the end, Ford subscribes to the theory, with some ironic detachment; and though Morgan travels to Egypt alone, the two become sole members of "The Pyramid."

In this famous fictional meeting, Morgan and Ford accept a theory of history as the eternal return which resembles the Nietzschean doctrines of the *Übermensch* and cyclical history set forth in *Thus Spake Zarathustra*. That Morgan sees himself as an *Übermensch* is suggested by echoes of the Nietzschean hero: "He knew as no one else the cold and barren reaches of unlimited success. The ordinary operations of his intelligence and instinct over the past fifty years had made him preeminent in the affairs of nations and he thought this said little for mankind. . . . I have no peers, Morgan said. . . . It seemed an indisputable truth. Somehow he had catapulted himself beyond the world's value system" (159, 161).

Morgan's philosophy of the eternal return is formidable indeed. Like Emma Goldman's anarchism, it has the potential—if endorsed by the novel—to justify such radical actions as the revolt of Coalhouse Walker or Mother's Younger Brother's terrorism. In addition, Morgan's version of the *Übermensch* could provide intellectual sanction for Harry K. Thaw's murder of Stanford White or for Tateh's abandonment of his earlier Hebraic code. In short, Morgan's Nietzscheanism proposes a transvaluation of values by which any individual action could be justified. With so much at stake for interpretation, the novel's treatment of Morgan's theory must be carefully evaluated.

The contradiction in Morgan's "practical Nietzscheanism" is made apparent in his meeting with Ford and in his trip to Egypt. In the meeting, Morgan says he suspected Ford might be an embodiment of a divine mission when he noticed a resemblance between Ford's features and the mask on the sarcophagus of Seti the First. In other words, an underlying belief in representation is a condition of Morgan's Nietzscheanism: an *Übermensch* must be discernible. The shakiness of this assumption is evident enough in the resemblance Morgan claims to have found. Ford's deflating reply—that the doctrine of transmigration may be apprehended without the trappings of Morgan's intellectualism—further gives the lie to the existence of the necessary signs, from manuscripts, pamphlets, or physiognomy, that Morgan valorizes.

Morgan's historical Nietzscheanism is undermined in the laughable account of his trip to Egypt. There, he spends the night in the King's Chamber of the Great Pyramid, hoping to learn the disposition by Osiris of his ka, or soul, and his ba, or physical vitality. These lofty aspirations are brought up short when the experience yields only two results: he dreams of a former life as a peddler, and he is bitten by bedbugs. Confused, Morgan reasons as follows: "He decided one must in such circumstances make a distinction between false signs and true signs. The dream of the peddler in the bazaar was a false sign. The bedbugs were a false sign. A true sign would be the glorious sight of small red birds with human heads flying lazily in the chamber, lighting it with their own incandescence. These would be ba birds, which he had seen portrayed in Egyptian wall paintings. But as the night wore on, the ba birds failed to materialize" (359–60).

Morgan's pathetic distinction between true signs and false signs recalls Blue's wish, in *Welcome to Hard Times,* for the "good signs" of spring that keep life going, and as with Blue, the wish is circular. Notice that Morgan's desultory gropings for meaning are prompted by previous representations, the ba birds in the Egyptian wall paintings. Of course, the fallacy that human destiny in history is readable in resemblances and recurrent signs is fundamental to many doctrines other than Nietzsche's; it is evident in Calvinist "signs of election" or the historiography of Thomas Carlyle, for example. Thus in the character of Morgan, the novel exposes the impoverishment of this tradition, that an "eternal return" can be read in history.

By contrast, the little boy's version seems less mystified; he is content to register the empty repetitions of the world without conferring meaning on them. In this aloofness—a kind of refusal to read—the boy separates himself from all of the other characters, not simply Morgan, who cannot tolerate a condition of uninterpreted redundancy. The boy resists the hermeneutic need to assign a meaning to repetition, preferring instead to see himself and the universe as part of history's dumb metamorphosis: "It was evident to him that the world composed and recomposed itself constantly in an endless process of dissatisfaction . . . the boy's eyes saw only the tracks made by the skaters, traces quickly erased of moments past, journeys taken" (135).

This cold, ontologically neutral view of change is also expressed in the boy's fascination with the eternal return in baseball: "[Father] turned to his son. What is it you like about this game, he said. The boy did not remove his gaze from the diamond. The same thing happens over and over, he said. The pitcher throws the ball so as to fool the batter into thinking he can hit it. But sometimes the batter does hit it, the father said. Then the pitcher is the one who is fooled, the boy said" (266).

The boy's acceptance of deception and pure repetition seems to fit the plot of *Ragtime*. Moments of insight, supposed climaxes, and turning points are revealed, in retrospect, to be hollow: Evelyn Nesbit seems to galvanize the lives of Tateh and Mother's Younger Brother, then runs off with a dance-hall musician; Coalhouse Walker brings official New York to a crisis, then dies, his confederates and Mother's Younger Brother dispersed to other causes; the marriage of Mother and Father gradually deteriorates; the obsession behind Houdini's quest to pierce the veil of death recedes, and he is last seen repeating old escape tricks; the sensational murderer, Harry K. Thaw, returns to march in an Armistice Day parade. Far from ratifying the idea that history has a meaning, the inconclusive action of *Ragtime* makes time appear random and open-ended, in keeping with the tradition of *Big as Life* and Doctorow's other novels.

But this conclusion is also incorrect, confounding character-narrator and author. Recall that as character in his California backyard, the boy served as a model for Tateh's misrepresentation, and that as narrator, the boy never learned. So the false impression of insight must be amended again. The boy's view of time, history, and change is no loftier than that of the other characters; it is only another illusion that reading, afterwards, discovers.

Chapter 6

Loon Lake
The World as Fiction

The main character in *Loon Lake* is Joseph Korzeniowski, known until the very end of the novel only as Joe, Joe of Paterson, or Joe Paterson. Joe lives with his working-class family in Paterson, New Jersey, until the age of eighteen and then leaves home to seek his way in the world. After a brief stay in New York City, Joe joins a traveling carnival as a roustabout. In the fall, he leaves in pursuit of a beautiful woman, Clara Lukacs, whom he had seen naked in a private train. Joe's quest brings him to Loon Lake, a huge estate in the Adirondack Mountains owned by F. W. Bennett, a multimillionaire who made his fortune in the mining and automotive industries. Mauled by dogs as he enters the property, Joe comes to resent Bennett's privilege and arrogance.

Joe finds Clara at Loon Lake in the company of Warren Penfield, a poet who has been allowed to stay at the estate for the past seven years. Clara is the mistress of Bennett when his wife, Lucinda, a famous aviatrix, is away; she is protected by Tommy Crapo, the gangster-president of an industrial-services corporation retained by Bennett. Joe tells Bennett that he is not interested in working for him, but Bennett gives Joe his unlisted telephone number. When Lucinda returns, Joe enlists Warren's help in arranging for Clara's escape with him.

Joe and Clara finally settle in Jacksontown, Indiana. They live together as man and wife while Joe works on the assembly line at a Bennett Autobody factory. Joe befriends Red James, secretary of the local union. After secret union plans for a strike are discovered, Red and Joe are beaten up; Red dies. At first Joe suspects union men retaliated against Red in the belief he was a turncoat. Then, Joe is questioned by the chief of police; during the interrogation, he advances a different theory of the crime: that Red was murdered by Tommy Crapo's gangsters when they understood that, as a double agent, Red may have been more dangerous than helpful to them. Joe now lies to the chief of police; he claims to have been sent to Jacksontown by F. W. Bennett to check on the Crapo organization. He gives the chief Bennett's unlisted telephone number and says that Bennett himself will verify his story.

Joe is released. After Clara deserts him for Tommy Crapo, Joe leaves Jacksontown for California with Red's widow, Sandy. Joe reads in a newspaper that Warren Penfield and Lucinda Bennett have been presumed lost in the Pacific on the first leg of their attempted round-the-world flight. Joe and Sandy decide to marry, but soon Joe changes his mind. Leaving Sandy on a train, he returns to Loon Lake. First he resolves to kill Bennett, but then, abruptly, he changes his mind and dives into Loon Lake. We learn that he became the adopted son of Bennett, who died in 1967, leaving Joe to perpetuate his legacy.

In the reading of the novel that follows, *Loon Lake* is seen as continuing *Ragtime*'s intuition of universal inauthenticity in two key scenes: Joe's fabrication of a story to the police and his dive into Loon Lake. Both moments acknowledge the world as only fiction. For the bulk of the novel, the main characters, Joe and Penfield, resist such a thought, which seems mad, but in the end they accept it. They are thus—inevitably thus?—two more deluded questers who take their place in the series that began with Blue. *Loon Lake*'s eternal return is disclosed in its narration, including its synechdochal title and its ellipses; in the characters Penfield and Joe; and in its allusions to Conrad, Williams, and Thoreau.

Loon Lake is Doctorow's second experiment in unconventional narration. In *Ragtime,* the narrator(s) render the question of their final identification undecidable. In *Loon Lake,* the narration is similarly complex: first- and third-person accounts of the life of Joe alternate with third-person accounts of the life of Warren Penfield; both are interrupted by passages that resemble computer printouts and by dialogue between Penfield and Lucinda over the Pacific, which presumably could be narrated only by an "omniscient" narrator. However certain assumptions yield more readily than *Ragtime* does a first, plausible hypothesis about the narrator. At the outset, there is Joe, who, like Daniel, writes of himself in the first and third person. (Like Daniel's narration, Joe's is sometimes elliptical and frequently violates chronology.) Having been given Penfield's papers, including some journals, Joe is in a position to reconstruct and narrate the scenes from his friend's past which interleave the account of his own life. The reader may also presume that Joe imaginatively narrates events for which he lacks any clues at all, for example, the dialogue between Penfield and Lucinda on their apparently fatal flight over the Pacific. Finally, it is possible that Joe as narrator has stored on a computer information concerning the lives of Warren, Clara, Bennett, and others. From time to time this data "interrupts" his narration; however, this kind of interruption could be explained as a kind of collage technique on Joe's part, the inclusion of documents without comment, in the same way Penfield's note delivering his written materials to Joe is included. Of course this hypothesis involves inferences, but accepting them will show just how radical Doctorow's experiment really is.[1]

Critics agree that, over the course of the novel, there seems to be a convergence of the various voices, especially Joe's and Warren's; indeed, some wonder whether Joe and Warren—born on the same day (2 August), but nineteen years apart—are somehow the same character.[2] Warrant for this speculation occurs near the end, after the narrator (seemingly, Joe, by context) tells of an almost mystical sexual experience, one that recalls many details from Penfield's life in Japan, a country Joe has never visited. The experience might be explained as a dream, but the narrator excludes this interpretation: "You are thinking it is a dream. It is no dream. It is the account in helpless linear translation of the unending love of our simultaneous but disynchronous lives" (291).

The trope "simultaneous but disynchronous" is an oxymoron. One resolution of its contradiction is that the lives of certain characters (Joe and the unnamed girl, Joe and Penfield)—although chronologically distinct throughout the novel—are in some other, still-to-be-defined sense "simultaneous." If true, the assertion now leads to this obvious question: If Joe is identical with Penfield and/or the unnamed girl, "who tells" *Loon Lake*?

The hypothesis of the ultimate joint identity of Joe and Penfield, at least, gains added credence by the many parallels between them: as children, each observes a woman holding up her infant daughter to urinate; later, each flees his working-class background; each suffers from the economic exploitation of Bennett's businesses; on separate arrivals at Loon Lake, each is attacked by dogs; each loves Clara; each flees Loon Lake with a woman Bennett prizes; each wants to kill Bennett but does not. At the very least, the oxymoron suggests the "eternal return"; but insofar as these parallels bear on the problem of narration, there is reason now to doubt the original hypothesis that the narrator is, at least solely, Joe.

This doubt raises the overarching issue of how readers attribute speakers to words and distinguish one speaker, or one source of writing, from another. In the case of naturalistic passages narrated by and about Joe, details of context confer the illusion of a single, continuous, present self. However, the arbitrary character of such contexts is exposed, not only by the blurring of Joe's character with Warren's, but also by the juxtaposition of such naturalistic passages with anonymous sources, perhaps including a computer.

The first such juxtaposition occurs during Joe's description of his love-making with the Scandinavian maid Hilda (or Bertha), whom Joe refers to as "it." Joe recalls:

> teasing it with a touch, watching it quiver, hearing its muffled squeaks, composing a fuck for it, the likes of which I like to imagine she has never known.
> Come with me
> Compose with me
> Coming she is coming is she
> She was very decent really and for my love gave me little presents. [6–7]

This three-line interruption of Joe's prose, like many that follow, cannot be ascribed to any certain source. At first glance it seems interjected into the narrative flow from an anonymous outside source. Now on the original hypothesis, the phrase "composing a fuck for it" may be read as a trope for "expressing a poem for her"; the words then introduce the doggerel lines that Joe thinks to himself and includes, collage-style, here. This labored reading shows that the Joe-as-source hypothesis is certainly not self-evident; on the contrary, it is only made possible by the interpretation of a trope and the substitution of the personal for the impersonal pronoun. Although such source- and face-creating moves seem almost necessary to the act of reading, they are also arbitrary. It is equally possible to assume, with some readers, that the anonymous computer doggerel appears spontaneously.[3] In this reading, the computer is an eerily autonomous conarrator, one that forces the reader to consider literally such sentences as "Computer data composes World War One poet" (12) or "Data comprising life F. W. Bennett" (183).

Quite apart from the undecidable source of these passages, their status as interruptions, their doggerel, and their punning play on "come" recall the similarly inexplicable interruptions on the theme of "ohm" in *The Book of Daniel*. While puns play an important part in plot details of each novel, they also portend the ever-present chance of the complete collapse of language into meaningless sound.

On occasion the "voice of the computer" seems to merge with the undecidable voice of the narrator. Twice, the source of the narration is referred to as "your register," once in the midst of a standard prose passage (158) and once in an apparent printout (183). This merging raises the question of how to decipher the difference between passages composed by human and nonhuman sources. A printout effect is sometimes created solely by random repetition, as in the recurrent "Come with me" passages, but of course these cannot ultimately be distinguished from human thoughts or from poetry. Occasionally the effect is created by wider than usual spacing between sentences, but there are three prose passages presumably written by a noncomputer (49, 103–4, 279) which also follow this practice, as does a quotation from Wordsworth's "Intimations of Immortality" (98). This method of undermining distinctions among poetry, prose, and their genres began in "The Songs of Billy Bathgate," but in *Loon Lake* its effect is more disturbing. Here one wonders whether the distinction between human and nonhuman sources of expression may be only a derivative of rhetoric. Or of typography.

On balance, the Joe-as-sole-source hypothesis cannot be sustained. Any attribution of a single source for the novel—to Joe, to an identical Joe and Penfield, to a computer—eclipses equally plausible unstated theories. Just as the narrator(s) in *Ragtime* always have the potential to destabilize an interpretation based on any single—on any uttered—attribution of source, so, in *Loon Lake,* the "convergence" of narrative sources, or the erasure of distinctions among them, creates a new undecidability. In the remainder of this chapter the word "narrator" will be used, without any true referent, as the misinterpretation necessary for the continuation of this discourse.

As in *Big as Life,* the title of *Loon Lake* is a synechdoche, naming both whole and part, here the novel and a poem, supposedly written by Warren Penfield. In fact Doctorow published the poem "Loon Lake" under his own name separately in *The Kenyon Review,* in 1979.[4] Of course, the appearance of excerpts from a work-in-progress is a common practice, but the separate publication of a synechdochal part intensifies the question of redundancy: will the subsequent work "add anything substantial," or will it, in keeping with the definition of synechdoche, be already contained by its part, already defunct? In "Big as Life" the inconclusive action forewarned of the novel's waywardness. In "The Songs of Billy Bathgate," the songs—when determinable as separate parts—miniaturize the narrative dilemma of the whole. On the other hand, the judgment of redundancy can never be made in advance.

The text of Penfield's poem "Loon Lake" differs only slightly from the version published in *The Kenyon Review,* but enough to dissociate Doctorow from it, and viewed from the reverse angle, the reattribution of the hardly changed poem, from Doctorow to Penfield, retrospectively undermines the authorship of *The Kenyon Review* poem.[5] These moves manifest the "death of the author," as first noticed in "The Songs of Billy Bathgate," in the metaphor of the writer as orphan, and the novel's version of the poem also erases its author in other ways. In the novel, Penfield wrote the poem in 1936, just before he disappeared, but his work is interleaved with four annotations by the "anonymous computer voice," which contain subsequent information Penfield could not have known. Thus "Loon Lake," the poem in the novel, is already intertextual; in this respect it is truly a synechdoche for the text.

The potential redundancy of whole and part is also suggested by the fact that most of the poem (57–70) narrates events that either have already occurred or will shortly occur: the arrival of Clara, Tommy Crapo, and Buster and their tour of the Lake (50–52, 61–62); the sound of the dogs that attacked Joe (46–47, 54–55, 68); details of the interior of the main house (60, 89); Lucinda's landing on the lake (64, 115). The accounts in both poem and novel are very close: as in the two versions of the poem, only minuscule features are altered: (from the novel) "The little flag in the stern flapped like a machine gun" (50); (from the poem) "while the small flag at the stern snapped like a machine gun" (62).

This order to the repetition creates an anachronism; the earlier poetic text seems a plagiarism of the later prose narrative. Now the Joe-as-single-narrator hypothesis would explain the repetition only as a lapse, an unconscious importing into Joe's narrative of a simile he had read sometime earlier in Penfield's poem. The tenuousness of that explanation makes more likely the otherwise dubious proposition that Joe and Penfield are "simultaneous but disynchronous"; Joe's expressions match Penfield's to such a degree that they seem one mind. The fact that Penfield's poem includes details that only Joe could have known—like the interior of the private railway car (30–31, 44–45, 58)—also suggests that the poem, like the novel, is somehow the product of joint authorship. Both the narrative in general and the poem in particular point to the lesson that literature is intertextual before it is textual. This is consistent with the view of writing expressed often before in Doctorow's works, in Blue's palimpsest, Daniel's use of his sources, and the *Ragtime* narrator's use of Kleist's "Michael Kohlhaas."

The least redundant section of Doctorow's-Warren's-Joe's-the computer's poem is its opening (57–59), a meditation on the lake as part of nature and as it may first have been perceived by the Adirondack Indians. The articulation of such a premodern, non-Western perspective appears in only one other part of the novel, the account of Penfield's short-lived career as a Zen novitiate. To the extent that Penfield is the poem's author, the poem shows his continuing interest in some alternative to modern, Western hermeneutics, even after his break with Zen Buddhism taught him the futility of one alternative. So Penfield's persistence may appear heroic or deluded or both simultaneously.

The poem paints the lake and its denizens with a detail and portentousness that at first may appear Thoreauvian:

> If you listen the small splash is beaver
> As beaver swim their fur lies back and their heads elongate
> and a true imperial cruelty shines from their eyes.
> They're rodents, after all.
> Beaver otter weasel mink and rat
> a rodent specie of the Adirondacks
> and they redistrict the world. [57]

Walden's correspondences mesh with a sympathetic imagining of the Indians' animistic, perhaps pantheistic, interpretation of the loon's flight and fall into the lake for prey: "which the Indian sees is what death is / the environment exchanging itself for the being" (59). Consistently with Penfield's interest in the nonmodern and non-Western, the poem finds in the flight of the loon a coherent, stable, harmonious understanding of death. If credible, that idea might become at last the authentic representation of death, sought for so long by narrators like Blue and Daniel.

Hope for such an answer is soon dashed by the poem, which abruptly replaces the Indians' faith with: "Well, anyway, in the summer of 1936 / a chilling summer high in the Eastern mountains / a group of people arrived at a rich man's camp." In fact, at this point the poem "Loon Lake" becomes indistinguishable from prose broken by spaces and computer interjections. So the hope for an autonomous text with a coherent representation of death collapses.

Death remains unrepresentable elsewhere, too. The death of the Fat Lady, the murder of Red James, the deaths at sea of Penfield and Lucinda—these unreported extinctions are also narrative gaps and absences. They are never the "environment exchanging itself." The Indians' view—that there is some representable way of understanding death—is stated but contradicted in the novel, just as the Zen Buddhist philosophy that Penfield temporarily espouses is later abandoned. The apparently nonredundant section of the poem "Loon Lake" becomes, after all, a synechdoche for the novel: in both, potentially true representations of death fly by and disappear, like the loon.

The defeated effort to understand death exposes a blind spot in interpretation, also experienced in the narrative's ellipses. Like Blue and Daniel, Joe as narrator of *Loon Lake* often omits scenes that are described—sometimes incompletely—only later. Coincidentally, the most conspicuous deferrals are moments of death: the gang-rape and murder of the Fat Lady and the attack on Joe and Red James. As with the omissions in *The Book of Daniel,* these gaps underscore the impossibility of representing death; they also draw attention to Joe's complicity—his misrepresentation of his own involvement—in the events he explains only after long delays.

The grotesque assault on the Fat Lady is described only after Joe begins his escape from Loon Lake with Clara. The second escape recapitulates the first: in each case, Joe steals a woman (Magda, Clara) who is prized by resented capitalist authority-figures (Sim Hearn, Bennett). The parallels suggest an analogy between the rubes' primitive gang-rape and murder and the violence, now hidden, that enabled F. W. Bennett to amass his wealth—his indifference to mining explosions and his suppression of workers through the use of the police and organized crime. Now Joe's revulsion at the gang-rape/murder of the Fat Lady is clear enough. His unsuccessful attempt at intervention, his cuckolding Hearn and flinging away his money show Joe's defiance of capitalist amorality, and a similar wish, to extricate himself from Bennett, motivates his escape from Loon Lake. In the second case, Joe's use of Bennett's money and car is symptomatic of the fact that he cannot so easily free himself from the larger, more glamorous world of Bennett, and his quest for autonomy ends in an assembly-line job for Bennett Autobody in Jacksontown. Joe's delayed account of his protest against inhuman violence may conceal a guilty recognition of his gradual adaptation to Bennett's world.

Joe's blindness is even more evident in the delayed account of the attack on Red James. In this sense, once again Joe attempts to intervene in a mass of bodies bent upon murder; once again he fails. Now the delayed narration of the event is more clearly understood as a "story" told to the chief of police. Joe assures the reader: "I have been very cooperative. Even though they did that to me I have told my story as completely and accurately as I can" (245).

The supposed (but unverifiable) completeness and accuracy of Joe's story cannot prevent the emergence of three different interpretations: that Red James was murdered by union men, by Tommy Crapo, or by Joe himself. As if he intuits this undecidability, Joe now effects his escape through his newfound ability to fabricate. The authenticity of his story cannot be established by any reference outside it. In claiming to be Bennett's son and challenging the police to disprove his story, Joe now enters a world in which the truth has become a wholly fictional construct.

Whatever the narrator's identity, the novel *Loon Lake* misrepresents in its formal features, even as it is told. In its redundancy of whole and part and in its blind ellipses, the narration stutters as it creates mysteries whose solutions are, in the end, deferred. If the narration misrepresents, then reading *Loon Lake* will misinterpret.

The idea that necessary misinterpretation shapes human destiny informs the lives of "simultaneous but disynchronous" narrator(s), Penfield and Joe, which are taken up here successively, faut de mieux, and thus erroneously. Like Red Bloom in *Big as Life,* Daniel in *The Book of Daniel,* or Houdini and Coalhouse Walker in *Ragtime,* the main characters in *Loon Lake* fight against such a destiny, but they fail.

A kind of prelapsarian phase of Penfield's childhood foreshadows his later fight: he can stand neutrally in the presence of his parents' raging counterclaims (25); he can make an impassive "inspection" of the effects of the Ludlow mining disaster (34); he can observe the nakedness of his playmate, the immigrant girl, and become "still"

(37). The hope for a still point, for some ideal peace seemingly promised by such moments reappears in his quest for tranquility in Zen Buddhism. Penfield's prelapsarian phase abruptly ends with the brutal repression of his family and the striking miners at the hands of F. W. Bennett, and he is expelled into a world of interpretation when his family is forced to leave their company house in Ludlow. In that moment, Penfield begins to see the world in terms of representation. As he loads boxes onto a wagon, the boy sees himself building a "model of a city" (38); the narrator makes an extraordinary, retrospective comment on this proclivity: "I have a comment here: I note the boy Warren Penfield's relentless faculty of composition. Rather than apprehend reality he transforms it so that in this case, for example . . . the pitiful pile of his family's belongings on the wagon bed is represented as a high vision of civilization. No wonder his father is angered" (38).

From Penfield's biography the reader learns that this beginning of representation is soon followed by his incarceration in the Colorado State Mental Hospital (21). Before concurring too quickly with the narrator's condemnation of Penfield's "faculty of composition," readers must remember that the narrator—Joe, Penfield, or whoever it is—also tries to represent while he condemns Penfield's misrepresentation. (Of course, the present discourse is not exempt, in seeking to represent, as it questions the narrator's questions.) In Paul de Man's phrase, the reader cannot escape questioning reference in language that refers.[6] This paradox may suggest how narration retraces the same errors it discovers.

The events of Penfield's mature life deepen the paradox by showing how misinterpretation compounds itself. At the Battle of the Somme, Penfield is dispatched to signal for an artillery attack. Frightened, he forgets his message and sends instead the first stanza of Wordsworth's "Intimations of Immortality"; however, the artillery barrage hits its target anyway. The dark comedy, reminiscent of Joseph Heller's *Catch-22*, is compounded when Penfield—perhaps understandably admitted for a second time to a mental facility—is awarded a Silver Star for heroism. (Is it possible that a different reading of Wordsworth might have made the guns pause at least momentarily? The question is moot. It is an odd parallel that misinterpretation of Wordsworth is featured so prominently in the texts of de Man and Doctorow, who returns to the subject in *World's Fair* and *Lives of the Poets*.) When the army recognizes Penfield's misrepresentation and the artillery's misinterpretation with a symbol of heroism, it officially endorses their delusions.

Penfield's journeys to Seattle and Japan record his search, consistent with his childhood memories, for some alternative. In Seattle he sheds his commitment to the working class, abandoning his defense of the general strike after he is smitten by the sight of his landlady's five-year-old daughter (257–58). For Penfield this child "deity" appears in the second of three such visionary moments that seem to reincarnate the immigrant girl. His apprenticeship at the Zen monastery introduces him to an ideal, clear-sighted harmony ("the endless serenity of the realized Buddha" [111]). Penfield sees the hope for such a state in the nonlinear consciousness, transcending all rational "yes" and "no," of the Zen master he tries to emulate, but Penfield fails for two reasons. First, he is constitutionally unable to accept the rigors of Zen discipline; this incapacity is implied by his personal koan ("If this is a religion for warriors, what are *you* doing here?"). Of course, the irascibility of his mentor may also cast doubt on the validity, for anyone at all, of the "realized Buddha" state. The second reason for breaking with Zen Buddhism is, however, even more important: Penfield meets the third avatar of the girl-deities, a Japanese girl (110, 140). After this girl dies in an earthquake in 1923, Penfield memorializes her death in his volume, *Child Bride in a Zen Garden*.

Though Penfield's three ideal visions have given him new aspirations, each ends in disillusionment. After four years of dissolute living, he returns to the United States, now with the vow to kill his family's enemy, Bennett; but in the light of his Japanese experiences and long detachment from the working class, this resolution is now an empty, romantic gesture. When Penfield becomes, instead, the poet-in-residence of Loon Lake, he fully reinhabits the world of necessary delusion that he had tried to escape. In this acquiescence lies the admission that his art is wholly co-opted, powerless to affect the world. Penfield's impotent poetry records his impossible wish to represent truly, a wish he reenacts in his melodramatic readings. Art colludes with the mystified world. Penfield's poetry becomes Joe's prose. It is against the background of his predecessor's failure that Joe's "simultaneous but disynchronous" career—the eternal return of *Loon Lake*—may be judged.

The lives of Joe and Penfield repeat each other in many ways, but one crucial overlap is the fact that, when each arrives at Loon Lake, he is viciously attacked by dogs. After Joe spies Clara, standing naked in a private railway car, he follows her to Bennett's estate. When this surreptitious vision and obsessive pursuit result in the attack, the reader is reminded once more of the myth of Diana and Actaeon. Clara's name and white robes evoke the purity and customary dress of the goddess, and when Bennett comments on the dogs' howling to his guests, he explains that "they took a deer" (100). The recurrence of this mythological allusion from *Ragtime* suggests an important way in which Joe's life repeats others' lives; like Mother's Younger Brother (with Diana/Evelyn Nesbit) and like Penfield (whose reaction to the three girl-deities anticipates his being "struck by lightning" when he first sees Clara [51]), Joe must confront the consequences of being blinded by an image of beauty and truth. Like his predecessors, he is driven to possess the radiance that blinds him, the significance that seems doomed to escape men.

Clara's elusiveness is obvious. Although she knows Penfield wants to leave with her, she first escapes Loon Lake with Joe. Later, after Joe comes under suspicion in Jacksontown, she abandons him and returns to her first lover, Tommy Crapo. Even in Joe's final vision of her (279–82), Clara holds herself aloof from Bennett. In these cases the flight of the white goddess seems just as fated as it is in Evelyn Nesbit's desertion of Mother's Younger Brother for a nightclub singer. The loss leads each man to submit to the influence of new, less dazzling, "mortal" women (Mother's Younger Brother/Emma Goldman; Penfield/Lucinda; Joe/Sandy)—all of whom offer them a more mundane destiny. In these parallels may lie an understanding of Joe's comment that his life was "simultaneous but disynchronous" with that of others; if possession of the goddess promises some present enlightenment—some Clara/clarity—her elusiveness and vengeance consign her votaries to blindness, to living, in Derrida's phrase, as exiles from the truth.

Joe is always an exile, in pursuit of the truth before and after Clara leaves him. His flight from Paterson is the first of several self-imposed acts of exile, of refusal to concede legitimacy to any arbitrary authority outside himself. Critics sometimes discuss Joe's acts of defiance in terms of an oedipal conflict, of the son against the paternal lawgiver.[7] This pattern holds for his rejection of his parents and his retaliation against the priest who catches him stealing money from the poor box; it continues when Joe cuckolds Sim Hearn; it is repeated when Joe steals Clara from the paternal figures Penfield and Bennett. But in these episodes Joe's rebellions reveal more than simply instinctual, filial, or generational conflict. They disclose a world without significance.

In the early sections of *Loon Lake,* it is money that confers the illusion of signification on all parts of society, even on those that nominally stand outside it, like the church or the carnival. In Joe's escapes from the church, Father, and the carnival, he demonstrates the arbitrary nature of their authority by flinging what they value—money—into the air. Joe's most important rebellion, however—against the secular, political world epitomized in Bennett—invalidates claims to signification even more deeply rooted than society's valorization of money. Thus Joe envisions his plan to live with Clara and work at Bennett's Jackstontown automobile factory as the moment of his final acquisition of some truth, as the confirmation of their personal identities in the achievement of independence from the owner of Loon Lake. Here Joe and Clara revive the dreams of Red Bloom and Sugarbush, of Billy Bathgate and Lovegirl. As Joe tells himself excitedly, "We could change, we could make our lives however we wanted!" (181), but Joe's actual experiences with Clara and Red James undermine this dream of love and autonomy. He cannot, after all, find in their lovemaking any affirmation of the truth he so desperately sought; on the contrary, love, like language, yields only illusion: "Our lovemaking was like song, or like speech. 'Don't you see,' I asked again and again, 'don't you understand?' And she shook her head from side to side in her distraction. I couldn't overcome this" (167).

Possession of Clara, the romantic spoils of Joe's oedipal struggle, does not bestow a new mutual identity. His experience is Billy Bathgate's or Mother's Younger Brother's. The identity they crave is not a presence capturable in the world but a fiction. For Joe, this discovery occurs when—to escape from Jacksontown, where he loses Clara—he embraces the arbitrary and becomes a storyteller himself.

In that moment Joe understands the world as fiction. Far from achieving independence through oedipal rejection of an father, Joe literally creates himself through collusion with, through an appeal to, that inauthentic father. Whether or not this scene signals the beginning of Joe's moral sellout, it is without doubt the constitutive moment of fiction-making, the moment at which Joe joins Blue, Billy, and Daniel as constructors in language. Neil Schmitz calls this moment an epiphany, in which Joe realizes he "is free now to write his own fiction, to make himself up as he goes along."[8] Joe describes his new insight as follows:

> It was an amazing discovery, the uses of my ignorance, a kind of industrial manufacture of my own. And the more it went on, the more I believed it, taking this fact and that possibility and assembling them, then sending the results down the line a bit and adding another fact and dropping an idea on the whole thing and sending it on a bit for another operation, another bolt to the construction, my own factory of lies, driven by rage, Paterson Autobody doing its day's work. I was going to make it! [263–64]

The pun "make it" in Joe's exclamation recalls Billy Bathgate's use of that phrase. It equates survival and success with the ability to construct a story, to manipulate his "factory of lies" and make them convincing enough to seem true representations.

Joe's epiphany compensates for the loss of Clara and emboldens him to try out new disguises with Sandy, until he tires of them. He now believes in his powers of "making it," of creating fictions that others—Sandy or the police—will interpret with reference to the world. This discovery on Joe's part aligns his joyful "wisdom" with Bennett's and with the Nietzschean idea of the *Übermensch*. At the end of the novel, both characters embody values similar to those of J. P. Morgan in *Ragtime*, although stripped of that character's ancillary beliefs in reincarnation.[9] Joe's absorption of Bennett's "wisdom" is hinted at when he returns to Loon Lake; he says that he greeted Bennett "like a complicitor while he stared at me quite astonished and then turned nodding as if he understood" (283).

This heady "insight" of Joe's is shown to be, after all, one more blindness when Joe finally understands that Bennett did not confirm his fiction to the Jackstontown police; in fact, the call was never placed. Now there is no way to distinguish lies from the truth; Joe's lie has *become* the truth. Now Joe can no longer attribute his survival to his story's correspondence to the "real world"; instead, he now sees how stories represent without referents at all. This ominous dimension of stories may prompt Joe to consider two mad alternatives as equally acceptable: to kill Bennett or to acquiesce in his world of fictional constructs. After Joe ponders the murder of Bennett, he leaps into Loon Lake, identifying himself with the novel's symbol of madness. With this gesture, Joe accepts a world so empty that a computer printout of the remainder of his life—telling that he follows in Bennett's establishment footsteps to become "Master of Loon Lake"—may suffice for the logical implications of his nonchoice, of his dive into Loon Lake.

Joe's leap into the water seems a baptismal gesture, since it leads to the revelation of his "true name," Joseph Korzeniowski, also the Polish surname of Joseph Conrad. This sudden, dumbfounding allusion has the effect of insuring that henceforth Joe must be understood intertextually, as a literary creation and not a person. Among reviewers the allusion prompted guarded speculation as to the relevance of the Conrad canon to *Loon Lake*. The novels' titles and their depictions of struggles against paternal authority are the most commonly cited parallels in Conrad's works to the action of Doctorow's novel.[10] Such speculation seems almost necessary in reading this text, but at the same time, the allusion again emphasizes the arbitrary character of this new hermeneutic exercise in understanding an ending as a preliminary to understanding the novel. Just as the several conclusions to *The Book of Daniel* undid the assumption that fixing the sense of the ending was a prerequisite to interpreting the text, so the wholly unanticipated allusion to Conrad is a reminder that "true name" is really "false name," of no help in interpreting character.

Consider one illustration. Joe's leap into the water may recall Jim's action in *Lord Jim*. If so, the reader might analyze whether Joe's action is a cowardly, guilty betrayal that later comes to haunt him, but no sooner does this line of inquiry occur than it is stopped by the computer biography, which prevents any access to Joe's later consciousness. Whether or not Joe is ever conscience-stricken is indeterminable. In other words, the allusion establishes the certainty of an intertextual relation, but withholds the "content" of that relation. Of course, Doctorow had produced this effect of "empty intertextuality" before, in the title of *Welcome to Hard Times,* and he creates it again in the title of his *Lives of the Poets.* It may be that this practice is a kind of literary analogue to the postmodern technique of "pure citation" prevalent in contemporary visual arts.[11]

In *Loon Lake,* other allusions also create this effect. In fact, the apparent "baptismal" allusion to Conrad forces the reader to acknowledge that, after all, even in his "false-true" name, Paterson, Joe has been "always, already" an intertextual creation. But the reference to William Carlos Williams is as empty as the allusion to Conrad.[12] Perhaps the most that can be said of both allusions is that they show Joe to be an offspring of literary modernism in English. Consistent with de Man's thesis is the observation that the reader of *Loon Lake* must forget, or become blind to, the intertextual dimension of Joe that was presented at the outset; the name "Korzienowski" only reminds us of this earlier forgetting. Thus the ending reveals the previously hidden cost of the reader's first "insight" into the novel.

Of all of the texts enmeshed in *Loon Lake,* none so powerfully anticipates its vision as Thoreau's *Walden.*[13] In *Walden* the account of the loon's incomprehensible movement seems a figure for the incoherence of both nature and art; of all beings at Walden Pond, the mad-seeming loon most defies the mind's presumptions of order. Even more threatening, the bird's flights, dives, and hurtles make a mockery of writing, with its hoary metaphors of eloquence, depth, and surface. The bird laughs at Thoreau's "I," in "derision of my efforts."[14] So in the light of *Walden,* Joe's plunge into the lake seems an identification with Thoreau's specter of the futility of reading and writing.

Of course, for Thoreau's "I," the loon becomes at last explicable: its laugh represents its position, prompting the following comment in *Walden:* "But why, after displaying so much cunning, did he invariably betray himself the moment he came up by that loud laugh?"15 It is obvious that narrative voice in *Loon Lake* cannot be located. Joe's quest for authenticity, echoing Penfield's, ends in the delusion of "making it." Like the world, the self is fictional. So Joe's decisive plunge into the lake mocks representation. Here the madness of the call of Doctorow's loon seems finer than Thoreau's.

CHAPTER 7

The Intertextuality of *Lives of the Poets*

Lives of the Poets consists of seven models of misrepresentation. All of its elements, from the collection's title to its parts, demonstrate the continuing struggle in Doctorow's texts between the attempt to make language represent and the enforced, belated recognition that it does not. *Lives of the Poets* exhibits this struggle in its preoccupation with intertextuality. While the collection may be read as the work of a single fictional author, the Jonathon of its first and last pieces, the reader must also ask whether and how these stories "represent" either this presumed author or any other coherent, signified presence. It is as if this volume were Doctorow's way of questioning whether there is a Doctorow behind his works. The collection begins with a story that extends Billy Bathgate's figure of the writer-as-orphan and ends with Jonathan turning over his typewriter to a child ignorant of English. In between, ostensibly autonomous stories become fully readable only in terms of others; hence, the collection directly confronts the issues of intertextuality and representation.

On the jacket, the subtitle of this text is *A Novella and Six Stories;* on the title page, *Six Stories and a Novella.* Subtitles always raise questions of redundancy. In addition, this subtitle's inversion is a trope, antimetabole, the literary analogue to mathematical equations such as {A + B = B + A}.¹ This antimetabole has the effect of calling its referents into question, since readers now must wonder for a moment which piece is the novella. Of course, "Lives of the Poets" would appear to be the novella, but the antimetabole calls attention to the fact that generic classification is relative. This unsettling of generic distinctions repeats questions asked in "The Songs of Billy Bathgate" and *Loon Lake,* and subsequent critical discussion of the collection's genre(s) has confirmed their arbitrary character.²

The antimetabole prompts another question: are the two versions of the subtitle the same? Of course in mathematics {A + B = B + A} is axiomatic, but as the above paragraph suggests, apparent linguistic identity may conceal difference. Following Nietzsche, Paul de Man argues that the almost universally accepted Aristotelian law of contradiction in philosophy is an illusion.³ Obviously, readers must bypass such threshold questions to start the process of reading and take for granted what the text has already questioned. But such understandable haste is slowed again when the main title is read as a trope or synechdoche, as in *Big as Life,* "The Songs of Billy Bathgate," and *Loon Lake*. Now the title and subtitle take the more complex form {synechdoche = antimetabole} or X = Y, expressions of new difference within apparent identity. The preliminary doubt of the principle of noncontradiction deepens before the reader can approach the sense of the words on the page. Doctorow's text seems to enforce what J. Hillis Miller called "slow reading," or reading that turns back upon itself to question the foundations of reading.⁴

Arriving at the apparent sense of the title, however, the reader is stopped by a third trope, exemplum (allusion), that is, the use of an older title, the magnum opus by Samuel Johnson, to name this new work. With this allusion, the subject of intertextuality moves to the fore. As in the case of the allusion to Conrad at the end of *Loon Lake,* a hermeneutic inquiry may ensue. The reader may ask questions about Samuel Johnson's age and our own; may compare Johnson's grounds for arriving at aesthetic judgments with those supposedly exemplified in the present text; may search for parallels in structure, organization, and theme between Johnson's chapters and Doctorow's "novella and six stories" (or, undoing this, its reverse); and may ask the same kinds of questions that spring to mind when reading *Hard*

Times or the biblical and contemporary versions of *The Book of Daniel*. As in those works, the mandated intertextuality discloses only the poverty and futility of such questions. Is it essential to locate Dryden in a story about a New England schoolteacher? Milton in a story of a terrorist bombing? Is there any connection more than phonic between "Willi" and Shakespeare? This collection's "empty intertextuality" is just as defeating as *Loon Lake*'s.

There is even a prior question: do we really know which entities to compare? "Samuel Johnson," the acknowledged source of the earlier *Lives of the Poets,* is a traditional icon of magisterial authorship. Will a comparison between his nonfiction and this fiction be valid? The question recalls *Loon Lake*'s suspicion of the fictional character of the world. If Jonathon is the fictional narrator of the entire collection, is it reasonable to compare his attributes as an "author" to those of the critic Samuel Johnson? These questions retard reading. After suppressing the doubts that interrupted the process of reading the title and finally wresting content from the title and subtitle of Doctorow's novel, the reader confronts only contradiction.

There will, of course, be parallels—the very breadth of Johnson's work and the variety of Doctorow's would seem to guarantee some, even some enlightening observations, but once again, hidden in this project are challenges to its validity which inhere in the reading process. Is not some, even some enlightening observation generable by an allusive titling of *any* text? Is not the act of "retitling" the essence of intertextual criticism itself? And if it is impossible not to bring, "after the first," some prior text to bear in the reading of subsequent ones, is not intertextuality necessary, whether or not a work bears an allusive title? Such an implication would seem to make "comparisons" both inevitable and futile.[5]

Although the title seems to have no obvious referents in the collection, it is true that poets are mentioned, both canonized poets (Delmore Schwartz [85]; Edgar Allan Poe [96]; Robert Lowell [126]; Rainer Maria Rilke [138]) and fictional poets (Rosen [123–25]; Jim Arlington [132–34]); however, the stories are hardly "about" them. Four of the seven pieces contain no writer whatsoever. Perhaps, then, the title suggests that the stories are "allegories of reading," in which schoolteachers, hunters, diplomats, and administrators may be "stand-ins" for those who express, like poets. Of course, the distinction between poetry and prose was of great importance to Samuel Johnson, but finding acceptable referents for Doctorow's title requires abandoning it—the necessity already encountered in "The Songs of Billy Bathgate" and *Loon Lake*. If "poets" are first considered as "writers" and next as "expressers," then the title applies to all of the characters and, especially, to Jonathon himself, who is supposedly the narrator of the first and last pieces and the author of those that intervene. This interpretation empties the title of meaning in an additional way: if all characters and narrators are "poets," then who is *not* a poet? Are "lives" and "poets" synonyms that make the title a redundancy? Is everyone engaged in the making of fiction?

That Jonathan is the author of all of the stories is the assertion made in the blurb on the jacket—the second instance of intertextuality (after the title or "first interpretation" of the text, which also precedes it). The blurb's interpretation—which Doctorow himself may share[6]—is worth exploring, though it is not infallible. The only textual evidence for Jonathon's authorship is his chance recollection, in "Lives of the Poets," of his friend Rosen's inquiry into when he might finish *Lives of the Poets* (123). The jacket's inference is the sort necessary to reading in general: that a single definable continuous consciousness, present at hand, is the author "behind" an assortment of texts. Such an inference is almost always made whenever assessing a writer's oeuvre: that "Johnson" or "Doctorow" is the presence that produced the otherwise arbitrary signifiers of a group of texts. The reason that Rosen's question cannot settle the issue is provided by the title itself; *Lives of the Poets* may refer to more than one work. In this way, the text verifies that a title, a signifier, never guarantees a signified author. If it expresses anything, Doctorow's title demonstrates only the alienability of titles.

Undecidability of authorship is apparent for another reason. Even if Jonathon is the presumed writer of the first and last pieces in the collection, since details of his family history match precisely in each text, the conclusion—that Jonathan is the imagined writer of the intervening stories—does not necessarily follow. Jonathan's authorship of these stories remains undecidable because in them new narrators have been imagined: for example, "Willi," in the third story, whose father is a farmer in Galicia in 1910, or the various "omniscient" voices of the other pieces. If Jonathon is supposed to be the "imagined writer of the stories" in the jacket's claim, he erases in his "second imagining" of new narrators his *own* creator. Willi and the leather man orphan Jonathon as Jonathon orphans Doctorow. In principle there is no reason why Willi could not imagine new narrators capable of continuing the process indefinitely, each new one killing the last parent. So Jonathan as author must remain an inference. The idea of the writer-as-orphan, begun in "The Songs of Billy Bathgate," recurs; the "imagined writer of the stories" remains a hypothesis of metaphysics.

The arbitrary character of the assumption of Jonathon's common authorship is demonstrated by two other species of "empty intertextuality" in the collection. First, stylistic repetitions among various tales might tempt a reader to conclude that Jonathon is the author. One example is the use of the word "compadre" in both "The Foreign Legation" and "Lives of the Poets." This is the hermeneutics of philology, but the paucity and triviality of such "common elements" warn throughout that, whatever the collection of "common elements" among disparate texts, they can never transform themselves into a signified "author." So *Lives of the Poets* may be viewed as an allegory of Doctorow's—or any other writer's—entire career, a set of diverse texts that seem to promise but in fact withhold the signified "author."

More striking are the obvious echoes of Doctorow's earlier works. The illusion of demystification in *Ragtime* is also felt in "The Writer in the Family"; the connection between prosopopoeia and death in "The Water Works" recalls the Bad Man from Bodie; the undecidability of motivation in so many works reappears in "The Hunter"; *Loon Lake*'s doubts of the subversive potential of art recur in "The Leather Man." These complex discourses are, in "Lives of the Poets," reduced to the level of trivia, and the result is that Doctorow's connection with Jonathon may become as ephemeral, perhaps, as Johnson's. So both writers—regarded as signified presences generating so many potentially crucial issues—may be reduced to the function of Conrad and Williams in *Loon Lake*: the empty acknowledgement of the stories' wholly intertextual provenance.

One disturbing implication of this argument is that it vitiates any attempt to understand common features among Doctorow's texts. Certainly *Lives of the Poets*, like *Ragtime*, implies the futility of all interpretation that seeks to make coincidence—stylistic or even "thematic" resemblances among texts—represent. But, of course, even that statement identifies a common feature.

"The Writer in the Family," a first-person recollection by Jonathon, narrates events that took place immediately following the death of his father Jack in 1955. At that time Jack's mother was still alive and in a nursing home. In order to spare her from potential trauma, her two daughters, Frances and Molly, concoct the story that Jack and his family have moved to Arizona. They enlist Jonathon's help by asking him to write letters to her, from time to time, as if from his father. These will be read to Jonathon's grandmother by his aunt Frances. For a time, Jonathon agrees to the ruse, but his letters soon disclose unpleasant family rivalries to him, especially those between his mother Ruth and his aunts. Putting this newfound knowledge to use, Jonathon composes a letter that, after Frances reads it, brings an end to the lie.

"The Writer in the Family" articulates again the values of the writer-as-orphan metaphor. Here writing begins with the creation of a persona that forever deprives the writer of "direct expression." The fact that Jonathon writes "in the voice of" his dead father makes writing synonymous with metaphoric orphaning, a misrepresentation from the start. Readers—in the form of his grandmother and aunts—gain consolation from writing only by misinterpreting it. This little story seems to crystallize in one place the writing dilemmas studied throughout this book.

A miniature *Künstlerroman*, the story undermines that genre's traditional expectation of enlightenment from art. For example, the ending—in which Jonathon unmasks the arrogance of his Aunt Frances—seems to affirm the capacity of fiction to demystify. Indeed, elsewhere in the story Jonathon's letters disclose to him the operation of family politics, and they teach Aunt Frances that her will to dominate has been observed and condemned, but in fact, the very purpose of Jonathon's letter is *mystification:* to keep his grandmother unaware of his father's death. Therefore any supposed illumination from art can come about only through the agency of a prior lie, insight begotten by blindness. To the extent that the writer persuades the reader that letters have an actual origin (a Cartesian subject and a magisterial author—Jack, Samuel Johnson, or Doctorow), and to the extent that the writer makes the reader believe in representation, "letters" can convey consolation. In assenting to the letters' representations, Jonathon's grandmother and his Aunt Frances can temporarily avoid confronting the absence or nothingness of death. Yet as soon as "letters" cease to provide this consolation—as soon as they subvert their own referent—they may suggest "real" death and readers will instantly reject them, as Aunt Frances vehemently rejects Jonathon's last letter. Once again, for Doctorow, the eternal return of letters and death.

The supposedly edifying nature of art is also undermined by Jonathon's misinterpretation of his own learning; even authors are not immune from the hermeneutic errors in reading their works.[7] Jonathon says his story teaches this: "I thought how stupid, and imperceptive, and self-centered I had been never to have understood while he was alive what my father's dream for his life had been" (17).

Jonathon sees his prior blindness as ignorance of his father's love of the sea and his sacrifice of this love for his family. Jonathon's discovery of Jack's naval documents led to this recognition, and now, as Jonathon rereads the last letter he wrote as "Jack," he finds new meaning, even consolation: "On the other hand, I had written in my last letter from Arizona—the one that had so angered Aunt Frances—something that might allow me, the writer in the family, to soften my judgment of myself" (17).

Before he searched for the naval documents, Jonathon could not know his father's "dream for his life." Yet now, *after* the discovery, Jonathon reads his earlier letter as reflecting an intention and a meaning he could not have possessed then. This is intertextuality at work: each new act of reading reverses cause and effect. The consolation Jonathon derives from his own letter occurs at the moment he attributes to it a meaning it could not have had. "The Writer in the Family" shows writing is born in two moments: in the creation of a persona that makes a fiction of the author and in that "author's" misreading of his text.

"The Water Works" is the most enigmatic of the collection. As the interior monologue of an anonymous narrator obsessed with a seeming "double," the story recalls Hawthorne or Poe; as the deadpan account of an extraordinary, surreal event, the story is reminiscent of Kleist or Kafka. In the light of recent criticism, these antecedents of the tale suggest that like them it may be studied as an allegory of reading.[8]

The plot is hermetic. The genderless narrator follows "my man" (or "my black-bearded captain") on his way to a waterworks, then inside the waterworks, where both observe the body of a dead child caught in a sluice gate. In a complex maneuver, the narrator's "man" (who also appears, perhaps, as "another of the water workers") recovers the corpse and takes it to the city in a horse-drawn carriage. Throughout the tale the narrator speculates about both the behavior of the mysterious "man" and more general matters. The limpidity of the plot tempts allegorical interpretation of the traditional hermeneutic sort: is "my black-bearded captain" who drives a carriage Death itself, a modern avatar of Chaucer's or Dickinson's personifications? At first such thematic interpretation seems plausible: the mysterious man's studied regard of a toy boat in the reservoir seems to make it disappear; his gaze into the sluice gates—"with a rapt expression of the most awful intensity" (23)—precedes the narrator's discovery of the corpse of the child. The air in the water works is "entombed." The churning of the water is "hellish." The man is associated with black and seems a spectral figure although his presence provokes no wonder in the workers comparable to the narrator's.

The story's obsession with death in the figure of "my man" recalls the association in *Welcome to Hard Times* between prosopopoeia and death in the Bad Man from Bodie. In pursuit of meaning, the narrator, "stalking death," must personify. The child's death is narrated in such a way as to emphasize that personification of death always precedes its occurrence; death cannot be "known" without personification. The referent of "death" escapes imperturbably from the writer's dogged, belated tracking. Death "sees" its object before the writer can; and the very effort to see, even belatedly, is a further distraction that permits death to effect itself elsewhere. After the disappearance of the boat, the narrator writes: "I was struck in the chest with the catastrophe as if I had stood on some cliff and watched the sea take a sailing vessel. When I thought to look for my man, he was running across the wide moat of hardened earth that led to the rear gates of the Water Works. I followed" (22).

This pattern of belatedness is then repeated inside the water works; the mysterious man sees the dead child just before the narrator does, then takes away the corpse, leaving the narrator with the distraction of the all-too-human water workers, who (like firemen or gravediggers) incarnate obliviousness to death through ritual.

As in *The Book of Daniel,* the attempt to "represent" death cannot escape the necessity for tropes, especially personification, inherent in all representational effort. In *The Book of Daniel,* this dilemma was implicit in the three versions of Susan's funeral, three "models" suggesting that each in the open-ended series was equally substitutable in the effort to represent death. As in *Welcome to Hard Times,* death seems to *require* personification. If death is "my man" or "my black-bearded captain," it already has a gender, it is already metaphor and personification even before its effects—arriving ahead of the narrator, distracting and occluding vision—are sensed in the world. As in both earlier books, it appears impossible to reach "beyond" metaphor in the attempt to represent death.

The narrator evidently acknowledges this ultimate impossibility in ruminations about water, the element that unifies the story. Death takes place "inside" the water works, but as the story opens storm clouds threaten outside; as the story ends, the rain begins. Oddly, the narrator reacts more strongly, more resentfully, to this ubiquitous water than to the dead child: "The rain had begun. I went back in and felt the oppression of a universe of water, inside and out, over the dead and the living" (24). In this summation, the narrator protests against something even more oppressive than death—"a universe of water." The phrase suggests the pervasive presence of water inside and outside the water works, but the phrase is also a metaphor and hyperbole. To parse the enigma, it may help to consider the passage formally, as an *example* of metaphor. In this reading, the narrator's protest is against metaphor itself, its inescapability, an oppression more egregious than life or death. Other details fit with this reading. Water is the element both inside and outside, like metaphor itself. The title "The Water Works" refers to a story, that is, to a man-made construction of metaphors and other figures. Are stories "metaphor-works"? Read in this light, the narrator's concentration on water even more than on death becomes understandable.

The association between water and metaphor is also arbitrary. It would appear that the pursuit of death could lead the narrator to any metaphor, as he seems to admit in the story's opening: "I had followed my man here. Everything he did was mysterious to me, and his predilection for the Water Works this November day was no less so" (21). Before the pursuit of death begins, the narrator realizes that its irruption into any particular place will be arbitrary: water workers are no more privileged than firefighters or gravediggers. "The Water Works" thus dramatizes the inescapability of troping in the attempt to represent death, to make a model of it; this is a truth known before the story begins and redundantly confirmed by it. An eternal return.

The fact that Jonathon may be the author of "The Water Works" only emphasizes the point made in "The Writer in the Family," that authors are not to be sought in their works. Jonathon's personal view of the relation between writing and death is so utterly banal as to mock the sophisticated story he supposedly wrote. In the beginning of his glib, complaisant monologue, Jonathon worries about his stiff left thumb and worries if "it is gout or arthritis unless, of course, death to the writer, it is that monstrous Lou Gehrig thing, God save us all" (81). In these two texts, the representations of "death to the writer" are at best incommensurate.

"Willi" recounts the recollection of a childhood "primal scene." As a boy, living on a farm in Galicia in 1910, Willi observed his tutor making love to his mother in a barn. He tries to disclose this knowledge to his mother but is unable. He goes to his father, a dog-breeder, who is, coincidentally, overseeing two dogs mate. In a sudden exclamation to his father, Willi compares the dogs to his mother and tutor. Later in the evening, Willi's father confronts his wife with his knowledge and beats her savagely.

Of all critical approaches to this story the psychoanalytic seems most profitable: Robert Towers, reviewing the collection, called the story "almost ostentatiously 'Freudian' in its content."9 The primal scene is presented from the standpoint of an adolescent boy; examples of animal and human intercourse are juxtaposed; the scene is repeated in dreams; the institution of repression in the father's revenge against his wife is registered in the young narrator, who recounts the events in the context of "initiation into manhood" (31). This recuperation of a Freudian *grand récit,* or "master narrative," recalls classic Freudian texts such as "A Child Is Being Beaten" or "The Wolf Man," in which visual spectacles are linked to the progress of the Oedipus complex.10 The story takes place in 1910, the year Freud published "Psychogenic Visual Disturbance According to Psycho-analytical Conceptions." The father's scientific aspirations and his Jewish background in a family that is "neither Jew nor Christian" also suggest the intellectual context of Freudianism. Invoking this tradition, a hermeneutic discussion might thematize the boy's internalization of the equation (in the repeated phrase "Give it to her") between violence (Willi's father hitting his mother) and the phallic thrust in coitus (the dogs breeding). This internalization marks the moment of repression.

These elements seem to point to a stable psychoanalytic referent for the tale. Willi seems to illustrate the excruciating processes of identification and rebellion attendant upon the oedipal moment. Even without the hypothesis that its author may be the thoroughly non-Freudian Jonathon of "Lives of the Poets," readers may begin to question such a theme, if only on the grounds of the ancient paradox of psychoanalysis: if repression like Willi's is real, can he express self-knowledge in narrative?

Skepticism regarding Willi's authorship and "insight" only increases after an examination of the story's chronology, through which it can be established that the most probable period in which he wrote his memoir is the late fifties.11 This is the period of the first impact of Freudianism on the study of literature, in the works of Lionel Trilling, Norman O. Brown, and Simon Lesser. Willi's interpretation of his experience reflects, therefore, the intellectual milieu of his day; indeed, his very selection and treatment of the episode reflects it. During the late fifties one of the writers frequently analyzed in Freudian terms was Wordsworth; in 1959 there appeared two well-regarded studies, David Perkins's *The Quest for Permanence* and David Ferry's *The Limits of Mortality*. Writing about both books, M. H. Abrams argued that the "major operative concept" of both was the "post-Freudian distinction between manifest and latent, conscious and unconscious content." Two years later, Harold Bloom wrote: "Wordsworth and Freud in their theories of artistic creation can be assimilated to one another." These quotations suggest the intertextual connection between Freud and Wordsworth which was popular at the time Willi composed his memoir.[12]

This moment of intellectual history is discernible in Willi's long introduction (27–28) to the time of his revelation. Willi precedes the narrative of the primal scene with an account of a visionary connection-to and separation-from nature that fits precisely with Freudian readings of Wordsworth in the late fifties. Intertextuality therefore defines his experience; interpretation precedes and governs it. Even Willi's later perception—for example, his hearing the prostitutes slapped in postwar Berlin—is determined by his prior sense of the supposed signification of the childhood scene.

The story's intertextuality does not end there. If Jonathon is accepted as the imagined author, the creator of Willi, then the story unfolds in a new way: it is a 1984 tale of "intertextual Freudianism" in the mid-fifties. The goal of interpretation now becomes not the intertextuality of the events themselves but Jonathon's construction of Willi's intertextuality. New questions arise. How do Jonathon's adulteries and sexual fantasies, depicted in "Lives of the Poets," result in a story like "Willi"? And vice versa: what can "intertextual Freudianism" tell of Jonathon's decision to move away from his wife? Articulated in these ways, the questions almost confess their unanswerability. It is clear from "Lives of the Poets" that Jonathon is no Freudian, for he never invokes Freudian categories when analyzing his own sexuality or that of his friends. Although he briefly mentions Wilhelm Reich (136), he cites him only as an example of an intellectual whom he admires for carrying his calling wherever it took him. (Jonathon himself hardly shares such a trait.) The most that can be said is that the story represents neither "intertextual Freudianism," nor its narrator, nor its supposed teller, Jonathon, but the way intertextuality severs the supposed connection between author and texts.

Reading "Willi" follows the familiar process of blindness and insight. It is worth noting, too, that its statement of empty intertextuality becomes apparent only after the story's chronology is computed. As noted before, the implication—that the blindness and insight of reading are repeated in the attribution of referents to numbers—appears often in Doctorow's "false chronologies."

In "The Hunter" the story's anonymous protagonist is a bright, imaginative young woman who teaches elementary school in a small northern town. Although enthusiastic in her teaching and care for the children, she suffers from depression and a nearly suicidal ennui. On a fall day, a bullet from a hunter's gun nearly hits her. Later, she drinks beer at a bar and is joined by the uneducated but affable young "local" who drives the school bus. She allows him to drive her home, but when he makes an overture toward her, she slams her door in his face. On the next day in school, the intensity of her renewed anxiety is apparent in her conversation with a school photographer.

The ambiguities of this story begin with its title's multiple referents: the orange-jacketed man whose rifle shot hits the side of an old mansion; the new school-bus driver, a "hunter" or prospective seducer of the schoolteacher; or the schoolteacher herself, whose groping to find some source of satisfaction outside her admirable job performance is evident from the story's beginning. The literal hunter's presence in the story seems so ephemeral as to urge acceptance of one of the metaphoric hunters, presumably the schoolteacher, as the proper referent. But the text does not resolve the ambiguity positively, so the "proper" referent becomes all three characters—and also the reader.

We cannot know if the hunter's shot is deliberate; near the window of the deserted house, the schoolteacher "wonders if he can see her from this distance" (44). This undecidability of motive is rendered in an ellipsis in the plot, in the tradition of *The Book of Daniel* and *Loon Lake*. Following the mysterious incident, the schoolteacher's behavior becomes manifestly more suicidal. She gulps Valium tablets and must run across a bridge to fight the temptation to leap from it into the river. Whatever the hunter's motive, his shot serves as a catalyst to, but does not originate, the schoolteacher's anxieties. Her subsequent arm's-length flirtation with the bus driver seems a desperate reaction to her plight. Her hurried conversation with the school photographer may presage an unspoken decision in favor of suicide. Her actions suggest that she may see her only authentic existence as, after all, the profession she has mastered so well as to find it wanting. So this story seems to portray a Camus-like fugue, deepened by an *acte gratuite,* the gunshot, strongly hinting at suicide as the only expression of freedom in the face of absurdity.

At this point, readers may reflect that they, too, have been "hunters" who have, in fact, supplied the object of the hunt in each case. Confronted with black marks and ellipses, readers assume that the orange-jacketed hunter is seeking a deer, that the school-bus driver is seeking the schoolteacher, that the schoolteacher is seeking the "meaning of life" or "authentic existence." Such assumptions are as necessary to the act of reading the story as supplying referents for its title. Just as the reader must ascertain the referent, so must the motives of the characters be pursued, motives that might be as undecidable as those of the orange-jacketed hunter. In its broadest sense, then, hunting may be a metaphor for reading or hermeneutics itself: the object of the endeavor is to locate and retrieve; the quarry is meaning. No sooner is meaning posited, however, than it is shown to be arbitrary; in fact, it cannot be understood to be arbitrary without first being posited.

If Jonathon wrote this story, it can hardly be said to represent him. Although "The Hunter" teaches that the attribution of motive is fictional, its author does little, in his own monologue, except to attribute motives: to his wife, lovers, friends, even to the non-English-speaking refugees he agrees to put up. Or even better, in "Lives of the Poets," Jonathon demonstrates the day-to-day necessity for what "The Hunter" shows to be fictional. So much for the notion that lucid authors write texts that illustrate their ideas.

In "The Foreign Legation," Morgan, a divorced museum curator, lives alone in his suburban house, alienated from his neighborhood through which he jogs every morning. He sees lovers parked in a car in front of his house. One day, jogging, he is inexplicably "given the finger" by a woman jogging. He jogs past a house where wealthy foreigners are staying. On another day, jogging by, he witnesses a bomb explode in their limousine, killing one of its occupants, a young girl.

The title refers primarily to the dark mestizo group, probably from Latin America, whose car is bombed, but other details suggest that the title may refer to all Americans, to a nation of foreigners. This secondary reference is implied by the account, almost comically exaggerated, of the diverse ethnic and religious affiliations of Morgan's family, his wife's family, the cleaning woman, the gardener, and the dry cleaner (61). The title thus resembles synechdoche, naming both some of the characters and, metaphorically, all of them. This kind of title is familiar to readers of Doctorow, but here it raises the issue of representation naturally, in the very idea of a legation.

Morgan's malaise in this land of acknowledged and unacknowledged foreigners resembles the schoolteacher's in "The Hunter." He is waiting "for whatever it was he'd always waited" (54); when he jogs near suburban homes, "he would see no sign that anything at all had happened" (54). Into the contemporary American scene of divorce and shopping centers, Morgan lives silently, signlessly, unenlightened by his binoculars, his local paper, his television, his mother-in-law's letter. It would seem that the bombing and its palpable bloody results might jolt Morgan out of his circular world of jogging and objectless waiting, but the result is the opposite: nothing can.

Morgan's blindness does not change. He obviously misunderstood the potential for ferocity latent in the Latin American mestizos upon two occasions: first, on his museum-sponsored trip to that region, when hungry beggars cried "trick or treat" outside the gates of the Embassy Halloween party; and, second, in his capacity as assistant curator of pre-Columbian art, through which he tries to understand culture through its represented artifacts. In these experiences he distances himself professionally from the violence that he understands, if at all, only abstractly. All the more reason, then, that the bombing should bring him some new, authentic awareness, but Morgan remains blind. Although he sees the mestizos as "leather" people (59, 60), that epithet may more accurately apply to Morgan himself; he sees nothing, though he is constantly depicted as a watcher, and he is nothing. The narrator indicates the full extent of Morgan's void: he "sincerely believed his house was not lived in" (58).

The bombing's failure to enlighten Morgan tells of his continued blindness, an opaqueness evoked by the story's flat style. Composed almost entirely of single-sentence paragraphs, "The Foreign Legation" presents experience as Morgan perceives it: as discrete, atomistic, unrelated events. He blurs the distinction between inner and outer reality, as when he mistakes his own breathing for the sound of the telephone, and his reaction to the bombing—"Did I do this?"—confesses only an inability to read.

Morgan's deficiencies are the effect of living in a world that seems to represent but does not, the condition rendered by the title's two referents. A foreign legation is a group of people who seem to represent, for whom the representative function is taken for granted. (In this regard it is worth remarking that the name of the country represented by the legation—its referent—is never mentioned.) As a corollary, the story shows that the ethnic identifications of all Americans likewise confer on them a spurious prospect of representation; Morgan's family (Calvinist of French Huguenot ancestry) is to Morgan as the unidentified mestizo people are to the foreign legation that represents them. The whole is supposedly represented in its part, but in fact Americans like Morgan and his former wife never represent their varied ethnic heritages. Just the opposite. America is the melting pot, the land that effaces all prior claims of ethnic representation.

The reader glimpses this vacuity over Morgan's shoulder as he reads a restaurant menu: "he could have the chili, or the chicken soup, he could have pigs' feet or Irish lamb stew or lasagna or souvlaki" (61). Perhaps Americans resemble these "ethnic foods," samples of other culture instantly rendered nonrepresentative as soon as they appear in America. Morgan "represents" his French Huguenot ancestry to the same degree that American lasagna "represents" Italy. America gives the lie to representation. Americans and their culture are like ambassadors without home countries, members of legations whose claims to represent can at any moment be exploded.

Morgan is unable to interpret because he has become the quintessential American, himself devoid of representation, in a signless world, standing for nothing, a living death ("His house was not lived in"). There are no "true homes." Everyone, not just the foreign legation, is foreign to this place. The bombing of the foreign legation car presents the reader with only a more graphic version of what Morgan already is: the possibility of representation exploded, a nothingness covered by misrepresentation, a "leather man."

The narration of "The Leather Man" is complex. It appears to be a monologue by an unnamed speaker who conducts a briefing or group meeting around a table. Among those in the group is an interlocutor, Slater, who is a young colleague of the man delivering the briefing. Mention of a lunch break (70) suggests that the setting is a formal conference or seminar. But more precisely, the piece is not a monologue; instead, it is narrated by an omniscient narrator whose voice on rare occasions is heard: "Slater, do you fuck around? A long time answering. No" (73).

The interruptions by the omniscient narrator are infrequent enough to call attention to the problem of narration, the question of who speaks, in the same way the computer interruptions of the narration of *Loon Lake* contributed to that novel's narrative undecidability. Here a related effect is created. Because the monologist, Slater, and the other listeners are given few defining attributes, and because of the run-on style, without quotation marks, these "interruptions" often blur the distinctions among the supposed characters and omniscient narrator. All seem to coalesce into one voice, one "leather man." This is only another way of saying that the story demonstrates the impossibility of a speaker's standing outside discourse, of seeking to isolate an extralinguistic signified, here the "leather man" phenomenon, which might thereby attest to the speaker's separate, different signification.

The story takes as its subject the attempt of the administrative mind to comprehend two threats to its preeminence: social dereliction and the aleatory. The briefer's seminar concerns contemporary social phenomena (including the counterculture, homelessness, and such social deviation as Peeping Tomism). He classifies these under the broad rubric of his neologism, "the leather man." His knowledge of contributions to this subject by social scientists suggests that the briefer may be an academic or a government bureaucrat; the ambiguity interestingly suggests *Big as Life*'s assumption that any large organization—business, government, university—may share the briefer's illusion that hermeneutics means control. His interest in the leather man phenomenon is administrative, and he analyzes social dereliction for the purpose of containing it. In his talk he seeks to show how pervasive the phenomenon is.

The inability of hermeneutics truly to grasp social dereliction is not a new subject for Doctorow. It was first broached in *Big as Life*. There, neither Creighton nor Kahn, despite their love of knowledge, investigated the survival of the criminal element in the city; Creighton's illusion—that history is only represented history—is exposed by Pinkeyes, the elderly fence with no record. Social dereliction is of interest to the NYCRAD researchers in *Big as Life* only as an instrument of social control, as it is in "The Leather Man." In Doctorow's fiction, social dereliction often gives the lie to the assumptions of referentiality in hermeneutics.

The briefer gives his most explicit definition of the leather man phenomenon as part of his discussion of adultery:

> What is the essential act of the Leather Man? He makes the world foreign. He distances it. He is estranged. Our perceptions are sharpest when we're estranged. We can see the shape of things. Do you accept this as a principle? All right, then, consider something as common as philandering. I'm an old-fashioned fellow and I use old-fashioned words. After a while your marriage becomes your cover. Don't laugh, I'm quite serious. Your feelings are broken down by plurality, you don't stop, you keep moving, it becomes your true life to keep moving, to keep moving emotionally, you find finally the emotion in the movement. You are the Leather Man, totally estranged from your society, the prettiest women are rocks in the stream, flowers along the road, you have subverted your own life and live alone in the wild, your only companion your thoughts. [74]

This definition comports well with the life of the vacuous, thick-hided Morgan in "The Foreign Legation." It also echoes accounts of estrangement and alienation in Camus and Sartre. So once again, the subject is intertextual before it is even articulated, and the briefer's hubris is his blindness to that. Referring to the degenerate astronaut James C. Montgomery, he claims that contemporary leather men are unable to articulate their own foreignness, even when they embody it (75). The undersurface of his arrogant, rambling monologue attempts to fix his own significance—as independent of texts, as a "nonleather" man, as authentic—but the end of the briefing proves the opposite.

Like Doctorow's other endings, this difficult one subverts closure. First, Slater challenges the briefer's claim to wisdom. He says there are "thousands of people in this country whose vocation it is to let us know what our experience is" (76). Their knowledge, Slater argues, should also be tapped, but the briefer warns Slater that their sources are suspect. Slater persists: "We'll know where they got their information. We gave it to them" (77). This dark exchange subverts the briefer's claim to authority while lumping together all of these analysts—Slater, the briefer, and all other sources—in equal delusion.

Slater's riposte destroys the "referent" the briefer sought to isolate. For Slater, the political subversions of art need not be feared, since its sources are not truths but, already, artificial constructs fed to writers by the "authorities," by writers of other texts. For Slater, representation cannot be subversive—it will never disturb society, even if it depicts a leather man. Because art can articulate only already constructed fictions, it can never affect the world it pretends to represent. Slater subverts the briefer's claim to authenticity in speaking about the leather man, but he does so at predictable cost: like the briefer, he becomes a leather man, himself. Their attempt to define their own authenticity by representing its opposite in language boomerangs. It ends by implicating them in the nonsignifying, aleatory world from which they wanted, all along, to distinguish themselves.

In retrospect it is possible to argue that Slater's critique of the briefer's neologism was always-already present in it. For example, the briefer, sometimes unknowingly, explains social deviation intertextually, under the auspices of prior "master narratives" or *grands récits*. The 1980s interest in introversion (or "cocooning") is only the recent reappearance of Thoreau (69). Morris Wakefield, the Peeping Tom from New Rochelle, finds his literary progenitor in Hawthorne (71–72). The interview with the astronaut ("Did the idea of space hold any terror for you?") echoes Pascal (75). In fact, the briefer's examples of the leather man phenomenon seem to bear out Slater's indifference to the subversive potential of art; the "information" in this briefing has already been given, in prior texts. The fact that the briefer's definition of the phenomenon recalls Camus and Sartre (as well as Jonathon or Doctorow, "author[s]" of "The Foreign Legation") now suggests that in the very attempt to articulate social phenomena, the recourse to prior fictions, constructs, or *grands récits* may be inevitable. In this light the coalescence of the briefer, Slater, and the omniscient narrator now seems an admission that identity itself is an intertextual construct.

"Lives of the Poets," at the end of the collection, is Jonathon's monologue. The reader is admitted into the presence of the "imagined writer of the stories." It is as if the hermeneutic quest pursued through six stories has reached its destination, the mind of the author, the source of all that preceded, and the simple irony is that, instead of finding a consciousness so profoundly complex as to subsume the six varied stories, the reader finds the successful author to be a gossip, the epitome of Heideggerian "idle talk." As if he were part of the world of John Updike's novels, Jonathon clucks over his friends' marriages, divorces, and adulteries, even as he has separated himself, without cogent explanation, from his own wife and family. His ethical concern exemplifies the dilemmas of liberal humanism in the 1980s: whether to provide quarters for illegal aliens, mestizos from Latin America. Prudently bourgeois, Jonathon fully explores his legal vulnerability before agreeing to house them. Like the leather man in his blindness, Jonathon enacts the contradictions of his characters without awareness that he is doing so. His final gesture, in turning his typewriter over to a mestizo child who writes nonsense on it, may be the closest Jonathan comes to acknowledging his stories' failures of articulation.

The relation between Jonathon's monologue and his previous stories casts doubt on the hermeneutic concept of an author harboring fixed motives and ideas that are then represented in his work. For example, Jonathon recollects his father (114–17), as he did in "The Writer in the Family," but now he does so only in the voice of literary appreciation, of the affectionate thumbnail biography, rather than in the hushed tones of discovery and epiphany—however contradictory—that marked his story. Other connections between the revealed author and his literary productions are equally disappointing, arbitrary, and tenuous; instead of adding to our understanding of the fiction, these details thwart it by exposing the artificial nature of earlier interpretations. The monologue suggests that adducing extra-literary evidence of authorial intention, in whatever amount, cannot succeed.

The elements that recur in his stories often trivialize their treatment of important issues. Like his protagonist Morgan in "The Foreign Legation," Jonathon reviews, in a kind of mock catalogue, the diverse ethnic and religious backgrounds of his friends (104); however, he does so because he wonders whether his wife Angel's oppressive urge "to mingle our souls," which has led to his decision to live alone, is common to all women. What suggested the philosophical issue of representation here becomes balm for a wounded ego. Also like Morgan, Jonathon eats at a diner with a "melting pot menu," where the counterman says, "Hey, compadre," but this incident only elicits a condescending reflection on the "sea wrack of waves of migrations, the detritus of vast tidal movements of impassive populations" (104). It may be the ugliness of this thought that prompts Jonathon to further trivialize and intertexualize the subject in recalling the relativistic lyrics of a popular song: "Maybe I'm right, maybe I'm wrong, maybe I'm weak, maybe I'm strong." (105).

The stories' portentous enigmas are here emptied of content. As he watches a violent storm over Houston Street, Jonathon recalls the specific image of the Mayan reservoir used in "The Water Works": "The skyline now is no higher than the 1930's, the era of my birth, this gets any heavier we'll be back in the last century with Melville's ironfronts. Cobblestones. Mayan reservoirs" (109). The echo of Hawthorne in the allusion to Wakefield in "The Leather Man" is picked up in Jonathon's reference to "Hawthorne, who taught me Romance" (134); however, this supposedly solemn literary indebtedness is acknowledged only in the midst of an extended recollection of an erotic tryst in the Berkshires. In Jonathon's memory of a Halloween party in Mexico City, the reader finds the author's experiential sources for Morgan's uneasy recollections in "The Foreign Legation" and for the narrator's menacing neologism in "The Leather Man":

> In October last year, going to a Halloween party in Mexico City at the residence of an American cultural attache, a house protected like all of them by iron gates, I pushed through a cluster of mestizos, leather-skin people of indeterminate age, some carrying infants in colored bindings slung from their shoulders, and they were holding out their fedoras, saying something in their soft toothless diction, and I figured it out, trick or treat, trick or treat, a murmur, no anger in it, trick or treat, like the sound of a gentle flock of ground birds. [131]

This blithe passage occurs while Jonathon considers a potentially serious, even radical, political point: that today's immigrants to American are driven here because of what we have done to their countries. But the very off-handedness of these thoughts—they are juxtaposed with recollections of laughter at a dinner party and of his friend Arlington's early morning poetry readings—is of a piece with Jonathon's detached, nonjudgmental, acquiescent voice. It resonates 1980s postmodernism, the desire for personal space, the easy hedonism of the Reagan years, the indiscriminate mixture of high and low, and above all the obsession with aging and the telltale signs of mortality. The weighty contradictions in interpretation exhibited in Jonathon's fiction are, for him, inconsequential. Whatever their supposed import in his fiction, the stuff of Jonathon's stories is present to his mind only ephemerally, as transitory as details of the weather or his hypocritical attendance at Crenshaw's publication party at the Dakota.

During the course of his monologue, certain events take place: Jonathon attends parties, reads his mail, receives unassembled bookcases; learns the details of a scandalous lawsuit for which he is, after all, excused as a juror; consults a priest supervising the housing of the illegal aliens; and talks with his attorney before deciding, finally, to accept them into his apartment. Throughout his monologue he watches the sights of Manhattan through his window: the heavy rainstorm engulfing the World Trade Center, a police drug-bust on

Houston Street, and the conversion of a clothing mill into a loft. In all of these activities Jonathon remains passive, not writing professionally, although there is mention of his friend Rosen's inquiry into the status of *Lives of the Poets*.

Jonathon never responds to this inquiry; thus it is impossible to know for sure if and when his manuscript was completed. If this collection is Jonathon's, it may well have been completed in the gap or silence following its last sentence. For this reason, then, it is not certain that even the just-noted trivial, gossipy "sources" of the stories gave rise to them. Who can know what occurred in the blank space between "Lives of the Poets" and *Lives of the Poets*? If Jonathon later became a committed late-fifties Freudian critic, would his story "Willi" become a true representation after all? And in that case, what of the other stories? Between any supposed evidence of authorial intention and the interpretation of literature falls an absolute nothingness such as this. It ensures the impossibility of reconstructing meaning as hermeneutics. Jonathon's final gesture—turning over his typewriter to the mestizo child—warns of this nothingness, as it allegorizes the removal of the author from the text.

In this way, "author" becomes a fictional construct, foisted upon the text by a reader who has little choice in the matter; on the other hand, what is true of author is true of any self: both are linguistic constructs. As he watches workmen remove the sign of the United Thread Mills building, Jonathon reflects on his condition:

> How do I feel? I don't care anymore. Maybe like that poet in Yeats who lies down to die on the king's doorstep because he's been kicked out of the ruling circle. Yeah, that's what this place is, that's what I'm doing here, and if I die, let the curse be on their heads. What else can this mean except I've been deprived of my ancient right to matter? Yes, you mothers, I of the Untitled Thread Mills, a mere man of words, will sit once more in the councils of state or a dire desolation will erupt from the sky, drift like a fire-filled fog over the World Trade Center, glut the streets of SoHo with its sulfurous effulgence, shriek through every cracked window, stop the singing voice of every living soul, and make of your diversified investment portfolio a useless thing. [143]

The "I" is not a self, but a letter derived from a prior word, one that can be taken down and rearranged (as "United" becomes "Untitled" to Jonathon). This realization results in the writer's dispossession, his being bereft of his "ancient right to matter." Here Jonathon sounds like the characters of his stories: himself, Willi, the schoolteacher, Morgan, the leather man. Creator and created never possessed autonomy or significance. They are by-products of intertextuality. The comic impotence of Jonathon's threats of vengeance for this dispossession make it all the more plausible. The lives of the poets—novella and collection, characters and narrators—are no more than the "I" of the "Untitled," who is their fictional father, the dead father, dead *archē* in whose name the writer in the family pretends to speak.

CHAPTER 8

Models of Misrepresentation in *World's Fair*

World's Fair narrates the childhood and family life of Edgar Altschuler, from his birth in about 1930 until 1941. (The novel's chronology is not exact.)[1] Some events of his parents' youth and courtship, which occurred in the early years of the twentieth century, are also reported. Edgar's narration takes place at some unspecified time after 1947. It is introduced and interrupted by short first-person recollections of family history told by Edgar's mother, brother, and aunt.

Edgar's parents, Rose and Dave Altschuler, are both children of Jewish immigrants to America; Dave's parents came from the Minsk district in Russia. The Altschulers live in the Bronx. Dave is co-owner of a record store in Manhattan; Rose is a housewife. Although there are intermittent references to the social dislocations of the depression and the rise of nazism in Germany, the novel concentrates on the events of Edgar's daily life: the games he plays in the neighborhood, his relations with his older brother Donald, and family problems with the relatives of Dave and Rose.

The family moves three times, adjusting themselves to Dave's changing financial condition. Edgar recalls the death of his senile grandmother. Just after entering school, Edgar is hospitalized with a ruptured appendix. Donald attends college briefly, then joins the Army Signal Corps. The 1939 World's Fair opens in Flushing, Long Island. Edgar wins second prize in an essay contest sponsored by the fair. The price consists of admission tickets for him and his family. He attends the fair twice, in June and September of 1941, just before it closes in October, and sees the time capsule buried on the premises. Then, Edgar buries his own time capsule, filled with various personal belongings, in Claremont Park. After the war, Donald returns to college and finishes his degree in 1947.

The straightforward autobiographical narration that comprises the bulk of *World's Fair* recalls the simpler narrative pattern of *Welcome to Hard Times*: like Blue, Edgar writes of himself only in the first person. This pattern divides the speaker into narrated and narrating selves, which converge at the end to valorize the idea of the writer as Cartesian self or presence. Like Blue's, Edgar's account offers the false promise that the convergence of Edgar's two fictional selves will authenticate a single representing presence behind narrative—Blue's palimpsest, Edgar's prize-winning essay or his longer narrative.[2]

Edgar's dream of a self disappears as he writes, though his illusion is particularly vulnerable in the intercalary chapters, written in the voices of Rose, Donald, and Edgar's Aunt Frances. Although it is not clear whether these chapters were delivered to Edgar orally, in writing, or by tape-recording, their conversational diction suggests Edgar's presence as a silent listener, studying oral history as he prepares to write. On the other hand, these monologues simply stand by themselves: Edgar does not introduce, rewrite, or judge them. Thus an uncertainty of their provenance—as of the interruptions from the computer in *Loon Lake* or the weak omniscient voice in "The Leather Man"—underscores the impossibility of establishing Edgar as the originating presence behind *World's Fair*. His is the primary voice, but the reader is never allowed to forget that the narrative as a whole is not his representation.

Indeed, the novel begins not with Edgar's discourse but with Rose's. In this preemption of her son's narrative, Rose's account reminds that discourse is never self-generated but already in place at birth, and it emphasizes that Edgar's "identity" in *World's Fair* is not as a self at all but as mere pronoun, the "you" to whom Rose addresses her short opening reminiscences. That Doctorow's principal narrator is constituted as merely a grammatical shifter becomes clear when Rose uses the second-person pronoun in its two ways, with both definite and indefinite antecedents: "I was by now interested in your father.... You played tennis in long skirts in those days... you didn't meet someone and go out and go to bed with them one two three" (3). The pronouns "you" and "your" in this case unsettle their own ostensible reference to (absent/present, listening/reading) Edgar, because they refer both to Edgar and anyone. This solecism—repeated throughout each of Rose's four chapters of reminiscences—exemplifies the inherent alienability of linguistic shifters.[3]

Even Rose is first known only as "you," in *her* recollection. This parallel usage suggests an infinite regress into the past of all spurious conferrals of identity by language. Indeed, Rose's father absorbs any singularity of her own identity into the pronoun's plural: "My father used to say to us, You think, you girls, you're beautiful? You should have seen your mother" (1). These passages set the stage for the most blatant instance of the linguistic construction of identity, the introduction of Edgar's name.

As in *Loon Lake,* the revelation of the narrator's "true name" is conspicuously delayed. For one-third of the novel, the narrator is referred to only by personal pronouns. A single, important exception occurs very early, as Dave shaves: "Good morning, Sunny Jim, he said. He had noticed early in my life that each morning I woke smiling, an act of such extraordinary innocence that he had ever since commented upon it" (9). Thus the narrator is "Jim" until much later, when at the Seder in Mount Vernon, Uncle Ephraim asks, "And how is Edgar?" (132). At that moment, Dave's "original" name for his son is revealed to be a trope, antonomasia. This pattern of transformation—of a supposed "signified" into a trope—recurs in *World's Fair;* however, the forced thought of the figurative nature of "Sunny Jim" prompts speculation about the nature of "Edgar," or any other name for that matter.[4]

Before leaving Rose's opening monologue, the reader may observe that she is, like Edgar, a writer of sorts, even a "recorder of voices." The suggestions generated from his parallel—to which Edgar remains oblivious—go far to subvert any claim for writing as the guarantor of a Cartesian self. Rose tells of her years as a typist; her account of her speed and ability provides an ironic prefiguring of that final "convergence of identities" Edgar seems to achieve: "I was a good secretary, Mr. Unterberg would dictate a letter to me and I could take it right on the typewriter, without an error, and so when he was finished I was finished and the letter was ready for him to sign" (2).

The words "when he was finished, I was finished," uttered before Edgar even begins his narration, mocks the "convergence of voices" central to the ruse of autobiography. It is instructive that Rose's writing, like Edgar's, results only in signs, in a letter; it should not surprise that Edgar's transcription—of many voices—yields no more.

On the cover of *World's Fair*, next to the title, are stylized renderings of the Trylon and Perisphere, which were built for the 1939 World's Fair and serve as the setting for the novel's climax. So even prior to Rose's monologue, then, the reader is confronted with double signs—in this case verbal and graphic—that may place in doubt the necessary relation of either to the referent, an event or a novel.[5] That such "double gestures" form part of the novel's design becomes clear from the protagonist's three meditations on the symbols.

Edgar's first interpretation of the shapes confidently assumes their representational function: "They represent the World of Tomorrow, which was the Fair's theme" (247). The representative function of predictions is, however, always open to question, and the World's Fair of 1939, with its complacent vision of social harmony, made social forecasts only more notorious than most. But these symbols are vitiated not only because the fair's predictions failed. In addition, the referent "World of Tomorrow" is itself a trope, a prolepsis, here capitalized as if to underscore its almost allegorical character. To the extent that it makes a promise of the future, the prolepsis also functions as a speech-act, a sign alleged to make something happen. On closer inspection, then, the presumption of any certain signified presence for the symbols is unsettled.

Edgar ponders the significance of the symbols a second time, when he reads the rules for the essay contest he is about to enter: "Under the printing of the contest rules were the palest, most meaningful shadows of the Trylon and Perisphere. Only gradually did I perceive them. They emerged in my mind as a message just for me, a secret summons, wordlessness, indelible" (303). Here the Trylon and Perisphere form part of a palimpsest, a first set of signs enmeshed in a second, which are legible only when the second is ignored; as such, they repeat the metaphor for writing used in *Welcome to Hard Times*. It is noteworthy that Edgar's Joycean interpretation of the symbols, as conferring a unique message or summons, omits any referent. Message of what? Summons to what? If a summons to write, the symbols become strangely self-perpetuating, since they only generate new signs—Edgar's autobiographical description of the typical American boy—whose representational value will in turn be called into question. In Doctorow's version of the Joycean portrait, the artist is not Daedalus or maker, but the by-product of the texts that generate him along with new signs.

Edgar's last encounter with the shapes occurs when he arrives at the World's Fair with Meg and sees the symbols' referent, the buildings themselves:

> Even from the elevated position I could see the famous Trylon and Perisphere. They were enormous. They were white in the sun, white spire, white globe, they went together, they belonged together as some sort of partnership in my head. I didn't know what they stood for, it was all very vague in my mind, but to see them, after having seen pictures and posters and buttons of them for so long, made me incredibly happy. I felt like jumping up and down. I felt myself trembling with joy. I thought of them as friends of mine. [321]

Edgar's ingenuous reaction to coming into the presence of "the signified" harbors ominous admissions: its meaning is still, after all, undisclosed and unknowable, except as trope, the prosopopoeia "friends of mine." Again the reader encounters the process of transformation by which signs are exchanged for ostensible referents that are then, belatedly, recognized as, after all, new signs, even tropes. Such a transformation was observed in the first sentence of *The Book of Daniel*. Here it accompanies the novel's symbols. As the cover's doubleness implies, Edgar's mistakes only repeat, as eternal return, similar errors necessary to the reading of *World's Fair*.

When a supposed referent becomes a sign or trope, discourse comes to resemble Heidegger's idle talk.[6] Edgar's earliest memories are of injuries and pains that produce howls; his mother's reply, "Oh, stop the nonsense. . . . You make a fuss over nothing" (6), defines a relation between utterance and object that is apparent in the major events and insights Edgar recollects from his childhood. At the beach in Far Rockaway, his experience of sand, bathers, and ubiquitous condoms results in a parody of the Joycean epiphany:

> Beyond any man's recognition, under the shouting and teeming life of the world's public on their tribal Sunday of half-nude ceremony, was some quiet revelation in me of unutterable life. I was inspired in this state of clarity to whisper the word *scumbag*. It was as if all the sound had stopped, the voices, the reedy cry of gulls, the sirens and the thunderous surf, for that one word to be articulated to illumination. I felt through my fingers the sand pour of bones, like some futile archeologist of a ground-up mineral past. I recognized that heat in the sand as some invisible power of distant light. And from the glittering blue water I took its endless motion and unimaginably frigid depth. All of this astonishingly was; and I on my knees in my bodying perception, wordlessly primeval, at home, fearful, joyous. [79]

The revelatory moment that aspires to transcend language, in which the protagonist might learn the authenticity of existence, is but the substitution of one series of tropes (simile, metaphor, hyperbole) for another (metaphor, personification). The concept that "learning" turns out to be only such a substitution has already been noted in *Welcome to Hard Times* and *The Book of Daniel*. Here, the substitution undermines the expectation of insight in epiphany: "illumination" is as empty as the word "scumbag."

The many senses of the emptiness-of-reference evoked by the scumbag-as-symbol recur in Edgar's reaction to his grandmother's death. The memorial candle for her is a literal sign of absence; the Hebrew letters on the glass label add new signs. Edgar associates these letters with others, on the window of the chicken market "where dead chickens hung on hooks by their feet" (124). Then, conflating the symbols, Edgar describes his grandmother's Siddur: "The cover had those Jewish letters on it that looked to me like arrangements of bones. In my room I played with my pick-up sticks to see if I could arrange them in Jewish letters, but they lacked bony width, they lacked the knobby thickness even of chicken bones" (125).

Words are like pick-up sticks—arrangements of mute, meaningless parts, whose putative referents could only be absence, emptiness, death; such passages recall the verbal obsession with death in *Welcome to Hard Times, The Book of Daniel,* and "The Water Works." After his grandmother's death, Edgar's mother takes her place in saying Sabbath prayers, and the world of empty discourse, the novel's version of Heidegger's *Sein-zum-Tode,* resumes. Of course Edgar, like everyone else in the novel, never perceives his own mortality in language. Heidegger explains how idle talk—language as constituted in "the they"—deprives one of an authentic relation even to one's own death: "If idle talk is always ambiguous, so is this manner of talking about death. Dying, which is essentially mine in such a way that no one can be my representative, is perverted into an event of public occurrence which the 'they' encounters."[7] Thus, even as Edgar unconsciously attests to the necessary relation between language and death, he sees death only as happening to others; "death is Jewish," he concludes, happening to his grandmother because she "spoke Jewish" (124).

The idea that language, once it is considered apart from representation in this Heideggarian sense, may block comprehension of even the minimal ontology of death is reinforced in the novel by the many occasions on which death is known only indirectly, through reportage: the parental white lie told to facilitate the death of the dog, Pinky (105); the news bulletin of the Hindenberg disaster (200); the accounts of the war in newspapers (251, 279) and newsreels (249); the *Daily News* report of the murder-suicide incident involving Donald's friend, Sigmund Miller (252–53). The eventless character of Edgar's childhood, about which some critics have complained,[8] is all the more discernible because it is delineated against a cultural background of incessant reminders of vulnerability and mortality. On the two occasions upon which Edgar does directly witness deaths, his writing reveals only the incapacity of language to grasp the experience in other than metaphorical ways. On seeing his dead grandmother in bed, he "felt the overall stillness of her, a declared inanimateness, the monumental event of death *recorded here for me as another kind of life*" (121-22; emphasis added). An even more dramatic instance of verbal *méconnaissance* is Edgar's recollection of the body of the woman killed in the accident on his school playground: "At night, before sleep, I remembered the arm of the dead woman bobbing up and down as she was carried in the stretcher, the hand limp, palm up, as if the arm were pointing to the schoolyard, indicating it repeatedly—so that I should not forget—as a place of death. For weeks afterward the strain of the blood was visible on the schoolyard ground, a darkening of meaningless shape on the sun-bleached cement" (194). The dead arm pointing is the first of two signs. Its "referent" should be the truth that existence may be defined, maximally, as a place of death. Yet this "lesson" never registers for Edgar—the referent remains unapprehended, and even the bloodstain, the second sign, is visible only as a "meaningless shape."

The reason the lesson cannot be learned becomes apparent later, in the account of Edgar's illness and hospitalization. His confidence in his recovery is based on his belief that forethought forefends, a conviction similar to one Freud described as "magical thinking" in children.[9] It is of interest that the presumed childish naivety of this doctrine is never retrospectively denounced by the narrating Edgar. His silence may be consistent with the fact that his youthful delusion does not differ, after all, from the prolepses and assumptions of referentiality made everywhere in the novel and most crucially, of course, by himself as narrator. Proximity to death appears to shake these assumptions; the dying children Edgar meets lose interest in their models, their toys and games. When Edgar himself is gravely ill, he, too, displays unwonted indifference to models, to the texts (*Wuthering Heights*, the Frank Buck comic, *Bambi*) that his father brings to the hospital. It is almost as if true immersion in life requires belief in referentiality, in the hope that fiction or other texts can "mean," but that imminent death may disclose the illusion of that idea.

Of course, to accept even this principle would be surreptitiously to reinstate representation, to find it in some epiphanic moment of closeness to death, and neither Heidegger nor Doctorow implies such a moment. Instead, the dying children—necessarily—cannot escape signs; they "enjoyed talking to one another" (231), and nearest to his own death, Edgar hallucinates a visit from his grandmother—demonstrating his ability to personify, to make the absent present—and refers to the experience in words that recall his earlier reaction to her death: "as if, becalmed and drifting to stillness, to inanimation, the mind sees death as life" (229). It is now evident that it is both necessary and explicable that Edgar "forgets" the lesson of the dead woman's arm pointing at the bloodstain in the schoolyard. Existence conceived even as Heidegger's *Sein-zum-Tode* cannot be represented. Like the black-bearded captain of "The Water Works," it always escapes discourse.

It is instructive in this regard that, when Edgar is gravely ill, his brother Donald presents him with a symbol of the World's Fair, the Heinz-57 pickle, and simultaneously makes him the promise that the whole family will attend the fair when he has recovered. Hope is seen as a function of the referentiality of signs, as in Blue's need for "good signs"; here, hope is associated with a speech-act, a performative, Donald's promise. It is as if existence depended on belief in such a speech-act. That the necessary operation of a performative is a delusion is apparent enough from the fact that the promise is "kept" only because Edgar enters and wins an award in the essay contest. Fulfillment of any performative is never inherent in it, but comes about arbitrarily (Edgar seizes the chance to visit the fair with Meg) or as a function of other signs (as in the case of Edgar's essay).[10]

Edgar's essay is a model of misrepresentation. That the assigned "theme"—the Typical American Boy—solicits fiction would be apparent if only from the intractable diversity of the novel's children. Even more fundamentally, the assignment solicits the fiction essential to novels: that an individual "self" can be represented and construed as "typical." The young Edgar, like the narrating Edgar, never questions this presupposition. His essay blends the empirical (drinking raw milk in the country), with retrospective wish-fulfillments (identifying himself publicly as Jewish), and with the purely imaginative ("In women he appreciates them all"). Many of Heidegger's doubts seem compressed in this sentence: "If he is anything he should say what it is when challenged." Here any essentialism, any "self," is momentarily suspended, but the inescapability of the act of articulation is also recognized ("he should say what it is"). So Edgar's essay becomes an exercise in prosopopoeia. It affirms not only the fiction of a typical American boy but also the necessity for personification. His last sentence tells the lie that Doctorow's narrators need to believe: "He looks death in the face."

Of course, Edgar's essay is not the novel's only model of misrepresentation: *World's Fair* recreates America in the thirties as a culture defined by consumer products that market meaning. Reviewers noted its plethora of commercial artifacts, such as Gee Bee racers or Little Orphan Annie Ovaltine mugs.[11] Now the multiplicity of such objects against the background of depression and imminent war creates initially a vertiginous effect, of capitalism's blindly self-replicating imperative, but beyond their function as icons of a culture of junk, these objects also serve as models, part of the world of idle talk. The most repetitive evoke the fair itself: the Heinz pickle, the Mr. Peanut, the DC-3 charm, the buttons and posters—these secondary representations deepen questions already asked about the Trylon and Perisphere. A survey of other "models" will show how all of them share those symbols' thwarted mission to represent truly.

Edgar's first literal model is his Railway Express truck, his favorite toy, which is praised for the accuracy of its representation: "The two rear doors unbolted and swung open *exactly* in the manner of the real ones. The steering wheel, *which actually worked*, was mounted at the *correct* angle, an *undeviatingly* horizontal on an *absolutely vertical* shaft" (20; emphasis added). Accuracy in representation continues to be Edgar's interest in praising Donald's igloos (37–40); his model airplanes (99); and his mechanical drawings, which are "like blueprints" (176). Edgar's insistence on faithful representation motivates his suspicions of the manipulative messages of fairy tales (119) and his exposure of Frankie, the sax player, for faking his part (184–86). In each of these instances models or representations are evaluated on the basis of their fidelity to some presumed authentic original.

The idea of fidelity to an original example is questioned, however, in Edgar's concern to assess the accuracy of movie versions derived from comics or radio shows (275–79). He compares different versions of Dick Tracy, Don Wilson, and Flash Gordon, but in a debate with his friend, Arnold, he reveals the fallacy of his own confidence in originals. Arnold believes the Green Hornet is "actually" the Lone Ranger's grand nephew, partly because they share the "real" name "Reid." To Arnold, chance resemblances imply some natural or necessary referent of signs, but after thinking about it, Edgar convinces his friend that both comic heroes may be simply the creations of the same writer. For Arnold, models are representations of true presences; for Edgar, the writer in embryo, signs (or better, the signs of *other* writers) are fabrications.

If models provide only the illusion of representation of an authentic original, the process of making or emulating them is so pervasive as to be inescapable. Donald and his band imitate the style of their jazz heroes (183); Edgar draws a cartoon based on Smilin' Jack (250); Meg's doll is modeled on Shirley Temple (210, 296); on the playground older children serve as models of wildness (139). Life consists of constructions of the arbitrary that imply presences. Edgar plays "baseball" with a deck of playing cards and dice: "Aces were home runs, kings triples, queens doubles, jacks and tens were singles. . . . I kept scoreboards and made up player names and kept batting averages" (351). Edgar's instinctive prosopopoeia—his attribution of human signification to the arbitrary signs of cards and dice—is his domestic version of the radio announcers' ability to evoke actual baseball games from telegraph reports. In both cases, artificial models of "real originals" actually supplant them. The world's surfeit of models, asking to be read, suggests that there is no alternative to "taking" them as representative, in the way Edgar's typical boy is taken: as narrative, as story.

The necessary futility of models is apparent in Edgar's narrative quest to understand his father. Dave's death predates Edgar's decision to write. (Once more the reader finds the writer as metaphoric orphan, first broached in "The Songs of Billy Bathgate" and *Ragtime*, developed at length in the filial quests of *The Book of Daniel* and

Loon Lake, and explicitly connected with the moment of writing in "The Writer in the Family.") In *World's Fair,* the intercalary chapters, especially, undermine Edgar's search for the truth of his father. It is clear from his relatives' asides (Donald's "You say he didn't use force" [308]) that the "absent" Edgar prompted these narrators to recall details of Dave's life (Donald's "I don't know much about Dad's life as a boy" [174], followed by Aunt Frances's "I don't know what to tell you about your father" [237]). These features of the intercalary monologues make Edgar's narrative resonate with faint echoes of that Joycean quest for the father-as-author, but the fact that no "true picture" of Dave emerges is less a function of his physical absence or of fallible and conflicting memories than of the act of representation itself. For example, Donald's conviction that his father was a philanderer is based on a signed photograph of a glamorous woman which he finds at the record store (283). Like the other photographs in the novel, this "representation" is a symbol mutely incapable of disclosing meaning of intent or context. Consider Dave's remark about the woman in the photograph: "she was wearing some sort of costume. I supposed she was some kind of singer, I don't know why I thought that" (284). His inferences are "based" only on other signs, like costumes, photographs, or signatures.[12]

John T. Irwin has argued that the futility of narrative attempts to define the father—especially as enacted by Faulkner's narrators—reflects the writer's belatedness, the anxiety of being secondary or derived, conscious of following an original.[13] Irwin analyzes this feature, which he finds pervasive in American fiction, in oedipal terms: the father's castration threat precipitates the son's idealization/aggression/narrative in an unending struggle that even third generations cannot resolve. In *World's Fair,* the grandiose, mythological dimensions of such a motive for filial narration appear demystified, stripped of psychological content, and attenuated to the point at which Dave functions for Edgar simply as one of many models, whose representative function—like the Trylon, Perisphere, or other symbols—the text subverts.

That Doctorow's fiction undoes the idea of narrative as filial quest may be apparent from the fact that it is Donald, not Edgar, who struggles with the model of Dave in oedipal terms. Donald says:

"Dad was a good model in one way—he didn't like working for anyone else. . . . But he was never satisfied to be what he had chosen to be. . . . And the funny thing is I thought I was getting away from him. And what did I go and do but get into a radio business of another sort, just like my father" (284–85).

Though Donald may believe in models, Edgar's narrative has called them into question. Despite all their efforts, Doctorow's "orphaned" narrators never find true fathers. Billy sees himself in the menacing clown; Daniel fails to solve the mystery that sent his father to the electric chair; Joe enlists in the cause of a fraudulent surrogate father. Despite Edgar's patient research, the essence of Dave escapes him. The writer begins and ends a figurative orphan.

The conclusion of *World's Fair* promises enlightenment to readers long stymied by the title. The fair is not even mentioned until the novel is more than half-finished; the first of Edgar's two visits does not occur until page 321. It is as if the referent of the title is suspended over the narrative of other, equally formative or insignificant events that constitute Edgar's childhood. This delay demonstrates how a title serves as a fallacious speech-act, promising but withholding future content. Yet the title, with its double symbols and puns, takes on new complexity when considered in the light of its "double referents": Edgar's two visits to the fair. The novel ends in repetition and anticlimax, which foretells, as so often in Doctorow's texts, eternal return.

The scenes themselves are new instances of Doctorow's habit of concluding his novels with enactments of fraudulent representations of America. *The Book of Daniel* ends in Disneyland. In *Ragtime*, Tateh's films celebrate a social harmony nowhere else visible; the Fourth of July parade is led by a wealthy madman who murdered with impunity. In *Loon Lake*, Joe's leap into the lake signals his acquiescence in Bennett's mad perversion of America. As in these novels, *World's Fair* ends with its characters inhabiting an unreal space in which their hope for meaning seems misguided. On his first visit to the fair, Edgar's coming to sexual knowledge is inseparable from the act of personification; acceptance of the fiction of Oscar the Amorous Octopus is the necessary condition for interpreting the scene as other than an empty spectacle of lust. As Edgar gradually understands the trope, he initially becomes sickened (345), but his "nauseating ache" becomes "bearable" (347) when, next to Meg in the car, he acknowledges his own implication and participation in sexuality with this simile: "I knew everything now, the crucial secret, so carelessly vouchsafed. . . . As I fell asleep the fireworks went off over and over again like me pounding my own chest and sending my voice to the heavens that I was here" (348).

Again, a Joycean epiphany is expressed only in a trope, here a simile that equates Edgar's affirmation of his own existence with the empty on/off markers of the fireworks. Even more important, Edgar's apparently triumphant cogito, or Dasein, is inseparable from an act of ventriloquism, from the art of throwing the voice; this metaphor is also the novel's flawed, residual concept of the writer.

If Edgar's first visit produced the false epiphany of sexual awakening, his second leads to an equally fraudulent political demystification. Dave presents the case against the World's Fair and its metonymy, the time capsule, for their distortions of American history and culture and their perpetuation of capitalist propaganda. Dave's critique underscores the arbitrariness of the World's Fair and time capsule as representations; in effect, Dave reads and disputes the meaning of "World's Fair" as "The world is just." On the other hand, Rose reads it differently. Her whisper to Edgar ("That may be so. . . . But it would be very nice to own a car" [367]) responds to the definition, "The world is beautiful." While voicing her hope, her future expectation, her prolepsis, Rose neutralizes Dave's political critique even as she demurs to it. The two interpretations, with mutually exclusive referents, cancel. As in the case of Edgar's sexual enlightenment, his political education ends with an acquiescence in the world of fiction.

However, the final ending of the novel is, of course, not the trips to the World's Fair, but Edgar's own creation of a time capsule, a seeming metaphor for writing a novel. This metaphor brilliantly unites the necessity for prolepsis and personification central to the act of writing. In order to write at all, the novelist must presuppose, even envision, a future reader, but even as he makes such an inaugural presupposition, the representative function of the "contents" of his work is called into question. The contents Edgar selects for inclusion are, like the contents of his essay, drawn from his life but misrepresentations of it. In fact, Edgar at first includes *Ventriloquism Self-Taught* "not because I had succeeded but because I had tried." Of course, it is obvious that no future "reader" of the time capsule could distinguish accomplishment from intent on the basis of this symbol. A future "reader" will have no more accurate a means of conjuring the absent Edgar than those who pray for his dead grandmother could derive from her memorial candle. As *Lives of the Poets* taught, the construction of an author behind a fiction is but another fiction.

Most revealing is Edgar's inclusion of "something I was embarrassed to let Arnold see, a torn silk stocking of my mother's, badly run, and which she had thrown away and I had recovered, as an example of the kind of textiles we used—although it was true that I had heard that women no longer wore silk stockings in protest against the Japanese, but now wore cotton or that new nylon stuff made of chemicals" (370).

This passage drastically divorces art from hermeneutics and restates the central discourse of Doctorow's works. Edgar has never until this time shown an interest in "textiles"; he even admits that the piece of silk stocking will not be representative. The inference is nearly inescapable that Edgar—like all writers?—may include material, even fragments of "texts," for reasons that are not well understood. (In this case, Edgar's embarrassment over the item leads to speculation: maybe the torn piece of silk is a harmless fetishistic object, connected with his sexual awakening?) The point is not whether Edgar "truly understands" his reason for including the silk, but whether there can be any "true understanding" of this detail, or of the novel as a whole, once the purport of the scene—that authors themselves may not know why they write—is granted. On this note of mutual incomprehension—Doctorow's, Edgar's, the reader's—the novel *nearly* ends.

Then comes a coda; Edgar retrieves the instruction book on ventriloquism from the time capsule, vowing to try harder to master the art. The implied artistic credo answers all grandiose, representative theories of art, like that of Stephen Daedalus. Writing is like ventriloquism in that it can consist of nothing but prosopopoeia, of "throwing the voice" in the illusion of representation. Most hearteningly, Edgar's retrieval of the book, in the midst of all this delusion, seems to promise, despite everything, another attempt, another in a series the endless, futile eternal returns. On this final note Edgar turns, through "dead leaves" (371) and disappears from the page.

On the other hand, endings mislead.

Edgar's renewed commitment to empty art is neither heroic nor foolish, but it is inescapable, since as a character he is inextricable from the fragments of the empty texts that define him. The network begins with the novel's epigraph from Wordsworth's *The Prelude*: "A raree-show is here, / With children gathered round" (Book VII, 174–75, 1850 edition). Wordsworth's raree show (or portable peep show) is part of the "living scene" (144) of London, especially the pleasure gardens of the Vauxhall and Ranelagh districts, and is noted in passing with such other exotic street sights as dancing dogs and a dromedary. In *The Prelude* such sights and sounds are part of the "thickening hubbub" (211) of the city, in the midst of which the speaker feels "the imaginative power / Languish within me" (468–69). It is of interest that the allusion to the raree show precedes a description of a fair, the St. Bartholomew's Fair (676ff), whose chaotic entertainments seem "blank confusion! true epitome / Of what the mighty City is herself" (722–23). Also pertinent is the fact the St. Bartholomew's Fair includes "Ventriloquists" (710).

In Doctorow's epigraph, the raree show may refer to the fair of the title or to the text itself. In either case, the epigraph from Wordsworth mocks the idea that this *Künstlerroman* might culminate in the discovery of a supposedly authentic voice, as the magisterial "I" of *The Prelude* is so often presumed to represent.[14] Further, it suggests that Edgar's painful adolescence is only a raree show, part of the blank confusion of the city. Since the novel's final figure for the artist is as ventriloquist—part of the fair that Wordsworth can imaginatively distance himself from—the epigraph hints that Edgar's artistic development is already subsumable under the master narrative or *grand récit* of Wordsworthian romanticism. If this is so, reading the novel after the epigraph is redundancy or even regression.

The epigraph also recalls two previous ironic allusions to Wordsworth. In *Loon Lake*, Penfield, the aspiring poet, signals a selection from Wordsworth's "Intimations of Immortality" in semaphore to his fellow-soldiers. His signal incites artillery fire, after which Penfield lands in a madhouse, where he is decorated for heroism. This act of reading Wordsworth surely mocks "official interpretation." In "Willi" the narrator's recollection of a primal scene is cast in terms that blend Wordsworth and Freud; he can represent it only intertextually. In both cases, the traditional heritage of romanticism is used against itself to imply an incommensurable gap between life and its interpretation. The allusions subvert themselves. Like them, the allusion to Wordsworth in *World's Fair* may most resemble the reference to Samuel Johnson in the title of *Lives of the Poets*. Teasing but empty, they state intertextual relations only to renounce them, or even better, they state only the necessity of intertextuality stripped of "content."

An even grimmer implication flows from the novel's references to Doctorow's own texts, especially to "The Writer in the Family." That story promises but withholds insights into the novel that resembles it so closely.[15] The reader of *World's Fair* may unavoidably recall Aunt Frances' request, in "The Writer in the Family," that her nephew fabricate letters written in the name of his dead father. Such a recollection would prompt speculation about Edgar's interview with Aunt Frances or the reliability of her comments, until the moment the emptiness of all such speculation is perceived; although similar, the texts are "separate" only because characters have been renamed. Such disappointed thought would be only another moment in the process of reading, the alternation of insight and blindness, the transformation of an apparent referent into a sign, that is exemplified throughout Doctorow's works. It may be simplest to accept that "The Writer in the Family" and *World's Fair* both do and do not allude to each other, or that they exhibit the likeness between reading and empty allusion.

World's Fair contains another disconcerting allusion—to *Ragtime*. After the funeral of his grandmother, Edgar describes her prayer book, "and the cover had those Jewish letters on it that looked to me like arrangements of bones" (125). This perception aligns Edgar with Evelyn Nesbit of *Ragtime*, who sees in the Lower East Side "stores with Hebrew signs in the windows, the Hebrew letters looking to her eyes like arrangements of bones" (48). Once again an allusion stirs speculation. Is there an important difference between "Jewish" letters and "Hebrew" letters? Does this difference help define the novels' different narrators? In what other ways does Edgar resemble Evelyn? Of course, the emptiness of all such inquiry into coincidences among texts was dramatized in *Lives of the Poets,* but it appears that dramatizations cannot prevent speculation attendant on recurrence in reading—again, eternal returns.

The most promising recurrence in *World's Fair* is Edgar's development of the metaphor of the artist-as-clown from "The Songs of Billy Bathgate" and the essay "False Documents." In "The Ballad of W. C. Fields (2:20)," the clown appears as W. C. Fields, whose crooked artistry discloses to Billy an apocalyptic vision of universal blindness; in "False Documents," acrobats disguise themselves as clowns and only gradually reveal their artistry. The clowns of *World's Fair* resemble those of "False Documents." When Rose takes Edgar to the circus, they watch a clown who is actually an accomplished artist in disguise. His artistry is rendered in a hushed, sustained mediation, so portentous as to seem a "true epiphany," words illuminated from within with meaning:

> It interested me particularly that in the circus there was one wistful clown who climbed the high wire after the experts were done, and scared himself and us with his uproariously funny, incredibly maladroit moves up there . . . he was actually doing stunts far more difficult than any that had gone on before. This was confirmed, invariably, as he doffed his clown garments one by one and emerged from the woeful little potbellied misfit as the star who headlined the high-wire act. In his tights and glistening bare torso he pulled off his bulbous nose and stood spotlighted on the platform with one arm raised to receive our wildest applause for having led us through our laughter, our fear, to simple awe. I took profound instruction from this hoary circus routine. It was not merely that I, the sniffer with the red nose, would someday in my good time reveal myself to be a superman among men. There was art in the thing, the power of illusion, the mightier power of the reality behind it. . . . You didn't have to broadcast everything you knew all at once, but could reveal it suspensefully, and make them

first cry out in fear, make them laugh, and above all, make them applaud, when they finally saw what an achievement had been yours by taking on so well and accurately the comic being of a little kid. [146–47]

The "wistful clown" is not a clown at all but a potent, skilled artist. The "profound instruction" Edgar takes from him concerns his "power of illusion": "he was actually doing stunts far more difficult than any that had gone on before." Here is a figure for the full potency of art, for the writer whose "far more difficult" stunts may include even allegories of reading or the decision to return to artistry when its hopelessness has been redundantly shown. All of this seems implied. The last sentence, especially, seems to be spoken by "Doctorow himself," justifying his high calling in this novel behind the voice of a child. The eloquence of the passage revives a thaumaturgical concept of the artist as a "superman among men." In such eloquence, can writing have finally reached the truth?

Probably not. The very next sentence, which begins a new section, shows that the wistful clown-acrobat only induces another false epiphany: "Of course that was a hard illusion to maintain once the show was over" (147). The clown, the disguised and potent artist, must take his place beside W. C. Fields and Houdini: all are mirages, false lures, will-o'-the-wisps for the writer, believable only by children, only as long as the show lasts, the raree show of *World's Fair*.

Chapter 9

Selected Essays and Interviews

Doctorow's essays and interviews are scrupulously crafted; each sets forth complex figures for artists and writers that invite extended exegesis in unavoidable counterpoint to Doctorow's evolving ouevre. Most important, each thoroughly interrogates the category "nonfiction" (hereafter without quotation marks only for the sake of convention). Just as relentlessly as *Loon Lake* and *Lives of the Poets* did, these works question that distinction. The number, variety, and density of Doctorow's nonfiction works makes full coverage of them impossible in this study, but the essays and interviews discussed here share certain features with his fiction. Often their arguments—whether on literary, cultural, or political subjects—break down. Underlying these local breakdowns is the major contradiction manifested in Doctorow's fiction: the assertion that the world as it is constituted is wholly arbitrary, but at the same time, the belief that fiction can give it meaning. An overwhelming aspiration to meaning, to the creation of the "new," animates the conception of characters like Blue, Red Bloom and Sugarbush, Daniel, and Coalhouse Walker; the novels also depict the collapse of these aspirations. In the same manner, Doctorow's nonfiction depicts the writer as engaged in a meaning-making enterprise that is, simultaneously, a delusion.

The nonfiction pieces offer no resolution to this contradiction but, instead, exemplify it again and again, just as the novels have, in eternal return.

This breakdown of meaning is manifested in new models of misrepresentation. In "False Documents," passages quoted from other writers subvert the claims they ostensibly support. In "The Writer as Independent Witness," the example of Dostoevsky invalidates not only the point under discussion—the political intent of literature—but the use of examples in general. A recurrent misrepresentation in the nonfiction is the persona or "I," which often calls attention to its created character and warns the reader against identifying it as Doctorow. A bold misrepresentation is the diametrically opposed interpretation of Ernest Hemingway's *The Garden of Eden,* in works published only a few months apart. This blatant contradiction seems part of a larger effort to show how readers may appropriate, incorporate, and supplant the authors they read. But as if even this position must be challenged, the late essays rebel against it and, in the name of the author, against deconstruction. But soon this protest—against a practice that Doctorow himself engaged in—also breaks down. Like the novels, Doctorow's nonfiction dramatizes writing as "a terrible, awful struggle," in the words of my epigraph.

Doctorow's best-known essay about literature, "False Documents" (1977), has often been cited in critical studies of his works, although its subject is literature in general. This essay is a major manifesto of American postmodernism, somewhat analogous to John Barth's "The Literature of Exhaustion," and it exemplifies the problems of representation discussed throughout this book. Many of its features lead the reader to question whether the essay should be classified as nonfiction at all and whether customary distinctions between fiction and nonfiction are valid.

The essay purports to be a discussion of the importance of the often-employed literary technique, or premise, of introducing a fiction with the claim that the tale that follows grew out of the discovery of certain real documents; Doctorow cites *Robinson Crusoe* and *Don Quixote* as two works that use this device, called "false documents" by the critic Kenneth Rexroth. This technical point is only the occasion, however, for a more broadly considered essay on contemporary aesthetics. In addition to Defoe and Cervantes, the essay alludes to Nabokov, Sartre, Benjamin, Nietzsche, Barthes, to name only a few. It ranges widely over such various questions as a text's credibility, the role of the artist in ancient and modern times, the place of fiction in Western and non-Western societies, and the use of techniques of fiction in the social sciences. The essay makes seemingly apodictic generalizations on these subjects in a fluent, assured style, but careful study of the essay's theses shows that they undermine themselves in ways not unlike the narratives of Doctorow's novels. As Joseph Valente first maintained, "False Documents" is itself a false document.[1] As such, the essay exemplifies, again, an eternal return, this time, daringly, in a nonfictional genre.

The essay distinguishes between the power of freedom and the power of the regime, between fiction writers in Western and non-Western countries, between fiction and nonfiction, but during the course of the essay, these distinctions break down, leaving Doctorow with the residual proposition, "there is only narrative" (26). The breakdown of distinctions and thesis development is sometimes signaled by breaks in the text and by both marked and unmarked ellipses.

The first distinction, between the power of freedom and the power of the regime, divides imaginative fiction from what Doctorow calls the consensus of realism or facts. At first this distinction valorizes the power of literature over other discourses, but no sooner has Doctorow made the distinction than he questions it ("Immediately I have to wonder if this formulation is too grandiose" [17]). Moreover, the power of the regime is determined to be "not from God but man-made, and, as such, infinitely violable" (17). If the second term in the distinction is so artificial, the whole distinction may collapse. An important quotation from Walter Benjamin is invoked to support the original contention of the power of art, but the quotation ends with this sentence: "The first great novel, *Don Quixote,* teaches how the spiritual greatness, the boldness, the helpfulness, of one of the noblest of men, Don Quixote, are completely devoid of counsel and do not contain the slightest scintilla of wisdom" (19). These words destroy the very claims for art made in the original distinction. They are followed by a break in the text, suggesting an impasse reached in the train of thought, after which the problem is reconsidered.

The literary device of false documents, Doctorow argues, enhances the authority of a text, no matter how transparent the premise: "in order to have its effect, a false document need only be possibly true" (20). To exemplify, Doctorow cites *Robinson Crusoe:* "all the English readers needed to know to read *Crusoe* and to believe it, was that there were others who could have had Selkirk's experience...." (20). Once again the text breaks off, here, even more tellingly, in ellipsis; further development of the argument has been suppressed or the narrative voice has simply trailed off. Has the argument reached a new point of contradiction? Is it really true that the transparency of the premise does not damage it? The essay itself may be said to have adopted a transparent premise, since it could not have been written without the discovery of the phrase "false documents" in a document by Kenneth Rexroth. Are there not now grounds for dismissing Doctorow's arguments?

At other breaks and ellipses in the essay, Doctorow's arguments approach new contradictions. For example, Doctorow invokes Benjamin again, to argue that literature recovers a state of wisdom that existed at a time before fact and fiction separated: novelists "pass on the collective wisdom in its own language" (21). But this argument blithely ignores the fact that Benjamin had earlier asserted that even *Don Quixote* contained "not the slightest scintilla of wisdom" (19).

Soon a new attempt to distinguish—between the power of literature in Western and non-Western countries—also founders. Doctorow first argues that, in repressive non-Western states, the seriousness of literature testifies to its inherently political character. He then writes: "Part of our problem, as Americans, in failing to apprehend the relationship between art and politics is, of course, our national good fortune." (22). This sentence has two meanings: first, that economic comfort leads to misunderstanding; second, that misunderstanding may be benign. In what sense might the second meaning be relevant here? Throughout the essay, misunderstanding the nature of literature seems to be taken for granted. The fact that distinctions collapse, only to be replaced by new, invariably vulnerable ones, is not salutary; these are the "hard times" of Doctorow's texts. So in such a situation, to acquiesce in misunderstanding, to give up the effort, may well be "good fortune," in the sense that it was for Joe Korzienowski.

The most instructive ellipsis follows a discussion of the next proposition: that criminal trials with disputed verdicts show that the apprehension of a factual world may itself by a convention. Here again, Doctorow undermines his original distinction between fact and fiction. Such trials as the Rosenbergs "[shimmer] forever with just that perplexing ambiguity characteristic of a true novel" (23). The question-begging oxymoron "true novel" dissipates into ellipses, into white space. At the conclusion of the essay, Doctorow entirely abandons the distinction between fiction and nonfiction and writes: "there is only narrative" (26). This position, which closely resembles the conclusion reached by J. Hillis Miller in *The Ethics of Reading*, prompts speculation as to whether the essay itself has all along been narrative, a story about a fictive contradictory entity, Doctorow.

That the essay is such a narrative becomes clear in the analysis of the constructed "I" that has all along been identified as Doctorow. To make "Doctorow," the essay constructs a conspicuous persona; the technique, which creates redundancy, is used frequently. The following are a few examples: "Certainly I know that I would rather . . . As a writer of fiction I could make the claim that . . . I have to wonder if . . . So what I suppose I mean [is] . . . I have to conclude that . . . I speak specifically of . . ." (16–20). The technique is hardly "characteristic" of Doctorow, since his other essays use it so rarely. In "False Documents," the fictivity of the "I" is also underscored by other means. For example, in the phrase "Perhaps I feel that" (23), the "I" seems oddly divorced from itself, and a few paragraphs later the dubious "I" is exchanged for an editorial "we" that begins four consecutive sentences and makes sweeping claims ("We all know examples of history that doesn't exist"), hyperboles that point to the rhetorical nature of the pronoun and thereby undermine its referent. (This procedure is similar to the one followed in the first chapter of *World's Fair*.)

The impression of persona-making is strengthened by two allusions that unavoidably raise the specter of *The Book of Daniel*. The

Rosenberg trial was invoked in support of the view that the existence of some discoverable world is only a convention, but acceptance of that argument would make Daniel's quest appear absurd, and his investigation into his parents' fate a delusion. This is precisely what the present study, after long analysis, discovers, but Doctorow's new analogy between the narrator of "False Documents" and Daniel only renders each work more dubious. To the extent that *The Book of Daniel* disclosed the writer's self to be an illusion generated by his discourse, so the essay "False Documents" creates a parallel illusory Doctorow.

A second similarity between Daniel and the "I" makes their fictive identifies more evident: their use of sources. Both narrators cite frequently; indeed, they share a source, the historian E. H. Carr. Daniel cites with approval Carr's analysis of the conflict between communism and nationalism in the Soviet Union (65–66). On the other hand, the narrator of "False Documents" cites with approval Carr's skepticism about the ultimate objectivity of history (24). Once again, the essay undermines the novel.

Most radically, the use of ellipses in the citation of sources by both Daniel and the "I" performs the same subversive function. Daniel used ellipses to omit material that might have refuted him; in a similar way, the "I" of "False Documents" often suppresses passages that raise potentially threatening questions of referentiality. Two instances are particularly egregious.

The first is an elided quotation from Jean-Paul Sartre's *Literature and Existentialism*. The purpose of the quotation *seems* to be to support a strong claim for art, made in the first paragraph of "False Documents," which culminates in the metaphor that a novel "is a printed circuit through which flows the force of a reader's own life." The passage from Sartre that follows is then adduced, with the omitted words restored below in brackets: "[Each painting,] each book, is a recovery of the totality of being. [Each of them presents this totality to the freedom of the spectator.] For this is quite the final goal of art: to recover this world by giving it to be seen as it is, but as if it had its source in human freedom."[2]

Inevitably, the suppression of Sartre's analogy between painting and writing raises the question of the relative degree of representation in both arts. Moreover, Sartre's version of *ut pictora poesis* retrospectively weakens the essay's claim for the power of art; Sartre saw art's recipient on the traditional hermeneutic model of a Cartesian subject face-to-face with a represented vision. By contrast, in the essay's figure, Sartre's hermeneutic is abandoned. In its place is an image far less stable, of a permeability between reader and the "printed circuit" that defines the reception of art intertextually. Indeed, "reading Sartre in support of Doctorow" defines even the reader intertextually. What began as "support" for art ends in showing its independence from the human.

After this elided quote, the essay shifts without comment to an entirely new subject.

The second instance of self-subverting ellipses in the use of sources occurs in the quotation from Walter Benjamin discussed earlier. It is even more egregious than the quotation from Sartre *because it is not marked as an ellipsis;* instead, like the quotation from the Bible on the last page of *The Book of Daniel,* the misrepresentation proceeds in silence. Now it was noted above that this quotation from Benjamin—in which the author asserted that *Don Quixote* did not contain "the slightest scintilla of wisdom"—ended the essay's first line of thought in apparent contradiction. However, that contradiction is deepened when the quotation's elided words are restored: "In then midst of life's fullness, [and through representation of this fullness,] the novel gives evidence of the profound perplexity of the living" (87).[3] This is, literally, misrepresentation of the concept of representation in art. The suppression leads to the unavoidable questions of whether novels can represent at all, and of what, if anything, is now being represented by the essay's "I."

By the end of the essay, the "I" of "False Documents" seems to be the creation, rather than the creator, of its argument. The pronoun becomes passive, directed, subordinate: "I am thus led to . . . And I am led to . . ." (26). The latter clause introduces a "pugnacious view—that the development of civilizations is essentially a progression of metaphors" (26). Hard upon this radical statement is a metaphor for writers as performers or clowns. Of course the metaphor is not new; it was introduced in "The Songs of Billy Bathgate" and later explicitly developed in *World's Fair.* This metaphor functions as the allusions to *The Book of Daniel* do, to make the narrator an intertextual entity, part of a progression of metaphors for the self created by a series of texts.

The essay's last sentences state its final metaphor, the fictive pronoun "we" that says it represents all novelists. The title's notion of "false documents" is here expanded to include whatever novelists write about: "But our right and our justification and redemption is in emulating the false documents that we universally call our dreams. For dreams are the first false documents, of course: they are never real, they are never factual; nevertheless they control us, purge us, mediate our baser natures, and prophesy our fate" (27).

In Doctorow's essays, an idealization of art ("The Passion of Our Calling") often appears at the end of the work, in the voice of "we" speaking as all writers. Its tone of exhortation increases with the imminence of silence, white space. Here, the hyperbole may be rhetorically analogous to the ellipses and break-offs noted in the body of the essay. But the ringing false eloquence of the ending of "False Documents" should not blind the reader to its insight: that the representations of life in novels are illusions, that fiction and nonfiction may be, alike, false documents.

Doctorow's interviews comment on his own work, and on literature and society, in tones more measured than those of "False Documents." That essay's "breezy I" became a persona almost manic in its uncompromising rejection of nonfiction and in its climactic, contradictory claims for art. In the interviews, such as "The Writer as Independent Witness" (1978), the eloquent "I" is replaced by a more cautious and tentative persona. In this new voice, the question of the political dimension of literature is often discussed, as are new metaphors for writing: in this case, the writer as "independent witness." But despite the modulated voice, contradictions similar to those of "False Documents" persist, at crucial moments, almost casually.

The most prominent in the interview "The Writer as Independent Witness" concerns the old relation between literature and politics (60–61): "I don't think this is anything new at all." Of course, political interpretations of literature are inescapable: "If you do a book about a boy and his dog, you're making a political statement." But this does not necessarily mean that works of literature represent their authors' political views: "And that leads to the interesting question of to what degree a writer can understand or know that he is political in order to get his work done. There's some kind of death that creeps into prose when you're trying to illustrate a principle, no matter how worthy."

It is remarkable that, in this passage, death inserts itself—"a kind of death that creeps into prose"—the moment representation is attempted; this fine statement of Heideggerian *Sein-zum-Tode* comports well with the many novelistic renderings of that relation. In what follows, it is crucially important to recall that, for Doctorow, death inserts itself at such moments of exemplification *not just in fiction but in all prose.*

Although the passage above implies that an author may remain oblivious to his own political intentions, the seeming corollary is denied: "on the basis of that, of course, to declare that art should not have political intent—or can't afford to—that's not justified." But sentences that follow show the contradiction: "One thinks of the intentions of writers, like Dostoevsky, who simply and modestly wanted to change the world. That didn't seem, somehow, to limit his capacity to express truth" (60–61). The reference to Dostoevsky may seem to occur casually in the course of the answer, until the reader recalls that it is *an example that tries to illustrate a principle,* the very operation that has just been warned against, and so the example is already an example of what not to do, a model of misrepresentation. Further scrutiny confirms this impression.

At the outset it can be observed that the passage says only that Dostoevsky's activist intentions did not limit his expression; the question as to whether that expression reflected intention is silently passed over. Even more noteworthy is the characterization of Dostoevsky's intent, and one wonders whether Dostoevsky was mistaken for Tolstoy. But most disconcerting is the fact that, as an example of political intent, Dostoevsky is surely of dubious relevance, since his novels finally subordinated the political and psychological realms to the religious. For all three reasons, this "example" turns on the immediately preceding principle, which it set out to illustrate.

What of the "principle" that one should not attempt to illustrate a principle? Can it be said that, like some double negative, this misexample turns out to exemplify the earlier warning, after all? What of Heideggerian *Sein-zum-Tode*? If the passage seems to illustrate that "idea," then does it contradict itself anew? Indeed, it may be that "some kind of death creeps into" the prose at this moment of the breakdown of representation; perhaps one thinks of violent death in *Crime and Punishment* or the rigorous attention to death in *The Brothers Karamazov*. These associations flicker to life and fade. In this intertextual abyss, nothing has been represented but the necessary failure of the attempt to represent. Doctorow's comments on this subject complete the circle they began, with added ambiguity from riddling pronouns: "So I guess my answer is, I don't think this is anything new at all." In the present reading, the otherwise indefinite "this" may mean the inescapable subversion of principles by examples, the eternal return of misrepresentation.

This discussion shapes a context for understanding the metaphor of the writer as "independent witness." It occurs at the end of the interview, after Doctorow again denies the distinction between fiction and history: "And I don't make any distinction any more—and can't even remember—what of the events and circumstances in *Ragtime* are historically verifiable and what are not. But I suppose that if you were to say to me, there's a danger in this sort of thing, I would have to agree. There is absolutely a danger. Except writers are independent witnesses and, theoretically at least, not connected to the defense of any institution, whether it be the family or the Pentagon or God" (69).

The common definition of "witness" is one who attests to the truth of events in the past, but that truth has just been declared inseparable from fiction, and it cannot be represented in examples. In this quandary, "witness" perhaps means less "authenticator of truth" than "sufferer of fiction." In either case, the emphasis of the phrase is on the adjective "independent," now separating writers from all other pseudowitnesses on the basis of the fact that writers do not depend upon and do not defend institutions. But this rescue of the phrase cannot succeed either, since the passage concedes that even the prized independence is true only "theoretically." It is as though such writers may exist "in principle," but any attempt to "exemplify" them will founder on the same problems that befell the naming of Dostoevsky as an instance of the validity of political intent in art. Writers are theoretically independent. No one would deny this assertion, which amounts to a tautology. In this way, the metaphor for writing drains itself of the content it seemed, at first, to profess.

The Paris Review interview (Winter 1986), entitled "The Art of Fiction," has two effects: first, it subverts the idea of the author from the perspective of the reader, designated here by the metaphor "the writer's younger brother;" second, it develops the view that Hemingway is repetitious in voice, which directly contradicts a book review Doctorow published only a few months later, "Braver Than We Thought." The two effects are related, since as reader (or younger brother) of Hemingway, Doctorow will seem to supplant him as writer.

In response to a question regarding the origins of his career as a writer, Doctorow comes close to saying that he was "always, already" a writer insofar as he was a reader. Comments on his reading at age nine introduce this subject, the metaphors of the younger brother, and the "printed circuit":

> Whenever I read anything I seemed to identify as much with the act of composition as with the story. I seemed to have two minds: I would love the story and want to know what happened next, but at the same time I would somehow be aware of what was being done on the page. I identified myself as a kind of younger brother of the writer. I was on hand to help him figure things out. So you see I didn't actually have to write a thing *because the act of reading was my writing*. I thought of myself as a writer for years before I got around to writing anything. It's not a bad way to begin. It's to blur that distinction between reader and writer. If you think about it, *any book that you pick up as a reader, if it's good, is a printed circuit for your own life to flow through*—so when you read a book you are engaged in the events of the mind of the writer. *You are bringing your creative faculties into sync. You're imagining the words, the sounds of the words, and you're thinking of the various characters in terms of people you've known—not in terms of the writer's experience but your own.* So it's very hard to make any distinction between reader and writer at this ontological level [35; emphasis added]

If each reader imagines characters idiosyncratically, reading is permanent misrepresentation, and each misrepresentation becomes a new writing. Since the printed circuit is both the book and the act of reading it, the "external world," in this figure, is nothing but reading. The younger brother becomes much more than a kind of assistant to the writer he reads: in fact, he takes his place. (The gender attributions here are Doctorow's.) Doctorow concludes his answer by claiming authorship of works written by others: "I wrote a lot of good books. I wrote *Captain Blood* by Raphael Sabatini. That was one of my better efforts."

The implication is that the reader—called larcenous in *Billy Bathgate*—can wholly co-opt or subsume the author, and as if in demonstration of this principle, Doctorow assesses Hemingway's *The Garden of Eden*: "in this as in the others he spoke with the same Hemingway voice." Even by itself Doctorow's verdict on Hemingway's repetition of voice would amount to a kind of annihilation of the author: only the creation of different voices in each book is what "keeps you alive as a writer" (29). An even more telling annihilation of Hemingway the writer by Doctorow the reader is effected when this offhand dismissal of *The Garden of Eden* is reversed in "Braver Than We Thought."

Doctorow's review of Hemingway's *The Garden of Eden*, "Braver Than We Thought" (May 1986), contradicts the view of that novel expressed in *The Paris Review* interview. A process by which readers replace writers is demonstrated in this "new reading," and its interpretation of Hemingway's literary strategy also intersects with figures for the artist in Doctorow's fiction.

According to this essay, Hemingway did *not* "speak with the same voice" in *The Garden of Eden;* instead, he bravely changed it. The title of the essay may imply a wry acknowledgement of this shift by the use of the editorial "we"—although Doctorow's earlier view is nowhere else implied. To the reader unfamiliar with *The Paris Review* interview, the title simply alludes to received critical opinion of Hemingway—"we" as mainstream readers. Readers of Doctorow must speculate how this phenomenon—generous praise for a novel published only a few months after an abrupt dismissal of it—"truly represents" the author behind the words. In any case, in this review Doctorow analyzes his famous predecessor's usual voice and his departure from it in *The Garden of Eden*. He finds in Hemingway the articulation of a serious writing dilemma not often noted by critics and also clearly relevant to Doctorow.

The essay begins by arguing that Hemingway's literary strategy dictated a kind of radical individualism, even hedonism: "The source of his material and spring to his imagination was his own life. Issues of intellect—history, myth, society—were beside the point. It was what his own eyes saw and heart felt that he cured into fiction. Accordingly he lived his life to see and feel as much as possible" (1).

It was writing that created the single-minded need to experience, not the reverse; the artistic imperative led to a life of unending "taking": "whatever he was he took what was available" (44). Carlos Baker's story of Hemingway, late at night, punching a dead marlin, is cited to show that "after he killed something it was not necessarily past his attention" (44). These remarks cast new light on the subject of taking and killing in Hemingway's works and in Doctorow's; they suggest that one writing dilemma may be the inability *not* "to take," in the sense of to interpret. Read in this light, Hemingway's tales of taking and killing may be allegories of reading. They anticipate Doctorow's *Billy Bathgate*, in which the writer is condemned to a life of taking, of appropriation, of "the rackets," because there may be no escape from such a condition.

Be that as it may, the essay claims to discover in *The Garden of Eden* a struggle *against* such a lifelong condemnation to taking. In the character of Catherine Bourne, Hemingway's text envisions a serious alternative to the traditional writer caught in the dilemmas of representation. The potential significance of this alternative shapes the speculation of the essay: "For there are clear signs of something exciting going on, the enlargement of a writer's mind toward compassion, toward a less defensive construal of reality. [Catherine Bourne suggests] in Hemingway the rudiments of a feminist perspective. . . . Perhaps Hemingway is learning to dispense his judgements more thoughtfully" (45).

The "something exciting" happening in Hemingway resembles the recurrent feature in Doctorow's texts: the "terrible, awful struggle" for the new, for some alternative to the eternal return. Variously in the characters of Red Bloom and Sugarbush, Billy Bathgate the singer, Daniel, Coalhouse Walker, Joe, Edgar, or Billy's mother, Doctorow's strong characters seek alternatives to fates that they cannot avoid. They seek to set themselves apart from the "eternal reiteration of all things." That such characters fail in their endeavor cannot obscure the fact that they exemplify the kinds of premises that for Doctorow make artistic renewal possible.

The tribute to Hemingway's *The Garden of Eden* finds an equivalent artistic courage, a new beginning after the exhaustion of old alternatives became evident in *For Whom the Bell Tolls:* "I would like to think that as he began 'The Garden of Eden,' his very next novel after that war work, he realized this and wanted to retool, to remake himself. That he would fail is almost not the point—but that he would have tried, which is the true bravery of a writer, requiring more courage than facing down an elephant charge with a .303 Mannlicher." The eloquence of this passage must remain in the mind as counterweight to the implications of its deadly word "almost."

In "Braver than We Thought," Doctorow destroyed the Hemingway of *The Paris Review* interview and created an astonishing new one. With this simultaneous destruction and creation, Doctorow seems to demonstrate the interview's radical proposition that readers may take the place of the authors they read.[4]

But in essays that follow, this claim, too, will be unsettled.

Of Doctorow's several essays on cultural criticism, "The State of Mind of the Union" (1986) is of interest for its indictments of contemporary intellectual life and of deconstruction. The essay considers both parts of the "secret story of American life under the bomb" (331).

The burden of Doctorow's cultural criticism is that American intellectual life in the 1980s has been debased by young writers seeking quick success and by neoconservative critics: both oblivious to the social dimension of art. This desultory milieu is represented in the figure of President Reagan as a deluding golem whom American intellectuals created for themselves. Their socially regressive values are the consequence of the same Faustian urge that led to the invention of nuclear weapons.

The essay's title and argument develop an personification, a "mind of the union." This first figure is then imagined as capable of creating a second: President Reagan, "a kind of golem sprung from national premises and fears" (328). Personification of nations may be inevitable in the writing of cultural criticism, just as, seen in *Welcome to Hard Times,* personification is surely inevitable in narrative. In Doctorow's essay national personification is related to another, as old as American literature, the writer-as-nation: "I take the writer as micronation" (328). On such reciprocal, Whitmanesque figures the essay's cultural criticism rests.

Of course, one implication is that the country's ills must also afflict the writer, so the indictments of culture soon turn against themselves. For example, the essay opens with implicit criticism of Norman Mailer for having invited George Shultz to address a meeting of the organization PEN, but on the next page, Mailer is defended as being the victim of unfair criticism. In another turn, "the estimable" John Updike is taken to task for his remarks to an audience at a PEN meeting, "reformulating in literary terms George Washington's conviction that this country should beware of foreign entanglements: he characterized his experience of the American state as pastoral" (328). Later in the essay, unnamed Eastern European intellectuals are blamed for criticizing American idealism, prompting the following baffling recommendation: "The rest of us should be as wary of this particular foreign entanglement as we are of the more generalized foreign insistence that we become *engagé*, but we are not." In its echoes of Updike, this sentence warns against the very literature of engagement it earlier seemed to advocate.

The reversal that most clearly implicates the essay in the evil it denounces comes at the conclusion. After having castigated young writers for their desire for quick fame and profit, the "I" begins a peroration: "I appeal to the traditional values of self-aggrandizement for which we artists and intellectuals are supposed to be famous" (332), but with these words, the writer as "micro-nation" confesses to the same faults of the "state of the mind of the union" he has just criticized. It is as though cultural faults can be discovered only in a covert appeal to them.

The essay's critique of deconstruction occurs in the following passage:

And what of our hottest school of literary criticism, which takes the concept of ambiguity to new heights, or depths? A book is a text or artifact whose meanings are to be disentangled and put alongside one another for examination. *This is a professional discipline worthy of a play by Molière. Its conclusion*—that the author of the piece is finally of no consequence and that the illuminations of the piece are simply a matter of supracritical excitations—*can be interpreted as meaning that the compositions of words have no or very little value. This is not too far from the conviction of illiterate teenagers* who roam the streets and subways of New York with their ghetto blasters booming. At least they know they live in a postnuclear world.

Everything I've noted here, from the young writers impatient of a long creative life to the deconstruction of our critics; every variety of intellectual retreat, of conformism, every small loss of moral acuity, *I see collectively as the secret story* of American life under the bomb. [331; emphasis added]

The sarcasm here recalls Susan's bitter protest against Daniel's preference for writing over political engagement; it recalls the tradition of the passionate insistence on meaning that animates such characters as Blue, Red Bloom and Sugarbush, Coalhouse Walker, Edgar. Like them, this "I" pleads for an alternative to a world without meaning, but also like these characters, this "I" cannot escape figuration.

It is of interest that the arguments made against deconstruction take the form of allusion and personification. The allusion to Molière seems to invite ridicule; on the other hand, among the professions Molière satirized was writing, especially his own art of the theater. The "profession" of literature and its criticism, of course, remains as unaffected as Molière by the allusion. Again, the passage protests that for deconstruction the author is of little consequence. However, *The Paris Review* interview adopted a position even more radical: that readers actually *replace* writers. An exemplification of that position is attempted in the shift from the interview to "Braver Than We Thought." In effect, this essay's protest on the author's behalf abjures a practice Doctorow himself just engaged in, as if to deny its validity only for others.

In this light, the ridicule through personification which likens the "conclusion" of deconstruction to the "conviction" of the illiterate teenager is equally self-subverting. The phrase "not too far from" calls attention to the trope; it concedes as much room for debate—over Doctorow's own practices, for example—as the claim that for deconstruction words have "very little" value. Such relativism militates against the polemic, even as it is uttered.

Of paramount importance is the statement that the social ills of which deconstruction is a prime example are all part of "a secret story." With this phrase, the essay reassigns its supposed nonfiction critique to the category of fiction. The essay now loses all pretense of being nonfiction.

The essay's end confirms and extends this suspicion. The reader is asked to "put aside the golem and consider the story of Faust" (331). The new legend is invoked to show the Mephistophelean character of the knowledge of nuclear weapons. The resulting threat of annihilation is attested to by a pastoral letter from the American Catholic bishops, which becomes the occasion for the essay's final appeal to writers. So the essay's arguments are reducible to two stories with mythical traditions, the legends of the golem and of Faust. By inviting the reader to exchange the first story for the second, the essay implies—despite all pleas—that cultural and literary criticism are species of fiction. And finally: the traditions encompassed by the two stories hint that this knowledge has even broader scope. The first story is readable only in terms of Judaism, the second, of Christianity. The two stories and their traditions therefore recapitulate, in miniature, the problem of canon-formation by which the New Testament seems to supplant the Old. The two stories in Doctorow's cultural critique are both incompatible and compatible, depending on their interpretation. Like the Old and New Testaments, the stories' "authors" are their readers.

In this way, "The State of Mind of the Union" implies that the contradictions in reading inherent in contemporary culture find antecedents in ancient texts. The state of mind of the union is a figure for inescapable stories, inescapable figuration.

"A Citizen Reads the Constitution" (1987) studies the work of the Constitutional Convention of 1787 and some of the major political issues confronted there. It also summarizes various interpretations of the American revolution and recognizes contradictions: for example, among those who support and oppose the thesis of Charles Beard. Of these conflicting positions, the following claim is made: "I think all of those theories are true, simultaneously" (216). This claim is allowed to stand without further remark. The essay goes on to assert that today the meanings of words are dissolving; it praises, by contrast, the belief in the value of words held by the framers of the constitution. Its conclusion valorizes the constitution's guarantees of democracy, especially the guarantee of free debate.

Like "The State of Mind of the Union," this essay expresses a concern for the apparent loss of meaning in language. The crucial paragraphs are as follows:

> And what of constitutional scholarship today, in the Age of Reagan?
> Well, my emphasis on text, my use of textual analogy, responds to the work over the past few years of a new generation of legal scholars who have been arguing among themselves as to whether the Constitution can be seen usefully as a kind of literary text, sustaining intense interpretive reading—as a great poem, say—or better perhaps as a form of scripture. *I have swiveled to embrace both of those critiques too,* but adding, as a professional writer, that when I see the other professions become as obsessively attentive to text as mine is, I suspect it is a sign that we live in an age in which the meanings of words are dissolving, in which the culture of discourse itself seems threatened. *That is my view of America under Reagan today: in literary critical terms, I would describe his Administration as deconstructionist.*
> And so, by way of preservation, text consciousness may have arisen among us, law professors no less than novelists, *as in medieval times monks began painstakingly copying the crumbling parchments to preserve them.* (216; emphasis added)

Once again there is an effort to criticize both culture and its interpretation that reveals, on closer examination, the inability to write without figuration. The debate among legal scholars is symptomatic of the loss of meaning; on the other hand, "I have swiveled to embrace both of these critiques too." This move may seem a desperate extension of the earlier, Whitmanesque attempt to contain con-traditions: with the metaphor of "embrace," the "I" aspires to stand outside legal debates and intense interpretive reading, in mastery of them. But the passage also concedes that the legal professions are now becoming as obsessively attentive to text as authors. If legal scholars are only now catching up with the text obsessions that have always been central to literature, then literature (even Doctorow's own) already harbors the degenerative implications that are now becoming manifest in Reagan-era legal studies. The attempt to extricate the writer from present or future loss of meaning only shows more clearly that such a loss was already there, in language and literature, before the attempt began.

The simile comparing contemporary text consciousness with medieval copyists unites novelists and legal scholars and assigns a cause for their common obsession ("by way of preservation"). In the simile, this cause applies, oddly, to both the copyists and their manuscripts: in an effort to preserve themselves and their texts, text consciousness arose among medieval monks and contemporary writers. It is, of course, unlikely that any interpretive effort can "preserve" a *self*. That much has seemed clear through the repeated expression, in Doctorow's novels, of abysmal, Heideggerian *Sein-zum-Tode*. If it discloses anything, writing possibly discloses only the absence or nothingness of death, and as to the preservation of *texts*, the simile finds literature and criticism as impotent as the art of copying. This is a telling analogy. It once again equates writing with the redundancy of Nietzsche's eternal return. Of course, the futility of any appeal to posterity has long been acknowledged in Doctorow's works. Blue's dying wish, that some future reader may pick up his blood-stained ledger, is an idealization of art that his own text showed to be hollow. The singer Billy Bathgate recognizes the fraudulence of fame. Edgar's time capsule is a poignant gesture, like Blue's, but his attempt to preserve art is vitiated by its nonrepresentative "contents." Throughout Doctorow's work, the novelistic motive of "preservation" is exposed as a delusion, although it may also be a necessary condition of articulation.

It is, finally, the necessary side of this paradox that Doctorow insists on in the idealizations of writing that follow this passage and are echoed in other essays and interviews. The emphasis is hardly surprising. In expository modes, writers may accept the convention that art may be discussed "from the outside." They accept, for practical purposes, the distinction between fiction and nonfiction that "False Documents" denied. Because of this convention, some idealization of art, however, contradictory, may be inevitable. Without the greater resources of fiction to illuminate the contradiction, expository writers can say, only, that writing is essential, that they write to preserve themselves. These may indeed be the idealizations that generate art and that expository writing and interview-responses almost always treat as truth.

My interview with Doctorow, published in *Michigan Quarterly Review*, put to the test many of the ideas set forth in this study. I had been prepared to encounter in Doctorow, in Victor Navasky's phrase, a "walking refutation of the intentional fallacy,"[5] that is, an author committed to the notion that authors' intentions—or even glosses on their works—were never privileged. The interview may have borne out at least that conventional sense of authorship; however, readers must determine its full application to other questions raised here. For example, this study's conclusions have understandably precluded quoting Doctorow in support of particular interpretations of his texts. On the other hand, some of his interview-responses seemed to comport well with them. The paradox can be resolved by examining such responses and by showing how their apparent concurrence with my thesis is, after all, new misrepresentation.

A simple instance concerns the idea of death in the novels. Although Doctorow denied any deliberate attention to the subject, he connected it immediately with narrative and hermeneutics: "It's a condition of narrative, just as it is of life . . . the preoccupation is not with death but with the meaning we make of it." Doctorow cited Walter Benjamin on the dignity death bestowed on an otherwise wretched life. He compared his own characters, especially his boys, to those of Dickens and drew a parallel—the sense of injustice that attaches to the deaths of their characters. "I couldn't think about the deathliness of these books without thinking of the life that qualifies the death."

These remarks may suggest a connection between death and the recuperation of meaning similar to the one traced here, but in the end they idealize writing. The list of examples that contradicts

Doctorow's hopes for writing is very long: Blue's attempt to find meaning in the Bad Man from Bodie; Daniel's quest for the meaning of his parents' deaths; the narrative silence after the death of Coalhouse Walker; the uninterpreted end of Penfield, or the boy in the water works, or the foreign legation. These deaths remain mute, and if they retroactively confer meaning on characters' lives, Doctorow's narrators never succeed in representing it.

A second answer that appears close to my thesis concerned *Ragtime*. When asked to comment on whether the character of Tateh was to be taken normatively or ironically—an acknowledged problem for hermeneutic critics—Doctorow called attention to that character's possibly humorous moral ambiguity. He said he would rather not "join in the critical understanding" of his works. He agreed that it was misguided to define a character as representative of a book's meaning; he pointed out flaws in Coalhouse Walker and Emma Goldman, too, who have been valorized on occasion by political critics. These replies seemed to confirm basic assumptions of this study. On the other hand, Doctorow's critique of character-based interpretations was founded on his view of the author's synoptic lucidity with regard to the whole work, knowledge that transcended any partial understanding of sociologists, journalists, philosophers (and, by implication, literary critics). Unlike them, novelists take all data as their resources, with the result that they "see more" than anyone else.

But if the first part of this response seems close to my thesis, the second contradicts the experiences of Blue, Daniel, the little boy—in fact, of all of Doctorow's writers and narrators. Their blindnesses are the subject matter of this study. In other words, Doctorow's interview-claim for authors is belied by the stories he tells about them. So if we are to believe Doctorow the interview-respondent, we cannot believe his texts. Put another way, it may be impossible for an interview-response not to idealize writing.

This suspicion was strengthened when the interview turned to the recurrent image of the orphan. Doctorow acknowledged its importance; he said that the sense of inconsolable loss was strong in several of his books; he wondered—since it had no biographical basis—whence it derived. He even agreed that there was a connection between writing and the condition of being an orphan. At first, he discussed this figure in psychological terms, as a way of acknowledging the relation between neurosis and art: "I've never found it necessary to deny the proposition of *The Wound and the Bow*." But on balance he found such psychological explanations "self-evident" and "useless as any kind of a critical tool." The connection between writing and being an orphan is, instead, a matter of redressing grievances, which "could include some sort of metaphysical disturbance or longing apart from any personal neurosis."

This response might seem to provide further evidence for this study's argument. The orphan/writer's grievance, on this view, would be the condemnation to write in the face of some intuition of its futility. The formulation is close to the argument made here concerning the putative orphan-figures of Billy Bathgate (singer and criminal), Joe Paterson, and Daniel Isaacson. But Doctorow's phrase "redressing grievances" makes its simple appropriation, in this spirit, problematic. The phrase refuses, after all, to move beyond the psychological problem it sought to supplant as "self-evident" and "useless": it implies a brave writer embarking on a Sysyphean quest; it implies that the completed work stands as a grievance redressed, if only in the effort; in so doing, it rebestows signification on art. On the contrary, this study argues that the dramatization, in fiction, of an "orphan of the mind" shows the consequences of writing that cannot achieve signification. Doctorow's fiction allegorizes that dilemma. So the interview-response, despite its seeming relevance, finally idealizes writing as the lives of Doctorow's poets never do. The discrepancy puts Doctorow the interview-respondent on the same side of the mirror as his readers, defining, in psychological terms, the act his fictions have shown to be impossible as a condition of writing.

It suggests, too, that interview-responses make new fictions, a proposition Doctorow explicitly acknowledged. Speaking of one of his replies to Victor Navasky, Doctorow said that fiction writers "continue to write after the book is written. But what you're writing now are fictions about the book." This answer aligns Doctorow's interview remarks, like the observations of any reader, with the process de Man called "secondary deconstruction."

The interview-response that seemed most startlingly close to my own reading of Doctorow's work concerned the function of the mother of Billy Bathgate the criminal. Doctorow insisted that her presence was crucial to the novel; he concurred with the idea that she stands as a "counter" or alternative to the world of words and numbers that otherwise pervades the novel. Doctorow saw her function as "prophetic." My own reading of this character, which emphasizes its very tenuous weight as such a new alternative, is set forth in the next chapter.

If an interview is a new, maybe a low-level, fiction, this one's most telling moment came in words that echoed my epigraph. Doctorow spoke about *Big as Life* and his six years of work on it to no avail. Conceding its failure, in Norman Mailer's words, to become excessive enough in its outrage, Doctorow said the novel's only value now was as a cautionary tale, one that teaches "what an awful struggle it is and what a risky way it is to live one's life."

CHAPTER 10

Billy Bathgate
Reading as Larceny

Billy Bathgate recounts the title character's rise in the world of organized crime through Billy's apprenticeship to the egregious Dutch Schultz, a twentieth-century incarnation of the same undisguised amoral violence that animated the Bad Man from Bodie. On board a tugboat, Billy witnesses Schultz's torture and murder of his former lieutenant, Bo Weinberg; in an empty restaurant, he watches Schultz spontaneously beat out the brains of a fire inspector; at home in the Bronx, he reads of Schultz slitting the throat of a gangland rival in a barbershop; in a hotel room in Onandaga, he watches the death agony of Julie Martin, president of the Restaurant and Cafeteria Owners Association, who has been murdered by Schultz. As verbose as the Bad Man was silent, Schultz speaks of his criminal career, without apology, as a business; his accountant, Abbadabba Berman, professionally manages the numbers of the organization. Schultz successfully defends himself in a trial for income-tax evasion. Billy steals Drew, a rich socialite moll, from Schultz, who had previously stolen her from Bo Weinberg. After Schultz dies in a shootout, Billy discovers a fortune that Schultz had amassed and hidden. After college and military service during World War II, the wealthy Billy settles into a position of some "renown," although he does not disclose whether or not his activity is criminal. Drew sends their baby to Billy's mother, who will care for it.

The threshold question is intertextual: what relation does this criminal Billy Bathgate, an adolescent during the thirties, have to Billy Bathgate the late-sixties folk-rock performer, titular hero of "The Songs of Billy Bathgate"? Separate characters with the same name, they share other similarities that stir the same speculation that was prompted by the "simultaneous but disynchronous" existence of Joe Korzienowski and Warren Penfield, in *Loon Lake,* or the conflation of narrator and character in "The Leather Man." Singer and criminal grow up in poverty in the Bronx. Both share a consuming passion for a white goddess (Lovegirl, Drew); both attack interpreters of their writing; both claim innocence and accuracy in their efforts at representation. But because these common features are so general, the intertextual relation may again be perceived to be as empty, or tautological, as were the allusions to Joseph Conrad or Samuel Johnson.

Both narrators are stand-ins for the writer. In fact, Billy Bathgate the criminal embodies the three values for the artist first articulated in "The Songs of Billy Bathgate": orphan, killer, and clown. The novel develops these three metaphors with even graver emphasis, more "hard times," than does the story. In the novel, interpretation is not merely a misreading or the passive alternation of blindness and insight as it was in the story; instead, it stands as a coercive, unjustifiable appropriation, like the rackets of organized crime. If for Doctorow hermeneutics has always been a delusion, it has never seemed as dangerous as it does here. In *Billy Bathgate,* reading is a larcenous, murderous "taking." Although this analogy was first worked out in Doctorow's volte-face in the interpretation of Hemingway, it finds very bold depiction here in Billy's acts of reading/taking: first in his model, Dutch Schultz, and next in his narrative, which recommits hermeneutic crimes. Billy taunts his readers' unacknowledged complicity in "the rackets," and like Billy, the reader strains, futilely, to understand. It is true that once more a seeming alternative to this dangerous world of delusion is contemplated. Billy's feckless mother holds forth the faint possibility of the new, of some way out of repetition and misreading, but as before, the hoped-for alternative fails.

His real father gone, Billy is a figurative orphan—like Joe, Jonathon, or Edgar—seeking out a surrogate father, in this case, Schultz. At the climax of the novel "the word of the father" is disclosed in an important scene of writing and reading, when Billy transcribes Schultz's deathbed monologue (308–10). What Billy records is apparently incoherent: he dismisses it at first as "disheartening babble" (313). This sample from the beginning of the monologue seems to bear out that judgment: "'Oh mama, mama' he said. 'Oh stop it stop it stop it. Please make it quick, fast and furious. Please fast and furious. I am getting my wind back. You do all right with the dot dash system. Whose number is that in your pocketbook, Otto: 13780? Oh oh, dog biscuit. And even when he is happy he doesn't get snappy. Please, you didn't even meet me. The glove will fit what I say'" (308–9).

When Billy reads it again, however, he understands enough to find two caches of Schultz's money (319). In this there is, literally, the reading moment hard upon the writing moment, when arbitrary signifiers seem to represent. Although the clues in Schultz's dying words that led Billy to find the treasure are not explicitly revealed, it is not hard, in retrospect, to establish plausible ones. In fact, with his comment that the "larcenous" reader will be able to "figure things out for himself" (320), Billy invites the reader to discover the clues, and readers may be drawn to accept. When Schultz cries, "My gilt edged stuff, and these dirty rats have tuned in!" (309), this may refer to the rat-infested basement of the beer-drop. There may be another buried revelation in "Money is paper too and you stash it in the shithouse" (310). That sentence tallies with Billy's discovery of the money "in the shit and refuse of Arnold's dreams" (310). The fragment "Look, the dark woods" may hint at the Park Avenue location of the beer-drop. Whether or not these, or other clues, "actually refer," the reader's acceptance of Billy's invitation means a duplication of Billy's own study of the transcript, so whatever becomes true for Billy forms an analogy for the reader. Because Billy sits behind a screen as he listens to Schultz's monologue, Schultz could not know his identity—just as an author cannot know the identity of his reader. So Schultz's narration is to Billy as Billy's is to the reader, and in both, the reader unavoidably becomes the taker.

(And what of the writer? Schultz's dying monologue seems uncontrollable language that reveals and conceals simultaneously: "pure" articulation, cut off from intent.)

Billy's initial incomprehension suggests the process by which some semantic sense that refers to a "referent"—in this case, society's most valorized, money—is literally deferred; speech is phonic and rhetorical before it is referential. "Otto: 13780? Oh Oh" is distinguishable as such only in writing. Understanding comes only later, after the dying man's words have first presented themselves merely as rhythmic signs. Reading, then, produces a profit, which Billy takes—as he has consistently taken, throughout his apprenticeship to Schultz. So the equation between reading and a necessary "taking," attendant upon the attribution of presence to signs, coincides with Billy's final independence, his assumption of adult powers, and Billy's formative act of appropriative reading is duplicated in the reader's: "That is almost all I will say of this matter although the larcenous reader will be able figure [*sic*] things out for himself, for herself, in fact anyone can put two and two together, it's all right with me, because of course I did go and collect it, it was just where I knew it would be" (320).

Reading is here equated with larceny, with an unjustifiable "taking," and so Billy's crimes (his taking Schultz's money here, his acts of complicity elsewhere) only reenact the reading process conceived as coercive appropriation. It is noteworthy that the sentence above makes this point only with an anacoluthon produced by an ellipsis, by which the reader must supply the missing word "to." In this way the sentence demonstrates as it asserts the reader's complicity, the reader's "taking." Supplying the missing "to" is as inevitable as "taking" the passage as real. These acts align the reading of *Billy Bathgate* with the "filling in" of ellipsis in *The Book of Daniel* and in the essay "False Documents."

(The cover of the paperback edition of *Billy Bathgate* gives these ideas visual form: Billy is a reader. In the cover are also two "real" holes and one "false" hole, supposedly bullet holes. The reading of the novel must proceed by filling in holes—as in "able figure things out"—and by trying to distinguish, lamely, true holes from false holes.)

If filling in an ellipsis illustrates the necessary "taking" of reading, Doctorow stresses its "unfounded" character by comparing it with larceny, even murder. Of course, the idea of reading as an enforced interpretive "taking" has always been present in Doctorow's texts, but in his interpretation of Hemingway, Doctorow maintained that readers replace authors, in effect killing them. In *Billy Bathgate* that idea is fully dramatized in the career of Billy, who "reads" Schultz well enough to replace him. This metaphoric killing is unabashed and untroubled, a far cry from Joe's gradual acclimatization to Bennett. Unlike Joe, Billy never has a qualm about following in the footsteps of his master-appropriator. Instead, he takes whatever he can, without apology, and, like Dutch Schultz, he ignores to his last word any distinction between legal and illegal. If Doctorow's previous works suggest the inevitability of "taking," then *Billy Bathgate* extends the trope by defining reading as larceny or murder.

Billy's *tour de force* in extending the trope is his story of the gangland murder of Bo Weinberg, told in chapters I and II. His first account is palpably elliptical; the actual killing is omitted, so when readers involuntarily imagine some scene of Bo's death, they become complicit and "commit the murder themselves." So the novel's first chapter teaches that in attributing presence to blank space, readers must "take," thereby, all unaware, appropriating. And readers must imagine not only murder but copulation: when Schultz removes Drew (known then only as Lola) to the aft cabin below, a second ellipsis occurs. Did Schultz rape Drew? Did Drew consent? Schultz's violations of Bo and Drew are repeated in Billy's account to the reader, since the reader must helplessly "take" the ellipses somehow.

And even when Billy "restores" the ellipses, in chapter II, he again forces the reader to "take." En route to Saratoga, Billy now narrates to Drew the omitted details of the night on the tugboat. However, while he protests the honesty of his account (153), his claim harbors contradictions. For example, he retells the tugboat incident in indirect discourse, addressing the reader and speaking of Drew, his listener by the waterfall, in the third person. Therefore his account is already a paraphrase of the original, a pseudopalimpsest that erases the "original." Even more important is the fact that Billy admits to having kept one incident in his story from Drew, his overhearing Dutch Schultz browbeat her into apparent sexual acquiescence. Thus Billy's narration to Drew contains a second ellipsis, and the reader—who must, along with Billy, decide on the basis of his account whether Drew actually acquiesced—is made to repeat the act of appropriation that launched the text *Billy Bathgate*. The reader must strain again, now for the unknowable act of will that was Schultz's and/or Drew's, but *again* be disappointed. In this the reader undergoes the doom of all reading, the ceaseless quest to read intent, the ceaseless failure.

So Schultz's "rape" of Drew becomes, via Billy, an analogue to the reader's "taking" of the scene: reading may presuppose such silent, invisible acts, and the interpretation that "follows" can only conceal that primordial "taking." So reading is already, in articulation, mistaken. Billy's seeming inability to avoid ellipsis suggests that it may be inherent in narration. The necessary filling-in of Billy's lacuna (here, imagining "willful" copulation) makes this example a preliminary to the major ellipsis in Billy's text, the question of whether he finally betrayed Dutch Schultz. That problem is taken up later, but Billy's narration implies throughout that the enforced making-decidable of reading—its larceny—consists of filling in gaps, making the absent present, privileging one referent at the expense of others it must suppress.

Thus *Billy Bathgate* tells of a world in which reading is always coercive "taking"; when it occurs—as in Billy's discovery of the meaning of Dutch Schultz's deathbed babble—reading will naturally create redundant "profits," only because it is, already, appropriative. Of course, Dutch Schultz, the Ur-reader, is the master of appropriation: "Mr. Schultz's urge to appropriate was stronger than his cunning, it was the central force of him, it operated all the time and wherever he happened to be, he'd appropriated speakeasies, beer companies, unions, numbers games, nightclubs, me, Miss Drew, and now he was appropriating Catholicism. That was all" (176).

Billy's reading consists of the continuous emulation of this model

Billy Bathgate

of reading, in which appropriation is inevitable but also pointless. In Onandaga, Dutch Schultz steals food from his men's plates; in the hospital, Billy steals food from Schultz's hospital tray. Dutch Schultz has acquired a vast fortune that, as Billy says, is never used. Likewise Billy's stash is hidden in Arnold Garbage's basement under piles of rubbish. Doctorow stresses the pointlessness of Billy's money in his memorable enumeration of the items in the junk-heap:

> It was three hundred and sixty-two thousand and one hundred and twelve dollars I had taken for my portion and stashed there under carriage parts and old newspapers and broken toys and bed slats and stovepipes, and paper bags of shoes, and clothing in bales, and pots and pans and panes of glass and machine gears and acetylene torches and screwdrivers without handles and hammers and saws without teeth and shoeboxes of bubble-gum cards, and bottles and jars and baby bottles and cigar boxes of rubber nipples and typewriters and parts of saxophones and the bells of trumpets and the torn skins of drums and bent kazoos and broken ocarinas, and baseball bats and chips in cracked bottles and bathing caps and Boy Scout hats and badges and campaign buttons and piggy banks and bent tricycles and molding stamp collections and tiny flags on toothpicks from all the nations of the world. [318]

The money is hidden under a pile of dysfunctional tools ("screwdrivers without handles") or signs ("Boy Scout hats and badges and campaign buttons"), suggesting this homology: cash, like a sign, is only junk temporarily assigned arbitrary meaning. All of Schultz's acquisitions, and all of Billy's narrative, come to this. The degeneration of words and things into an empty heap becomes evident when the heap itself is seen as a trope, synathroesmus or word-heap, which is in turn composed of other tropes.[1]

The apprehension of cash and objects as empty signs makes Billy's "taking," like the reader's, futile. The criminal careers of Billy and Schultz are driven independently of—in spite of—their accumulation of banknotes or signs. In them the reader witnesses "pure" appropriation divorced from all context, use, or application to the world. In them is figured a condemnation to appropriate that is inevitable, like the necessity to read.

Other scenes exemplify the parallel between reading and appropriation. As a busboy at the Embassy Club, Billy reads the importance of the matchbox left by Bo Weinberg's companion and retrieves it from the garbage. For this act of reading trash, Berman gives him an instant reward of twenty dollars (85). Billy absorbs the barbershop killing on two occasions, first by reading a newspaper account (104–5) and next from Schultz's monologue (108–11), which Billy retells rather than quotes. Billy's version of Schultz's explanation supplants both the newspaper and Schultz, so it is already an appropriative interpretation of events: "you sometimes don't hear the details just looking at the face that speaks, you wonder at your own great recklessness to have put yourself in his line of vision, you hope he won't see that it is your deepest desire to conform your mind to his, to speak in your own mind with his voice, which means you cannot" (108). In this passage, Billy—like Blue and Daniel—admits that his narration is cut off from representation. It is all interpretation, all larceny.

The relation between Billy and Drew suggests that love, like narration, is also a wrongful appropriation. For Billy, the pursuit of Drew is one more instance of the appropriative discourse that marks his emulation of Dutch Schultz. Schultz's fierce appropriation of Drew, acted out almost in front of the humiliated Bo Weinberg, becomes Billy's model. With his "success"—their rapturous intercourse on the trip to Saratoga—Billy betrays and replaces his model, thereby demonstrating the futility of all such imitation. One act of larceny merely replaces another, in eternal return, and the actual possession—here of Drew, but equally of money, loyalty, or any other referent—only belatedly appears a mistake. Billy's decision to rescue Drew from gangland murder and to return her to Harvey Preston illustrates for the reader, although only in retrospect, the mistake that governs Billy's emulation of Schultz: that in acquisition lies signification. (Of course, this "learning" may also be considered the reader's own acquisition, the profit derived from reading. Readers, once more belatedly, may turn the undoing of the text into their own reading, as in de Man's second step.) In this way the experience of love, too, is a redundancy, a repetition of knowledge that should have been known from the outset but was not.

The redundancy of Billy's love is also clear in its intertextuality: *Billy Bathgate* comments on the long sequence of white goddesses in Doctorow's fiction and classical mythology. Like *Loon Lake*'s Clara or *Ragtime*'s Evelyn, Drew shares the man-destroying vengeance of Diana observed. On the other hand, she is also closely associated with the goddess Aphrodite, a fact that connects her with Lovegirl in "The Songs of Billy Bathgate." The introduction of Drew recalls the image of the birth of Aphrodite in the earlier fiction: "And up she came, her marcelled blond head, and then her white neck and shoulders, as if she was rising from the ocean" (15). Aphrodite was married to Hephaestus, but becomes the lover of Ares, the amoral god of indiscriminate killing; so Drew is married to Harvey, but becomes the lover of Schultz. Like Ares, Schultz was acquitted of a notorious crime; like Mars, the Roman counterpart of Ares, Schultz receives a kind of public homage at the horse races. The Praxiteles statue of the goddess shows her laying down her garment before her bath; in Onandaga, Drew lays down her skirt before diving into a mountain gorge and then resurfaces in the manner of Venus rising: "at this moment the water shook and she broke into the air, her head and shoulders rising, and she shouted or drew a great gasping breath that was like a cry of pain as the water poured off her shoulders, and she threw her arms behind her" (165).

With her "helmet of hair" (46), Drew also recalls the tradition of the armed Aphrodite, goddess of war. As Billy watches her dress, he observes that "it was the practiced efficiency of the race of women dressing, from that assumption they had always made that a G-string was their armor in the world, and that it would do against wars, riots, famines, floods, droughts, and the flames of the arctic night" (45).

The many parallels with Aphrodite mean ancient stories are being retold here. That Drew is stolen twice, by Schultz and by Billy, emphasizes the redundant nature of desire. Like Doctorow's earlier goddess-figures, Drew is never to be fully apprehended by the men who pursue her, and in returning their son to Billy, at the novel's end, Drew emphasizes her independence from all claims on her. If she incarnates a truth, it is unpossessable. The "signified" of appropriation escapes.

The novel's most somber link between reading and an inevitable, larcenous appropriation appears in the recurrent figure of the juggler, which continues the tradition of writer-as-clown established in "The Songs of Billy Bathgate," *World's Fair,* and "False Documents." It is as a literal juggler that Billy first attracts Schultz's attention; later, Schultz's ability to manage his gang is compared to juggling (147). Here juggling appears to be a metaphor for the desire to control. Billy himself sees in it the virtue of dexterity: "[M]agic was not the point, it was never the point, dexterity was to me the point, the same exercise as walking like a tight-rope walker on the spear fence points while the trains made their windy rush under me, or doing the backflips or handstands or cartwheels or whatever else arose in my mind of nimble compulsion" (23). The metaphor of the juggler is used to describe Billy's efforts to protect Drew (238) and even to portray God at the center of the universe (26). These contexts align juggling with an aspiration to absolute control.

A rich, complex passage applies the figure of the juggler directly to narration. It occurs as Billy tells Drew about talking to Bo Weinberg on the tugboat. Bo claimed to be classier than Dutch Schultz and described his ideal of reliability, illustrating it with an anecdote about his murder of Salvatore Maranzano. The story made Billy laugh; he tells Drew how the story took him out of himself, leading him to imagine both the scene narrated and the place he associates with both Bo Weinberg and class, the Embassy Club. The end of Bo's story elicits Billy's comparison between storytelling and juggling:

> I became the object of his baleful stare. And what are you laughing at, he said, you think it's funny, wiseass? The story was clearly over, as in juggling when the ball you throw up finds the moment to come down, hesitates as if it might not, and then drops at the same speed of that celestial light. And life is no longer good but just what you happen to be holding. (160)

Here the metaphor of the juggler suggests that Heideggerian relation between storytelling and death so evident in *The Book of Daniel,* "The Water Works," and *World's Fair:* narration and its illusion of representation provide a momentary distraction from the apprehension of death. The story is to the teller as a ball tossed in the air reaching its apogee; once it has lost its momentum—its capacity to hold attention achieved through a claim to representation—it falls. The story ends when it is apprehended that it is fiction, not life, and this ending coincides with grim disillusionment, hard times: "And life is no longer good but just what you happen to be holding." The sentence suggests that the goodness of life, like the laughter of Billy and Bo at the end of his anecdote, is a by-product of illusions created by storytelling. "What you happen to be holding" may mean "fate," whatever is, whatever is left over after illusions of representation have been dispelled, but there is no word for any entity that does not already harbor claims of representation. It cannot be said. It is "what you happen to be holding": nothing or another ball, another story that will rise and fall in endless repetition, eternal returns.

The juggler is a figure for the eternal returns of all of Doctorow's fiction. The circulation of words continues until death.

The fact that Billy applies his metaphor to the doomed Bo on the tugboat makes its effect devastating. Billy listens to a man with cement hardening around his ankles, tactilely apprehending the imminence of death, minute by minute, under an implacable sentence. The anecdote briefly functions to distract teller and listener, writer and reader, from their mortality, but as the story ends they are returned to it. The scene recalls the situation of Edgar and the "truly" dying children in the hospital in *World's Fair*. At first it appears as though readers "closer to death," like Bo and Billy, have a finer instinct for the misrepresentations of art, for the lies of the world of idle talk. For example, Bo concludes his monologue with new, wild exaggerations of his killings. His angry boasts of having killed Dutch Schultz, of having "killed them all" (160), seem to acknowledge the emptiness of his apologia. As he is led to certain death he moans, "Mama, mama" (21); these traditional first and last words, redundancies, suggest the futility of those between. (They are also uttered by the dying Dutch Schultz.) In these ways, Bo's moment of death seems to put him on the verge of this "true" understanding: that the world is inescapably fictional.

And Billy, too, in imagination, seems to have a heightened awareness of the truth of this moment. As he watches Bo by the rail, just before Schultz kicks him into the sea, he imagines the hapless victim singing "the song, it is blown away by the sea wind, his farewell chant, the song in his mind, all anybody ever has" (162). Billy's limpid sentence seems to crystallize the ontological situation of this novel and so many others by Doctorow; it suggests the delusion of possession, of the rage to appropriate, to appropriate verbally, which is Billy's fate. And so by proximity to death, Billy and Bo, both jugglers, seem to achieve some perspicuity.

But these moments also pass in illusion. The reader recalls that the insights of Billy and Bo occur during the course of his narration to Drew, next to the waterfall, at a moment of seduction. They take their place in a narrative full of ellipses and suppressions. In short, these are "representations of misrepresentation" that can claim no more truth than any other. In retrospect it is easy to see the fraudulence of such expressions as "truly dying" or "greater proximity to death." If language cannot represent, then it cannot get any closer to death than it can to the "wills" of Schultz, Drew, and Billy himself. Even the juggled balls of Billy's narration fall, eventually.

So, in the end, the metaphor of juggling confers only the illusion of meaning, of authorial control, of the eternal return as signified presence. It may be one of the last illusions of an understanding at the center of signs spinning round.

Interestingly, the metaphor is exchanged, at the novel's end, for another, which is its antithesis. The opposite of a juggler's art is indifference to objects tossed in the air; at the end of his narrative, Billy uses this antijuggling metaphor to concede that his own efforts to locate truth in narrative have been deluded: "I will confess that I have many times since my investiture sought to toss all the numbers up in the air and let them fall back into letters, so that a new book would be written. . . . But I have done it and done it and always it falls into the same Billy Bathgate I made of myself and must seemingly always be, and I am losing the faith it is a trick that can be done" (321).

Here it is evident that the gangster's, the juggler's, and the writer's illusions of control and dexterity are exposed; instead of manipulating the discourses of the world like the juggler, the writer is superfluous. However arranged, Billy's signs can produce only the pseudonymous title and the accompanying text. Renouncing words circulating in the air is Billy Bathgate's acquiescence to necessity.

If the metaphor of the writer-as-juggler ends in futility, the metaphor of the writer-as-killer extends that futility from writing to reading. Although Billy never directly kills anyone, a critical question, raised by his ellipses, is whether he set up Schultz and the rest of the gang for their slaying at the Palace Chophouse. The possibility that Billy's narrative may conceal collusion and self-interest puts it in the tradition of Blue's, Daniel's, and Joe's. Reviewing the evidence on the possibility of Billy's betrayal of Schultz seems essential to reading the novel; at the same time, it demonstrates the way readers may come to resemble the killers they seek.

Of course, Billy never narrates conclusive evidence that he betrayed Schultz, but many details in the novel suggest that he did. In the following passage, Billy includes himself among potential betrayers who seem to be the inevitable consequence of Schultz's way of life: "Here I will say about Dutch Schultz that wherever he went he created betrayals of himself, he produced them perpetually from the seasons of his life, he brought betrayers forth from his nature, each in our manner shape and size but having the common face of betrayal" (194). At another point, Billy wonders if Berman is planning betrayal (144), and later, Billy overtly states his own desire for revenge (202). That Billy has motivation enough to betray the gang is clear in his resentment against Berman for tricking him out of twenty-seven cents (60) and against Lulu Rosencrantz for punching him in the nose (202). In J. J. Hines's refusal of the bribe and in Schultz's wild plan to assassinate Thomas E. Dewey, Billy reads clear evidence of the imminent end of Schultz's power (281). Schultz's spontaneous rage against Billy for withholding information suggests that he, for one, considers Billy a possible traitor, and Billy's "candor" in telling Schultz of Drew's knowledge (of the sallow-skinned man, Schultz's apparent ally but eventual assassin) masks his own disingenuousness. He never tells anyone that, in the church in Onandaga, he made sure the sallow-skinned man never noticed him (185, 314). By concealing himself on that occasion, he is later able to "maintain deniability," to preserve to the end the fiction that he was an unimportant member of Schultz's gang; later, this deception helps Billy find Schultz's money. Suspicion of Billy's betrayal is strengthened when he survives the otherwise wholesale slaughter of the Schultz gang at the Palace Chophouse.

Further doubts about Billy's loyalty appear after that massacre. In his deathbed monologue, Schultz says "the boy came at me. Yes, he gave it to me" (309). Of course, Billy states unequivocally that the man with the sallow skin ordered the murders of Dutch and his gang (317), but however consistent with events this conclusion may be, it must remain only a hypothesis to the reader as long as it is possible that Billy may be suppressing other guilty knowledge of his own role in the orchestration of the murders. Finally, it is unclear that Billy's association with this man ends with his deportation in 1942, for, as Billy says, "by then I was myself patriotically employed overseas" (320). Did the two become wartime partners while in Europe? Taken in the light of his continued refusal to name this notorious criminal, these hints of collusion between Billy and the rival gang raise the issue of whether his narrative suppresses a deliberate act of betrayal against Shultz, one that eventually made him at least coequal in money and power with Schultz's killer.[2]

Hints do not amount to a case, however, and Billy is careful never to let his narrative definitively implicate himself. As he puts it, "I knew while I held something of these events in my hands, I would not have them bloodied" (296). The hole at the center remains. Doctorow's treatment of this issue recalls the question of the Isaacsons' guilt or innocence in *The Book of Daniel*. Daniel's attempt to solve the mystery entails ellipses that conceal his self-interest; Billy's attempt to maintain clean hands serves only to call attention to what has been unexpressed. It would be tempting to distinguish the two narrators on the basis of their apparent motivations. Until the end, Daniel seems oblivious to the self-serving nature of his ellipses, while Billy—if truly a traitor—surely suppresses his guilt in a conscious act of exculpation. Yet this is precisely the hermeneutic conclusion that is suspended in Doctorow's texts: whether "conscious" or not, narrative ellipses *cannot* disclose a narrator's (much less an author's) intention. Nothing cannot generate something; absence cannot generate presence. Billy's narrative would be the same whether or not he betrayed Schultz, or, as he said before of his narrative: "I have done it and done it and always it falls back into the same Billy Bathgate I made of myself and must seemingly always be" (321).

If Billy's ellipses make it impossible to call him an "actual" killer, as an interpreter of Schultz, he remains a metaphoric killer, as the reader is of Billy. In absorbing his teachings and interpreting him, Billy supplants and kills Schultz just as surely as Billy Bathgate the singer imaginatively killed Lovegirl, just as surely as Doctorow, the writer, imaginatively killed Hemingway, as the reader kills Doctorow. Killing is the ultimate "taking," the final appropriation, the necessary making-fictional of the world for one's own ends. This is the track left by the writer, which is followed—belatedly, necessarily—by the reader. The reader must so often "take" absence as presence, ellipses as meaning (guilt? innocence?), that his necessary larceny may come to resemble killing, too.

The present study turns again to that part of Doctorow's fiction which seems to give it life, the imagination of the new, of some relief from the world of interpretation—the futile, necessary taking of "the rackets"—that seems so unavoidable. This is the struggle to say "things you haven't said before" in Doctorow's words. The love of Red Bloom and Sugarbush or Billy and Lovegirl, the passion of Daniel or Coalhouse Walker, the quests for authenticity of Penfield and Joe—these moments hold out some hope of a meaning that is separate from, and outside, the tenacious delusions of reading and writing. In *Billy Bathgate*, the possibility of such a moment may be perceived in the character of Billy's mother, who seems to stand apart from the world of misrepresentation he thrives in. In her is imagined the possibility of a turning away from reading, a refusal to participate in its lures. To the extent that the novel succeeds in portraying such a mode of existence as plausible, it suggests an authentic alternative.

Billy's mother is known only by her maiden name, Mary Behan.[3] She is introduced in a scene that becomes, for her, habitual: sitting at her kitchen table, gazing at numerous memorial candles. Billy describes her as follows: "She stared into the lights as if she was reading them, as if each dancing flame made up a momentary letter of her religion. Day and night winter and summer she read the lights, of which she had a tableful, you only needed one once every year but she had all the remembrance she needed, she wanted illumination" (29).

Mary's "religion" is of her own making: although she is an Irish Catholic, Billy says she would rather go to temple than church (180). Her "reading" of the candles seems direct, as if unmediated by language: the lights are letters that provide instant illumination. As though in confirmation of this seemingly nonverbal apprehension, her first words to Billy ("something's wrong, what have you done" [29]) show her intuition. When they have tea together at Schrafft's, she closes her eyes and fingers the place mat "as if she was blind and was reading it in Braille"; when she speaks, in a voice "not quite hers," Billy wonders whether he spoke for herself "or had read it off the dots of the embossed place mat" (93). She seems uninterested in completing sentences (92). She seems to speak by things, not words: for example, her placing the baby carriage and rag doll in Billy's room may imply her urging him to marry and have children (90–91). In Mary, these details suggest that some relation to signification may be imagined which is fundamentally different than hermeneutics.

Mary's actions seek to subordinate hermeneutics, or the interpretation of meaning, to something else. After Schultz orders a telephone to be installed in Billy's kitchen, Mary begins to cement tiny seashells to it; later, she buys a fishtank and submerges the phone in it (313). Her actions suggest that the idea of the transmission of meaning may be "containable" within some larger entity, perhaps associated with the life-giving properties of the sea. It is obvious that Mary seeks to distinguish herself from the aggressive world of misrepresentation embodied in Schultz. When she places a newspaper photograph of Dutch Schultz in the carriage and pulls a blanket up to it (257), she may indicate the inferiority of hermeneutics, perceived as aggressive, to some larger maternal or instinctual principle.

If Mary's character may be read in this way, the ending of the novel, in which she agrees to care for the child of Billy and Drew, might then be interpreted as an endorsement of the alternative she offers to the discourses Billy cannot escape. Mary's supposed craziness might be sanity. In opposition to the wholesale destruction wrought by larcenous, murderous reading and writing, Mary's "religion of direct illumination" might stand as a creative counterweight.

Mary's alternative to the eternal return, compared to earlier ones, is attenuated: gone is the playful dialogism of Red Bloom and Sugarbush; gone is the passion of Daniel or the rage of Coalhouse Walker; gone is Penfield's interest in the non-Western or Joe's impulse to kill Bennett. In Mary Behan the alternative takes its most marginalized form, as if these options are becoming harder to imagine.

But her momentary alternative disappears, too. She accepts and appropriates Billy's criminal profits, despite her intuition concerning their source. Her move to a new apartment is made possible by Billy's reading of Schultz's deathbed monologue. Thus the viability of a "nonreading" alternative seems to depend, after all, on reading. Mary may suggest a metaphysical prospect of nonreading only in her son's verbal world. The final tableau of Billy and his mother, pushing his son's carriage in the park, seems to present the dilemma pictorially: Billy the redundant reader and writer, walks with Mary, some future alternative. Which one is mad? Perhaps the scene explains the sense in which Billy's mother serves as a "prophet," as Doctorow put it, in his interview with me. Interpretation and the hope of escaping it—of "saying things you haven't said before"—are linked, as they have always been in Doctorow's texts. Together, Billy and his mother travel one path, which the reader follows, too.

Afterword

Doctorow's texts warn of the futility of conclusions but concede their inevitability; nowhere is such a warning more crucial than in those specialized models of misrepresentation—summaries or afterwords—that recur in literary criticism. The words that follow take notice of Doctorow's warning in attempts to generalize about his rendering of America, his place in literary history, and his career to date.

Consider for a moment the novels' collective, devastating critique of America and its received values, as if that critique might be paraphrasable, in New Critical terms, in "themes." This consideration reveals an attack so savage that certain activists among social moralists—should they attend to the subject—might become uneasy about the presence of these texts in local libraries. In *Welcome to Hard Times,* Blue's pathetic (but also self-serving) adherence to enlightenment and constitutional ideals is a delusion so dangerous as to hasten apocalyptic destruction. In *Ragtime,* America as the beacon of immigration is like those "phony" mediums Houdini exposes—spiritual frauds that exploit the credulous. In *Loon Lake,* Bennett's corporate America shares the ethos of Sim Hearn, who profits from gang-rape and murder of the weak; as a CIA official, Joe Korzienowski is the perpepuator of the politically respectable version of that legacy. Likewise in *Billy Bathgate,* America is Dutch Schultz and his protégé Billy: a land of rapacious criminals, oblivious to conscience. These thematic depictions of America may startle readers who look to novels for moral edification.

But coincident with this thematic turning is another, away from America and toward the reader, toward the process of reading itself.

This turning may deepen any initial shock, with this result—the loss of any initial safety readers may have felt in making confident condemnations of something outside themselves, even of the object of attack, America. Now readers must see themselves not only as complicit with corruption but also as false creations, models of misrepresentation. The larcenous reader is just as much an invention of the text as Doctorow's America and his criminal narrators are. This second turning neutralizes, for a time, the novels' frightening attacks in states of deep indeterminacy.

A similar indeterminacy results from the effort to place Doctorow's oeuvre in the larger context of American literary history. Nevertheless, some temptation to "place" Doctorow may be inherent in any study of his works.

The temptation is all the more understandable because from its beginning—from the discussion of Blue's palimpsest—this study has shown that reading a single Doctorow novel "separately" is possible only at the sacrifice of seeing its relations with others. So now consider that a corollary may also be true: that the attempt to compare one writer's oeuvre with those of others can proceed only at the cost of eradicating individual distinctness of texts that first gave rise to the illusion of separability. If so, generalizations about Doctorow's oeuvre will be misrepresentations. In what follows this hypothesis is tested in the light of some premises of literary history.

The most popular of these may be referred to as the literary history of the anthologies, a conception of a canon of texts divisible into historical periods, sometimes corresponding to nations or geographical regions. Each period is defined by characteristics also exhibited by works of literature that represent it. This paradigm of literary history was first conceived by Hegel; in America it was developed by such twentieth-century scholars as Perry Miller, F. O. Matthiessen, and R. W. B. Lewis. It persists in the heuristics of many widely used collections of American and world literature.[1] According to this paradigm, literature represents intellectual dilemmas also discernible in society and in the evolution of theology and philosophy. For example, American literature progresses from the era of Puritanism, through the enlightenment, transcendentalism, realism and naturalism, to modernist reactions to these systems of ideas. Literary historians sometimes adopt the categories modernism and postmodernism to divide the twentieth century roughly in half. But whether it treats earlier or later periods, the paradigm presupposes a Hegelian hermeneutic of history—as a sequence of *Zeitgeists*—and explains literature as conveyors of them.

In this kind of literary history, if Doctorow's oeuvre may be said to exemplify either American modernism or postmodernism, several problems ensue. First, the difficulty of distinguishing these two terms is notorious.[2] Second, the doubtful notion that a peculiarly American postmodernism exists must be presupposed.[3] Most fundamentally, Doctorow's works themselves reject the hermeneutics of history as early as *Big as Life*. For the purposes of this test, one can ignore all of these problems and simply stipulate a name and definition for our literary period—for example, postmodernism as a playful subversion of art brought about by ridicule of its traditional claims, including those to textual autonomy. In fact this definition synthesizes various parts of recent theories.[4]

Now to test the idea that Doctorow's works might "represent postmodernism" according to such a definition, just as, say, John Barth's or Philip Roth's might. An argument of this sort would require, first, the analysis of a "second order" of intertextuality—of the relations between two or more intertextual relations—so as to establish a common denominator among the writers studied. Does Doctorow's *Billy Bathgate* stand in relation to "The Songs of Billy Bathgate" as Roth's *Zuckerman Unbound* does to *The Ghost Writer*? As Barth's *Letters* does to his earlier works? As Pynchon's *Vineland* does to *V.*? In what way is Doctorow's work "playful" like Roth's? Like Barth's? Like Pynchon's? Questions like these fascinate, until one recognizes that postmodernist features of the works obtain only to the extent that differences among individual texts, which might make the ratios uneven, are ignored. As a result, this generalizing procedure leaves only the most vapid residuum: that American postmodernists sometimes playfully take their own prior works as the subjects of new texts—a form of Doctorow's "empty intertextuality." Doctorow's works anticipate and deflect literary criticism that subordinates texts to such extralinguistic signifieds as history. Advocates of the periodization of American literature would have to show that the second-order, playful interextuality of postmodernism was definitively distinguishable from the patterns of repetition in contemporary non-American writers or in the oeuvres of, say, James and Wharton or Chopin and Twain. Because few studies examine this immense subject, grouping Doctorow with other contemporary writers as American postmodernists is problematic. Such difficulties lend impetus to movements in contemporary literary theory to abandon the concept of periodization entirely.[5]

If patterns of writers' lives are created by their works, then one of the most familiar is that of the artist-in-despair, seeking salvation. Having articulated ultimate contradictions so compulsively and so often, seeing no chance of surpassing work already created, the writer enters into a phase of negation—of self-parody, bitterness, or silence—in a desperate search for artistic renewal. Such a paradigm underlies studies of nearly all great writers: of Americans, for example, Hawthorne, Dickinson, Melville, Twain, Hemingway, Plath. (It would be worth knowing how much of this design is attributable to the examples of Dante's persona or of Shakespeare's "development" from the histories and comedies, through the tragedies, to the last romances. Perhaps its conformity with the template of Christianity makes the design a common master narrative, or *grand récit*, of much Western art, although the exception of Homer may caution readers to remember its legendary nature.)

It would be tempting to assign Doctorow a place in the tradition of the American version of this *grand récit*. Like his American predecessors, he seems bent upon a course of ever more audacious confrontation with the apparent principle of writing so insidious to creation, to life, to well-being: Nietzsche's "eternal reiteration of the same." His career begins, in *Welcome to Hard Times,* with a clear acknowledgement of the threat of such a principle to both life and art. The works that follow imagine various new ways of thinking—in Red Bloom and Sugarbush, Daniel, the little boy, Penfield and Joe, Billy's mother. These creations may suggest, somewhat, Frost's metaphor of art as a "momentary stay against confusion"; the deployment of such characters may be brave recourses, strategies to contest the feared victory of the alternative—silence or succumbing to the deathlike principle of repetition.

The succession of Doctorow's works may persuade some readers to emphasize the word "momentary" in Frost's phrase, since over the course of his career, Doctorow's alternatives have become weaker, more marginal, less plausibly conceived as bearers of the intellectual burden they assume; each seems less capable of fighting the world of dead redundancy that always prevails in the end. A biographical critic might be concerned at a sequence of texts that seems to point only in the direction of defeat for the prospect of "saying things you haven't said before," of continued artistic renewal. Such a worry can be intensified by interview responses, like the following, in which Doctorow describes desperate expedients necessary to sustain writing:

> You know, you do all sorts of things to get your work done. For instance, you can see just how shaky a writer is and just how far over the edge of the cliff he is, by how much the title keeps pulling him back; he says the title of the book to keep himself from falling. And so you use anything you can to get yourself through the day, and to get the book done. You can use the title, you can invent an aesthetic, you can write a manifesto, you can go to a bar and talk to other writers.

Unquestionably, Doctorow saw danger of this kind in the career of Hemingway, who was "braver than we thought" in turning to a new voice, as he did in *The Garden of Eden,* instead of to his rifle; in this light Doctorow may have understated the case in his interview with me when he said that creativity is born of despair. But it is precisely at this point—when the artificial patterns of artistic development threaten to shift to the other, to the "real" side of the mirror—that the fictional nature of criticism and interpretation must be reiterated; the pattern traced above is no more than another prosopopoeia, another personification of signs, one that temporarily inserted a signified, despairing Doctorow behind his words. Such a pattern is always made afterwards, of afterwords. In fact, the subject of artistic renewal, discussed lucidly in the essay "Braver Than We Thought," is never finally separable from its paradoxical—from its bright—expression.

Appendix

Language and Death in Heidegger

In the first part of Division Two of *Sein und Zeit* (sections 46–53), Heidegger discusses the relation between Being and death using his neologism *Sein-zum-Tode*. Most commentators interpret this concept existentially, as an apprehension of the irrevocability of death which has the effect of disclosing the inauthenticity of the "everydayness" (*die Alltaglichkeit*) or "idle talk" (*das Gerede*) that constitutes life.[1] In this way, *Sein-zum-Tode* is interpreted as an authentic experience that momentarily demystifies a superficial world. In truth, Heidegger's text may give some warrant for such interpretations; existentialist interpretations of *Sein und Zeit* form a substantial tradition. On the other hand, the concept of *Sein-zum-Tode* is less often analyzed as part of a single moment in the larger, ongoing, unfinished argument of *Sein und Zeit*. Read in such a way, sections 46–53 study a relation between Being and death that is not necessarily grounded in human anxiety over mortality. Instead, Heidegger's point is that *Sein-zum-Tode* is inherent in the temporality of Dasein (the subject of Division Two, which these sections initiate), and Dasein is not synonymous with the human.

Instead of defining a momentary human apprehension of death, Heidegger's discussion of *Sein-zum-Tode* tests that experience, in an instance of a Husserlian *epochē*, as one hypothesis among many in his investigation of the question as to whether authentic Being is possible for Dasein. In fact it is *Sein-zum-Tode* that raises just this larger issue of whether Dasein can attest to an authentic potential-for-being. In the context of Heidegger's larger exploration, it is possible to see that *Sein-zum-Tode* may illuminate the condition of idle talk and everydayness without, however, accepting the seeming corollary that *Sein-zum-Tode* must name some authentic entity related experientially, through the human, to Being. In fact, the unfinished *Sein und Zeit* never defines authentic Being or authentic Dasein. A definition of Being as *aletheia*, or unconcealment, does not appear in Heidegger's work until his lectures of 1935 (not published until revised in 1953) and of 1943.[2]

In *Sein und Zeit,* the examination of *Sein-zum-Tode* is part of an open-ended inquiry into the possibility of authentic Being. Consideration of this topic in sections 46–53 enables Heidegger to define more precisely the *separation* between Dasein and Being. By the time Heidegger begins to define authentic Being, it is further purged of even the tentative connections with the human, which prompted interpreters to conclude that, in the serious contemplation of death, some human authenticity would reside which was distinguishable from the inauthenticity of everydayness and idle talk.

Of course, *Sein und Zeit* does warn of that potential misinterpretation in Section 53, where Heidegger firmly rejects the condition of "dwelling upon" (*sich aufhalten*) or "pondering" (*Verhalten*) over death as promising in any way a fruitful outcome for philosophy: "Thus, if by 'Being towards death' we do not have in view an 'actualizing' of death, neither do we mean 'dwelling upon (*sich aufhalten*) the end in its possibility.' This is the way one comports oneself when one 'thinks about death', pondering (*Verhalten*) over when and how this possibility may perhaps be actualized."[3]

Heidegger's denial of signification to the merely human apprehension of death is clear in this and other passages.[4] What remains, however, is the question taken up later in his career: if the intrusion of death can illuminate everydayness without implying any authenticity in human experience, in what way, then, is death itself ontologically authentic?

Heidegger answers this question by finding death, or human mortality, to be a function of language. This connection is first made in the lecture "Die Sprache" (1950), in which Heidegger expounds his famous apothegm, *Die Sprache spricht.* The elaboration of this maxim, which is also central to the work of Derrida, de Man, and Miller, dissociates language from both the human and the representational.

Appendix

The difficulty and the austerity of this enterprise—Heidegger's willingness to consider language apart from *any* prior presuppositions—is evident in this statement of his purpose:

> To reflect on language thus demands that we enter into the speaking of language in order to take up our stay with language, i.e. within *its* speaking, not without our own. Only in that way do we arrive at the region within which it may happen—or also fail to happen—that language will call to us from there and grant us its nature. We leave the speaking to language. *We do not wish to ground language in something else that is not language itself, nor do we wish to explain other things by means of language.* [emphasis added][5]

In his maxim and in the essay as a whole, Heidegger dispenses with the presupposition that language must have ground or reference. As he later puts it in the same essay, "In its essence, language is neither expression nor an activity of man. Language speaks."[6] Once the inquiry into language is divorced from human representation, Heidegger can introduce a definition of *Sprache* that unites it with mortality: "To reflect on language means—to reach the speaking of language in such a way that this speaking takes place as that which grants an abode for the being of mortals."[7] This definition makes no presuppositions about man as Cartesian subject or initiator of language. It assumes nothing about the referential capacity of language. In 1958 Heidegger returned to this subject; while admitting that the relation between language and death is elusive, he still found it necessary: "The essential relation between death and language flashes up before us, but remains still unthought. It can, however, beckon us toward the way in which the nature of language draws us into its concern and so relates us to itself, in case death belongs together with what reaches out for us, touches us."[8]

In these late texts, Heidegger comes close to saying that death can be conceived only as a function of nonrepresentational language, which confers upon man a space (or an "abode") to die.

Notes

Abbreviations Used in the Notes

EC   Richard Trenner, editor, *E. L. Doctorow: Essays and Conversations* (Princeton: Ontario Review Press, 1983)

DP   Herwig Friedl and Dieter Schulz, editors, *E. L. Doctorow: A Democracy of Perception* (Essen: Die Blaue Eule, 1988)

Introduction

1. Critical discussions of Doctorow's misrepresentations as inaccurate models are exemplified in the articles that follow. In "Rage and Order in Doctorow's *Welcome to Hard Times*," *South Dakota Review* 22 (1984): 79–85, Stephen L. Tanner argues that Doctorow misrepresents the Old West in *Welcome to Hard Times*. In "Historicizing Fiction and Fictionalizing History: The Case of E. L. Doctorow," *Prospects: An Annual Journal of American Cultural Studies* 5 (1980): 423–37, Cushing Strout accuses Doctorow of "tinkering with history" in *Ragtime:* his historical details are "in a contemporary idiom at odds with the era of ragtime" (431, 432). The result, for Strout, is corruption of "the veracious imagination" (435). Writing about *The Book of Daniel* in "Some Shapes in Recent American Fiction," *Contemporary Literature* 15 (1974): 539–61, Earl Rovit complains that "when the novel departs from documented history . . . the narrative becomes strained and banal" (547). Joseph Turner, in "The Kinds of Historical Fiction: An Essay in Definition and Methodology," *Genre* 12 (1979): 333–55, classifies *The Book of Daniel* as a "disguised historical novel" that "cannot be read without taking the Rosenbergs into account;" but at the same time, "confusion"—as manifested, for example, in the complaint of Earl Rovit—arises because the

novel also subverts the "disguise" of the Rosenbergs (348, 349). For a use of the word "model" closer to my own, see my discussion of Paul de Man on page 6 and in Note 14, below.

2. John T. Irwin, *American Hieroglyphics: The Symbol of the Egyptian Hieroglyphics in the American Renaissance* (Baltimore: Johns Hopkins University Press, 1980). Doctorow's allusions to Whitman and Poe are discussed in chapter 4; to Thoreau in chapter 6; to Hawthorne in chapter 7; to Hemingway in chapter 10.

3. Bibliographies of and excerpts from basic texts concerned with the twentieth-century literary and philosophical challenges to representation are collected in Hazard Adams and LeRoy Searle, editors, *Critical Theory Since 1965* (Tallahassee: Florida State University Press, 1986) and Robert Con Davis, editor, *Contemporary Literary Criticism: Modernism through Post-Structuralism* (New York and London: Longman, 1986). These collections summarize contemporary critical controversies, including Marxist, psychoanalytic, and feminist approaches. Summaries and assessments of deconstructive criticism are available in the following: Jonathan Culler, *On Deconstruction* (Ithaca: Cornell University Press, 1982); Christopher Norris, *The Deconstructive Turn: Essays in the Rhetoric of Philosophy* (London: Routledge, Chapman and Hall, 1984); Vincent B. Leitch, *Deconstructive Criticism: An Advanced Introduction* (New York: Columbia University Press, 1983). For the argument that Derrida's writings have little relevance to literary studies, see Rudolphe Gasche, *The Tain of the Mirror: Derrida and the Philosophy of Reflection* (Cambridge: Harvard University Press, 1986). Of course it is true that Derrida argues against the Heideggerian privileging of poetic discourse, for example the poetry of Holderlin, but discussions of literature do not necessarily imply privilege. Even on its surface Gasche's argument seems difficult to accept, since Derrida himself analyzes such crucial literary figures as Rousseau, Poe, Blanchot, Ponge.

4. Friedrich Nietzsche, *Werke, Grossoktavausgabe,* 2nd ed., 20 vols. (Leipzig: Kroner, 1901–13), 15:65, trans. David Farrell Krell, in his three volume translation of Martin Heidegger's *Nietzsche* (San Francisco: Harper and Row, 1984), 2:5.

5. Richard King, "Between Simulteneity and Sequence," DP, 49. In another essay in this volume, "Power and Degradation: Patterns of Historical Process in the Novels of E. L. Doctorow," Herwig Friedl argues that one of Blue's final statements is "not to be confounded with Nietzsche's idea of the eternal return of the same as the pattern of will triumphant in willing itself endlessly" (22). These two positions are not

in contradiction, since King's observation concerned only the course of history. Friedl's caution is well-taken, since it distinguishes Blue from Nietzsche's "gay" philosopher. Friedl finds the bleakness of Doctorow's novel closer to Schopenhauer than to Nietzsche.

6. As noted in the text, this interpretation of Nietzsche's doctrine of the eternal return owes much to Heidegger's lectures on Nietzsche, three volumes of which are available in David Farrell Krell's translation. But the interpretation advanced here also comports well with other recent readings of the doctrine, notably David B. Allison's in his introduction to *The New Nietzsche: Contemporary Styles of Interpretation* (Cambridge: The MIT Press, 1985), xi–xxviii. Allison argues that the eternal return should be understood in the context of Nietzsche's denial of "the fundamental correspondence between the signifier and the signified" which produces a "system" that consists wholly of "metaphor-metamorphosis" (xv, xvi). Another interesting analysis of the eternal return is Pierre Klossowski's "Nietzsche's Experience of the Eternal Return" in the same volume, 107–33. Klossowski interprets the eternal return as entailing the loss of meaning and goal: "They are *everywhere* and *nowhere* in the vicious circle, since no point of the circle can be both beginning and end at once" (119).

7. Martin Heidegger, *Nietzsche,* trans. Krell, 2:191.

8. Ibid, 43.

9. Heidegger cites Nietzsche, *Werke* 16:414. See *Nietzsche,* trans. Krell, 2:25.

10. Martin Heidegger, *Einfuhrung in die Metaphysik* (Tubingen: Max Niemayer, 1953), trans. Ralph Mannheim, *An Introduction to Metaphysics* (New Haven and London: Yale University Press, 1959), 100. In his *Heidegger and the Language of Poetry* (Lincoln and London: University of Nebraska Press, 1978), David A. White concludes: "the whole burden of Heidegger's investigations into language as a medium of representational thinking is to indicate the presuppositional character of representation and the metaphysics on which it is based" (151). Heidegger's critique of Being as *Vorstellung* is foreshadowed in his essay on historiography, "Die Zeit des Weltbildes" *Holzwege* (Frankfurt: Vittorio Klosterman, 1950), trans. Marjorie Grene, "The Age of the World View," *Measure* 2 (1951): 269–84. Rpt. *Boundary 2* 4 (1975): 341–55. For the relevance of that essay to the treatment of history in Doctorow's *Big as Life,* see chapter 2.

11. Gerald Bruns, *Heidegger's Estrangements: Language, Truth, and Poetry in the Later Writings* (New Haven and London: Yale University

Press, 1989), xix. Bruns compares the work of the late Heidegger with that of John Ashbery and Thomas Pynchon and provides a groundbreaking account of the relation between language and death in Heidegger's late collection of essays *Unterwegs zur Sprache.* He describes this relation, and Heidegger's ambition in these lectures, as follows: "Language, like death, is the limit of the human. Heidegger wants to disconnect man and language in order to reconnect them in the archaic way in which he reconnects us to our mortality" (157). My only reservation with this account is that it confers the power of reconnection on the philosopher, rather than on *Sprache,* to which—in my own reading of Heidegger—the philosopher merely responds. In Bruns's view of Heidegger, the writer/philosopher/poet still retains the power to articulate these reconnections; in my view of Heidegger, if the power to articulate exists at all—and I believe Heidegger never assumes it does—it belongs to *Sprache* and not to mortals. For a very different account of the theme of mortality in Heidegger—one that ultimately connects death with care and love—see David Farrell Krell, *Intimations of Mortality: Time, Truth, and Finitude in Heidegger's Thinking of Being* (University Park and London: The Pennsylvania State University Press, 1986). For a caution against the use of the terms "postmodern" and "postmodernism," see note 2 of the "Afterword."

12. Paul de Man, *The Rhetoric of Romanticism* (New York: Columbia University Press, 1984), 80–81.

13. Paul de Man, *Blindness and Insight: Essays in the Rhetoric of Contemporary Criticism* (New York: Oxford University Press, 1971), 141.

14. Paul de Man, *Allegories of Reading: Figural Language in Rousseau, Nietzsche, Rilke, and Proust* (New Haven and London: Yale University Press, 1979), 205. Notice de Man's careful, ambiguous use of the word "model" in this passage, which creates an open-ended sense I would wish for the use of the word in my title.

15. Two recent volumes that acknowledge the import of Derrida's opposition between hermeneutics and deconstruction are *Hermeneutics: Questions and Prospects,* ed. Gary Shapiro and Alan Sica (Amherst: University of Massachusetts Press, 1984) and John D. Caputo, *Radical Hermeneutics: Repetition, Deconstruction, and the Hermeneutic Project* (Bloomington: Indiana University Press, 1987). In their introduction, Shapiro and Sica discuss work by recent philosophers which colors the meaning of the word "hermeneutics" in various ways: as edification, as interested in the past, as founded in phenomenology, as harboring the antipodal tendencies of respect and suspicion. In contrast to these recent

redefinitions, the older sense of the word "hermeneutics"—as defined in this paragraph of the text—will be retained here.

16. Jacques Derrida, "Structure, Sign, and Free Play in the Discourses of the Human Sciences," *Writing and Difference* (Chicago: University of Chicago Press, 1979), 292. In my estimate Derrida's work has been the most influential in analyzing the illusions of hermeneutics. At the same time, he is not the only one of these five writers to challenge hermeneutics. For the argument that the late Heidegger abandoned hermeneutics, see Hubert Dreyfus, "Beyond Hermeneutics: Interpretation in Late Heidegger and Recent Foucault," in Shapiro and Sica's *Hermeneutics*, 66–83.

17. Jacques Derrida, *La Carte Postale* (Paris: Flammarion, 1980).

18. Caputo's *Radical Hermeneutics* is one such attempt to reinstate hermeneutics after an assessment of the challenge posed to it by Derridean deconstruction: "Deconstructive criticism is for me the gateway through which radical hermeneutics must pass. . . .Radical hermeneutics makes a pass at formulating what the French call *la condition humaine,* the human situation . . . And I call this 'hermeneutics' just because I think there is something liberating about all this, not dehumanizing" (97).

19. For J. Hillis Miller's discussion of storytelling in Kant and Kafka, see *The Ethics of Reading* (New York: Columbia University Press, 1988), 13–39, and *Versions of Pygmalion* (Cambridge: Harvard University Press, 1990), 16. For the argument that even de Man could not free himself from the necessity for prosopopoeia, see "'Reading' Part of a Paragraph in *Allegories of Reading*," in Lindsay Waters and Wlad Godzich, eds., *Reading de Man Reading* (Minneapolis: University of Minnesota Press, 1989), 155–70. For the concept of "varnishing," see "The Ethics of Reading: Vast Gaps and Parting Hours," in Ira Konigsberg, ed., *American Criticism in the Poststructuralist Age* (Ann Arbor: Michigan Studies in the Humanities, 1981), 34.

20. J. Hillis Miller, "Stevens' Rock and Criticism as Cure, II," *Georgia Review* (1976): 330–48.

21. J. Hillis Miller, "The Critic as Host," *Critical Inquiry* 3 (1977): 439–47.

22. The case for Doctorow as a radical Jewish humanist is made by John Clayton in "Radical Jewish Humanism: The Vision of E. L. Doctorow," EC, 109–20. It is worth noting, however, that other hermeneutic criticism disputes this categorization. See Carol Ianone, "E. L. Doctorow's 'Jewish' Radicalism," *Commentary* 81 (1986): 53–56. In reply

to an interviewer's question about Clayton's thesis, Doctorow responded with the following equivocal metaphor: "to get back to the idea of a radical Jewish humanist tradition, if I was not in that tradition, I would certainly want to apply for membership." EC, 54–55.

23. Paul de Man, "Genesis and Geneology in Nietzsche's *The Birth of Tragedy*," *Diacritics* 2 (1972): 50.

24. Turner, "The Kinds of Historical Fiction," 347.

25. John G. Parks, *E. L. Doctorow* (New York: Continuum, 1991), 127.

26. Geoffrey Galt Harpham, "E. L. Doctorow and the Technology of Narrative," *PMLA* 100 (1985): 84–85.

27. Jacques Derrida, "The Law of Genre," *Critical Inquiry* 7 (1980): 55–82.

28. Paul de Man, *Blindness and Insight*, 106.

29. The classic defense of the validity of performatives is J. L. Austin's *How to Do Things with Words* (New York: Oxford University Press, 1962). Derrida outlines his differences with Austin in "Signature Event Context," in *Margins of Philosophy,* trans. Alan Bass (Chicago: University of Chicago Press, 1982): 307–330. In *Allegories of Reading*, 127–28, 281–83, de Man analyzes the failure of speech acts in Rousseau.

CHAPTER 1   Construction/Destruction/Construction:
            Welcome to Hard Times

1. David S. Gross, in "Tales of Obscene Power: Money and Culture, Modernism and History in the Fiction of E. L. Doctorow," in EC, 120–50, sees the novel as demystifying the truly exploitative nature of capitalism, which is concealed in most Western fiction. Frank W. Shelton, in "E. L. Doctorow's *Welcome to Hard Times:* The Western and the American Dream," *Midwest Quarterly* 25 (1983): 7–17, argues that the novel attacks the shortsightedness and competitive ethos of capitalism.

2. In *E. L. Doctorow* (New York and London: Methuen, 1985), Paul Levine says that Blue expresses not only "his own frustration over the inadequacy of his narrative but perhaps also Doctorow's misgivings about the ability of fiction to convey the truth about life" (30). Arthur Saltzman, in "The Stylistic Energy of E. L. Doctorow," EC, 73–108, believes that behind Blue "we detect Doctorow himself questioning the legitimacy of his own craft" (81).

3. Paul Levine quotes Blue in support of the view that the novel is governed by an "almost classically tragic view of history" (29).

4. In *Ragtime* the newly successful "Tateh"—a nickname bestowed

on a character whose unpronounceable last name is never revealed—changes his name to "Baron Ashkenazy." The revelation that Joe "of Paterson" or Joe Paterson, in *Loon Lake* is really Joseph Korzienowski is discussed in chapter 6. The confusion created by the nickname "Sunny Jim" for Edgar Altschuler, in *World's Fair*, is discussed in chapter 8.

5. For discussions of the fallacy of "proper names," see Jacques Derrida, *Signeponge/Signsponge*, trans. Richard Rand (New York: Columbia University Press, 1984), 8, 24–30, and J. Hillis Miller, "The Triumph of Theory, the Resistance to Reading, and the Question of the Material Base," *PMLA* 102 (1987): 289.

6. Saltzman, "Stylistic Energy," 76.

7. Marilyn Arnold, "History as Fate in E. L. Doctorow's Tale of a Western Town," in EC, 207–16.

8. Shelton, "E. L. Doctorow's *Welcome to Hard Times*," 9.

9. Blue first mentions the letter to Molly in the evening. On the next day he unsuccessfully tries to persuade Jimmy to take a job with Isaac. This conversation teaches Blue his "unending futility," but just at this point in the narration, Blue's sense of time becomes blurred: of his attempts to retain his integrity he asks, "How long was I able to do that? One week? One hour?" (168). Afterwards the narration shifts to an account of life in the spring (169–70); it is impossible to know whether this account implies elapsed time, although that effect is created by the position of the account. Afterwards, chronology resumes with the otherwise disconnected phrase "One morning." Blue finally tells Angus Mcellhenny about the letter on a Saturday night. This blurred chronology emphasizes Blue's hesitation in delivering the message. As the introduction makes clear, false chronologies that make reading recoil on itself are common to Doctorow's novels.

10. For the image of the palimpsest in the poetry of William Carlos Williams, see Joseph Riddel, *The Inverted Bell* (Baton Rouge: Louisiana State University Press, 1974).

11. For discussions of the place of *Welcome to Hard Times* in the tradition of the American western, see Kevin Starr, Review of *Welcome to Hard Times*, *New Republic*, 6 September 1975, 25–27; David Gross, "Tales of Obscene Power," 133; and John G. Parks, *E. L. Doctorow*, 22–23.

12. Marilyn Arnold discusses the novel's biblical allusions in "Doctorow's *Hard Times*: A Sermon on the Failure of Faith," *Literature and Belief* 3 (1983): 87–95.

13. J. Hillis Miller, *The Ethics of Reading* (New York: Columbia University Press, 1988). In *Versions of Pygmalion* (Cambridge: Harvard Uni-

versity Press, 1990), Miller sees prosopopoeia as a figure that fills the blank of death with a fictive person (125). This seems close to the function of the Bad Man from Bodie.

14. Arnold, "Doctorow's *Hard Times*." In this article Arnold argues that the novel depicts the destruction of the town as a function of the decline of religious values.

15. John Clayton, "Radical Jewish Humanism: The View of E. L. Doctorow," *EC*, 109–19.

16. J. Bakker, "E. L. Doctorow's *Welcome to Hard Times*: A Reconsideration," *Neophilologus* 69 (1985): 472.

17. Stephen L. Tanner, "Rage and Order in Doctorow's *Welcome to Hard Times*," *South Dakota Review* 22 (1984): 84.

18. Carole Ianone, "E. L. Doctorow's 'Jewish' Radicalism," *Commentary* 81 (1986): 54.

19. Paul de Man, *Blindness and Insight: Essays in the Rhetoric of Contemporary Criticism* (New York: Oxford University Press, 1971), 140.

CHAPTER 2 *Big as Life:*
The Dead-End of Hermeneutics

1. There has been very little criticism of *Big as Life*, and most of it is evaluative. For example, John W. Hattman in *Best Sellers* 26 (1966): 86–87, argues as follows: "Unfortunately [the novel] is also marred by numerous overly graphic passages of description of sexual action and by the implied and finally stated position that religion in general and the Catholic Church in particular has nothing meaningful to say in the face of such a crisis" (87). In "Nude Giants in Fun City," *New Leader*, 24 October 1966, 25–26, Thomas J. Fleming accuses Doctorow of banality. Paul Levine's strictures are as follows: "With its predictable plot, lifeless characters and confusing resolution, *Big as Life* is the problem child among Doctorow's novels. In contrast to his first book, it fails to subordinate its political vision to its imaginative structure or to exploit the possibilities of the popular formula in an original way" (*E. L. Doctorow* [New York and London: Methuen, 1985]), 33–34. An interesting analysis of the novel appears in Barbara Cooper's "The Artist as Historian in the Novels of E. L. Doctorow," *Emporia State Research Studies* 29 (1980): 5–43. I find myself fully in agreement with her conclusion about Creighton, that "all his efforts to understand what is happening are futile;" however, our reasons for reaching this same judgment are different. Cooper sees Creighton's problem as being overwhelmed with data; I

see in Creighton's incapacity a Heideggerian critique of the hermeneutics of contemporary history.

2. Arthur Saltzman, "The Stylistic Energy of E. L. Doctorow," *EC*, 82.

3. Levine, *E. L. Doctorow*, 32.

4. Martin Heidegger, "Die Zeit des Weltbildes," *Holzwege* (Frankfurt: Vittorio Klostermann, 1950), trans. Marjorie Grene, *Measure* 2 (1951): 269–84.

5. Jacques Derrida, "The Principle of Reason: The University in the Eyes of its Pupils," *Diacritics* 13 (Fall 1983): 9–10.

6. Martin Heidegger, *Der Satz vom Grund* (Pfullingen: Gunther Neske, 1957). In "The Principle of Reason" Derrida often refers to this work, as he develops a critique of contemporary research similar to Heideggers's.

7. Levine, *E. L. Doctorow*, 32.

8. Jacques Derrida, "The Principle of Reason," 12.

9. Martin Heidegger, "The Age of the World View," *Measure* 2 (1951): 269–84. Rpt. *Boundary 2* 4 (1975): 341–55, 346.

10. Michel Foucault, *Les Mots et Les Choses* (Paris: Editions Gallimard, 1966), translated as *The Order of Things* (New York: Random House, 1970), 322–28.

11. Jacques Derrida, "Signature Event Context," in *Margins of Philosophy*, trans. Alan Bass (Chicago: University of Chicago Press, 1982), 315ff.

12. Roman Jakobson, "Shifters, Verbal Categories, and the Russian Verb," Russian Language Project (Cambridge: Harvard University Press, 1957). For a discussion of the impact of Jakobson's work on shifters to Heidegger's philosophy in particular and poststructuralism in general, see Anthony Wilden, *The Language of the Self: The Function of Language in Psychoanalysis by Jacques Lacan* (Baltimore: Johns Hopkins University Press, 1968), 180–85.

13. The names Red Bloom and Sugarbush almost too conspicuously clamor for allegorical interpretation of the older sort, perhaps along lines that stressed the organicist values inherent in Red's music. But the stability of that line of interpretation would be threatened by the intertextual resonances of "Bloom" that evoke Joyce's music-loving urban wanderer, who returns after a barroom brawl to a sexually bountiful wife. Other character names recall the multiple-referent pattern in *Welcome to Hard Times*. Creighton, sometimes "Dr." and sometimes "professor," is irritated when he receives a telegram addressed to Captain Irving Croton; he recalls that in the past he had often been confused

with an N.Y.U. professor of law named William Crawford (66). Red calls the owner of Harry's Music Supply "Harry Supply" (128). Mr. Giotto, the fence to whom Red sells his diamonds, is called "Pinkglasses" for most of the novel. Names that are either puns or antonomasia (the substitutiopns of epithets) emphasize the rhetoricity of naming and call into question the "proper name."

14. Nietzsche, Heidegger, and Derrida develop notions of philosophical "play" as antidotes to the intellectual aporia their works disclose. Nietzsche's most celebrated embodiment of this notion is Zarathustra. Derrida seems to valorize play as an alternative to interpretation in the passage from "Structure, Sign, and Free-Play in the Discourses of the Human Sciences"; on the other hand, as always with Derrida, the extent of the valorization is open to question. The most obvious examples of intellectual play are wordplay, evident in Derrida's well-known puns. In his *Poetic Thinking: An Approach to Heidegger* (Chicago: University of Chicago Press, 1981), David Halliburton discusses the valorization of music in Heidegger's late writings (197) and concludes that "music, together with dance, bids fair in Heidegger's total 'style' of thought and discourse to carry language to a higher realization" (218). He also notes a similarity between Heidegger and Derrida with regard to the notion of play (202–9). For a discussion of the importance of the pun in Heidegger's late writings, see Gerald Bruns, *Heidegger's Estrangements: Language, Truth, and Poetry in the Later Writings* (New Haven and London: Yale University Press, 1989), 140–49. To the extent that all three philosophers seek to valorize play or music as an alternative to the aporia of hermeneutics, they surreptitiously attempt to reinstate a metaphysics of presence that their work elsewhere denies.

15. Levine, *E. L. Doctorow*, 33. For the argument that Red Bloom's music should be considered an authentic alternative to Creighton, see Cooper, "The Artist as Historian," 17–18.

16. In *The Birth of Tragedy from the Spirit of Music*. However, the precise extent of Nietzsche's valorization of the Dionysian has been a subject of debate among Nietzsche's critics.

17. Certain commentators on Heidegger believe that his writings endorse a species of "conversation" modeled on his interpretations of poetry. For example, Gerald Bruns argues that Heidegger's "relationship to a poem is like a relationship to the other in a conversation. The elucidation of the other is like picking up on the words in play rather than like giving an interpretation of what someone means or laying bare the structure or madness of another's discourse" (*Heidegger's Estrangements*, 67). To the extent that Red's conversations with Sugarbush ap-

pear to be different in kind from the interpretations of Creighton, Putnam, and Rockelmayer, they seem to pose the kind of alternative to the failures of hermeneutics that Bruns finds in Heidegger. Another writer frequently associated with the concept of conversation as alternative to interpretation is Mikhail Bakhtin. In *The Dialogic Imagination: Four Essays by M. M. Bakhtin* (Austin: University of Texas Press, 1981), Bakhtin opposes the freedom of "dialogic" discourse to the dead-ends of "monologic" interpretation. In *E. L. Doctorow* (New York: Continuum, 1991) John G. Parks argues that Doctorow's entire ouevre should be read in terms of Bakhtin's idea of culture "as polyphonic, as a heteroglossic dialogue or conversation" (18). Interestingly, his discussions of *Big as Life* treats "improvisation" as an alternative to "the doom of historical repetition" (33). As noted in the introduction, Parks's thesis confines the threat of repetition to history, and this chapter argues that the conversations of Red Bloom and Sugarbush are themselves part of a redundancy in discourse that is also evident in the novel's formal organization.

18. We learn of other benedictions prior to the title of Part III. Standing with his fellow musicians, Red ignores the benediction that concludes the morning ritual of the Army of Redemption (97); we later learn that the musicians' stations are given out after the benediction (100). The interpretation of the giants' arm in its initial position, "as if in benediction" is made by the narrator (121). As Creighton drunkenly turns toward the city he repeats the giant's gesture by lifting "his arm slowly, as if blessing the darkness" (144). These iterations undermine the authority of the traditional religious speech-act and make more plausible the idea that the title of Part III refers mockingly to the novel's own words.

CHAPTER 3   "The Songs of Billy Bathgate":
            The Writer as Orphan, Killer, Performer

1. Roland Barthes, "The Death of the Author," in *Image—Music—Text,* ed. and trans. Stephen Heath (New York: Hill and Wang, 1977).

2. Paul de Man, *Blindness and Insight,* 2d ed. (Minneapolis: University of Minnesota Press, 1983).

3. Robert Graves, *The White Goddess* (New York: Farrar, Straus and Giroux, 1966).

CHAPTER 4   Ellipses and Death in *The Book of Daniel*

1. Mas'ud Zavarzadeh's *The Mythopoeic Reality: The Postwar American Nonfiction Novel* (Urbana: University of Illinois Press, 1976) analyzes the

work of other American writers. A well-informed discussion of *The Book of Daniel* in the genre of historical novels is Joseph Turner's "The Kinds of Historical Fiction: An Essay in Definition and Methodology," *Genre* 12 (1979): 333–55. In his article "Telling Tales on the Rosenbergs," *Literature and History* 12 (1986): 48–57, Peter Humm discusses *The Book of Daniel* and works of fictionalized history by Norman Mailer and Kurt Vonnegut. Humm's interesting conclusion is that Doctorow "forces his readers to pay attention to the deceptions involved in writing as well as in making history. Like [Mailer and Vonnegut], he deconstructs narrative in order to destabilize history" (54).

2. At times Daniel seems to exhibit a historian's concern for accurate chronology, as in his statement that in 1954 he was fourteen and Susan nine (86). More often, however, he is indifferent to the subject, as in this sentence: "We moved there in 1945 when I was four years old. Or maybe in 1944 when I was five years old" (108). There is never any attempt to reconcile these contradictions. The overall effect of Daniel's handling of dates is to entice the reader into a chronological reconstruction of events only to mock that attempt. This "teasing chronology" recurs in *World's Fair*.

3. Paul Levine, *E. L. Doctorow* (New York and London: Methuen, 1985), 35.

4. Michelle Tokarczyk's *E. L. Doctorow: An Annotated Bibliography* (New York: Garland, 1988) lists 75 entries for *The Book of Daniel* to 115 for *Ragtime*. When brief notices, reviews, and novel/film studies are deducted from these totals, the number of full-length articles devoted to each work is roughly equal. At this writing Doctorow's oeuvre consists of seven novels if *Lives of the Poets* is excluded, eight if it is included. In my interview with him, Doctorow referred to "The Songs of Billy Bathgate" as record liner-notes. Doctorow lent some support to classifying *Lives of the Poets* as a novel with his remark that it should be regarded as a "novel about a guy who has written six stories" (quoted in James Wolcott, "Rag Time," *New Republic*, 3 December 1984, 31). For more on the question of the genre of *Lives of the Poets*, see chapter 7, note 2.

5. Geoffrey Galt Harpham, "E. L. Doctorow and the Technology of Narrative," *PMLA* 100 (1985), 87. In his stimulating section on *The Book of Daniel*, Harpham sees Daniel's text as exemplifying Hayden White's claims for the authority conferred upon history by narrative. For another link between Daniel and Hayden White, see below, note 11. This view comports well with the argument of this chapter, but Harpham also contends that *The Book of Daniel* develops electricity as a metaphor for "force" and for a "master principle of narrative," extending its au-

thority to history only by means of "closure," which he sees as completed in the electrocution scene (87, 88). My own view—that the importance of the novel's open-endedness (not closure) is stressed by the codas that follow the electrocution scene—is set forth on pages 83 and 84.

6. Susan E. Lorsch, "Doctorow's *The Book of Daniel* as *Kunstlerroman:* The Politics of Art," *PLL* 18 (1982): 395.

7. Sam B. Girgus, "In His Own Voice: Doctorow's *The Book of Daniel*," DP, 84.

8. John Stark, "Alienation and Analysis in Doctorow's *The Book of Daniel*," *Critique* 16 (1975): 110.

9. Robert Forrey, "Doctorow's *The Book of Daniel:* All in the Family," *Studies in American Jewish Literature* 2 (1982): 173.

10. Barbara Cooper, "The Artist as Historian in the Novels of E. L. Doctorow," *Emporia State Research Studies* 29 (1980), 27.

11. Barbara L. Estrin, "Surviving McCarthyism: E. L. Doctorow's *The Book of Daniel*," in EC, 196–206.

12. Daniel's title introduces a short, discursive reconstruction of policy-making in the early years of the Truman administration; this account accurately paraphrases the interpretation of these events by Daniel's acknowledged source, William A. Williams (248–51). For the argument that Daniel's view should be identified with Williams's, see Daniel L. Zins, "Daniel's 'Teacher' in Doctorow's *The Book of Daniel*," *Notes on Modern American Literature* 3 (1979): Item 16. Several critics have noted the contradiction between "objective" history and the use of the subtitle "raga," which means a form of Hindu music characterized by structured improvisation. See Winifred Farrant Bevilacqua, "Narrating History: E. L. Doctorow's *The Book of Daniel*," *Revue Francaise d'Etudes Americaines* 12 (1987): 59. Bevilacqua, like Harpham, sees Daniel-as-historian as enacting the relativistic historiography of Hayden White (59).

13. In this chapter and henceforth, the word "ellipsis" is used in both its broad and narrow senses. In the broad sense the word can mean "leaving something to be understood by the reader" (OED); this is the sense implied by Daniel's refusal to describe the cigarette-lighter scene or the "shameful" letter he wrote to Robert Lewin. The two narrow senses of the word are derived from rhetoric and the conventions of punctuation: (1) the "omission of a word or of words which are readily implied by the context" (Edward P. J. Corbett, *Classical Rhetoric for the Modern Student* [New York: Oxford University Press, 1971], 468); (2) "marks indicating the omission of letters or words" (Webster's *Third International*).

14. Lorsch, "Doctorow's *The Book of Daniel* as *Kunstlerroman*" 394. In

"E. L. Doctorow and the Technology of Narrative," Harpham makes the same point, in a way that suggests his concerns, and my own, for the relation between narrative and meaning: "The juridical question of whether the Isaacsons were guilty or innocent has become tangled up with the technical question of whether there can be any reconciliation between sequence and repetition, temporality and structure, that will produce a genuine noncontradictory form of meaning" (85).

15. Heidegger describes the way in which death robs Dasein of representation: "If idle talk is always ambiguous, so is this way of talking about death. Dying, which is essentially mine in such a way that no one can be my representative, is perverted into an event of public occurrence which the 'they' encounters" (*Being and Time,* trans. John Macquarrie and Edward Robinson [New York: Harper and Row, 1962], 297.

16. The interminable oscillation between attributions of selfish and unselfish motives to characters creates a local instance of undecidability: some motive must be attributed, just as the independent existence of some author must be assumed, but the very act of attribution in "groundless" figuration will in the end render such judgments fictional. This phenomenon is apparent in Blue in *Welcome to Hard Times* and in Billy Bathgate's "Garden of Adding." For a discussion of this dilemma in the works of George Eliot, see J. Hillis Miller, *The Ethics of Reading* (New York: Columbia University Press, 1988), 79–80.

17. To the contradictions in chronology may be added these baffling sentences: "I think this was in 1949 or 1950. I was seven or eight." (114).

18. Paul de Man, *The Rhetoric of Romanticism* (New York: Columbia University Press, 1984), 70. For de Man's use of "of" as metaphor, see his *Allegories of Reading: Figural Language in Rousseau, Nietzsche, Rilke, and Proust* (New Haven and London: Yale University Press, 1979), 205. J. Hillis Miller discusses this usage as a double genitive in "'Reading' Part of a Paragraph in *Allegories of Reading*," in Waters and Godzich, eds., *Reading de Man Reading,* 168–69.

19. "The Habit of Perfection," in *Poems and Prose of Gerard Manley Hopkins,* ed. W. H. Gardner (Middlesex, England: Penguin Books, Ltd. 1953), 5. It is impossible to rule out that the citer of the line is "Doctorow," in which case it denotes the absolute inaccessibility of the author behind his text. The poem's pun on "habit" may suggest a parallel between Susan's "starfish" condition and vows of asceticism and silence taken by certain nuns. This dimension of the allusion would make it even more offensive to Susan.

20. The irony of most of these subtitles should be apparent, although BINTEL BRIEF may require some explanation. The Yiddish phrase "Bintel Brief" means "bundle of letters." It gained currency in the early part of the twentieth-century as the title of a feature resembling "letters-to-the editor" in newspapers written for the Jewish-American community. Letter writers often brought up financial and ethical questions, to which newspaper editors would make specific responses. An English translation of a collection of letters and responses appeared in 1971 under the title, *A Bintel Brief: Sixty Years of Letters from the Lower East Side to the Jewish Daily Forward*, ed. Isaac Metzker (Garden City: Doubleday and Co., 1971). The introduction discusses how the term came to take on the meaning of "a remarkable story" (14). Most letters in this collection are much shorter than the one written by Daniel's grandmother; its length and excesses make it appear a parody of the genre. Also, her letter is broken off in mid-sentence, an abrupt ellipsis that raises new intertextual questions.

CHAPTER 5   Illusions of Demystification in *Ragtime*

1. The time of narration is established by the sentence "Today, nearly fifty years since [Houdini's] death, the audience for escapes is even larger" (8). Houdini died in 1926. The fact that the narrator is American is established by his many references to various times "in our history;" see for example pages 30, 103, 150, 177, 100, 230, 298, and 300.

2. In "Between Simulteneity and Sequence," *DP*, Richard King provides an excellent analysis of the narrator's shifting irony and tone. A typical sarcasm is the following: "There seemed to be quotas for death by starvation" (46). In the introduction to her *E. L. Doctorow: An Annotated Bibliography*, Michelle Tokarczyk argues that *Ragtime*'s prose mocks that of history books (xv). The narrator's sometimes disconcerting rhetorical flourishes are especially evident in the beginning of new chapters, for example pages 109, 225, 279, 287.

3. In "The Stylistic Energy of E. L. Doctorow," *EC*, Arthur Saltzman writes that the narrator is "revealed at the conclusion of the novel as the Boy grown to adulthood" (95). In "Recomposing Time: *Humboldt's Gift* and *Ragtime*," *Denver Quarterly* 17 (1982): 16–31, Barbara L. Estrin contends, "We realize in the intrusion of the 'I' that the parent we had known all along as an archetype was a father to the writer" (19).

4. In "The Artist as Historian in the Novels of E. L. Doctorow,"

Emporia State Research Studies 29 (1980), Barbara Cooper argues that the narrator is anonymous and achieves aesthetic synthesis by adapting the techniques of photography (34). In "Between Simulteneity and Sequence," King argues that "the narrative voice of *Ragtime* is the voice of mass historical consciousness, but that voice is ironized by imaginary inverted commas standing, as it were, at either end of the narrative" (55). In "Doctorow's *Ragtime:* Narrative as Silhouette and Syncopation," *Dutch Quarterly Review of Anglo-American Letters* 11 (1981): 97–103, Susan Brienza also distinguishes the narrator from the little boy. Other readers acknowledge doubt about the identification. Mark Busby, in "E. L. Doctorow, *Ragtime,* and the Dialectics of Change," *Ball State University Forum* 26 (1985): 39–44, writes that the little boy is "possibly the narrator" (41). Bettina Friedl, in "The Stability of Images and the Instability of Things in E. L. Doctorow's *Ragtime,*" DP, 91–104, says that the boy is "the central intelligence of at least parts of the novel" (101). In this section I use the words "narrator(s)" and "they" in the exploration of narratological uncertainty. Later in the chapter I revert to the words "narrator" and "he" where the possibility arises that the boy narrates. It is clear, however, that this usage is just as fictional as "narrator(s)."

5. The following sentence appears to endow the children with a unity so transcendent as to surpass physical separateness: "What bound them to each other was a fulfilled recognition which they lived and thought within so that their apprehension of each other could not be so distinct and separated as to include admiration for the other's fairness" (304). A statement of such extreme unity provides evidence for identifying the narrator as the two children speaking together. But this identification, like other nonanonymous ones, is vitiated by the possibility that the narrator may also be anonymous; see note 9, below. In addition to literary analogues in Goethe or Shelley, the relationship between the two children may evoke Jungian concepts. For example, Bettina Friedl finds in the play of the little boy and the little girl the articulation of Jung's *anima* or archetype (97).

6. Geoffrey Galt Harpham, "E. L. Doctorow and the Technology of Narrative," *PMLA* 100 (1985), 89.

7. See for example Busby, "E. L. Doctorow, *Ragtime,* and the Dialectics of Change," 42–43.

8. The association between Evelyn and Diana is made explicit in the fact that Evelyn served as the model for the Gaudens statue of Diana, with her bow drawn, that Stanford White had put at the top of the

tower of Madison Square Garden (30). That Mother's Younger Brother's furtive espial of Evelyn recalls the story of Diana and Actaeon is suggested when Emma Goldman, unlacing her, remarks: "You have no more need of stays than a wood nymph" (68); Actaeon discovered Diana at her bath accompanied by nymphs. Ovid tells this legend; his stories are told to the boy by his grandfather, the classical scholar (132). Following his espial of Evelyn, Mother's Younger Brother seems to become suicidally driven. Like Actaeon, he undergoes a metamorphosis—the blackface he uses as his disguise in Coalhouses's gang. The idea that Actaeon is destroyed by his own thoughts is not new: Shelley employs it in *Adonais* 31. In one of the novel's many coincidences, a Flemish tapestry of Actaeon being torn apart by dogs hangs in the home of Mrs. Stuyvestant Fish (36).

9. In a similar way, the other possibilities—that Sha narrates alone or that Sha and the boy narrate together—become unreliable even in their own terms. If Sha narrates, she is oblivious to the inconsistency between her father's denunciation of Mameh and Evelyn Nesbit and his flirtation with Mother. Sha does not see that as the model for her father's popular films, including *His First Mistake* and *A Daughter's Innocence,* she helps perpetuate his misrepresentation of American childhood. The possibility that both narrate together would at first seem to endorse the ideal of "dialogism," noted before in Red Bloom and Sugarbush, in *Big as Life,* but that prospect is canceled by their obliviousness to the intertextual side of the Coalhouse Walker story, which gives the lie to all such ideals. Of course both identifications are finally vitiated by the continuing possibility that the story is told by an anonymous, sardonic cultural historian. There is no escape from the conclusion that the narrator always consists *simultaneously of two entities,* whose existences are mutually exclusive.

10. Cooper, in "The Artist as Historian," and Busby, in "E. L. Doctorow, *Ragtime,* and the Dialectics of Change," believe the novel endorses Tateh without qualification. In *Fiction and Historical Consciousness: The American Romance Tradition* (New Haven and London: Yale University Press, 1989), Emily Miller Budick argues that Tateh's shift from silhouette-making to movie-making is accomplished by a realization about art and history that also informs the novel as a whole. John G. Parks, in *E. L. Doctorow* (New York: Continuum, 1991), agrees, seeing the marriage of Tateh and Mother as the representation of "a new historical composition" and Tateh's films as a "regenerative and morally responsible" vision (69). However, other readers think the novel treats

Tateh with irony. In *E. L. Doctorow* (New York and London: Methuen, 1985), Paul Levine points to Tateh's "corrupted sensibility" in exploiting the myth of success (59). Saltzman, in "Stylistic Energy," believes Tateh's success is satirized because it is so conspicuously the result of "blind luck" (94). In "Historicizing Fiction and Fictionalizing History: The Case of E. L. Doctorow," *Prospects: An Annual Journal of American Cultural Studies* 5 (1980), Cushing Strout argues that the novel condemns Tateh for embodying the "entrepreneurial energy" of Henry Ford (433). Phyllis Jones, in "*Ragtime:* Feminist, Socialist, and Black Perspectives on the Self-Made Man," *Journal of American Culture* 2 (1979): 17–28, makes the case that the novel condemns Tateh throughout as the character "most objectionable in his sexism," which is evident in his treatment of Mameh, his denunciation of Evelyn Nesbit, and his pedestal-elevation of his daughter "that makes her more property than person" (25, 26). In critical discussions of Doctorow's texts, interpretation of Tateh is one instance of the uneasy coexistence of opposite views.

11. In "Incorporating the Text: Kleist's 'Michael Kohlhaas,'" *PMLA* 105 (1990): 1098–1107, Clayton Koelb says that Kleist's story stages a drama of deep ambivalence about texts (1105). In *Versions of Pygmalion* (Cambridge: Harvard University Press, 1990), J. Hillis Miller sees in "Michael Kohlhaas" the "perhaps necessary injustice involved in any attempt to make oneself the emissary, intermediary, or interpreter of God's judgment" (124). This remark seems applicable to Coalhouse Walker. Paul de Man, in *Allegories of Reading: Figural Language in Rousseau, Nietzsche, Rilke, and Proust* (New Haven and London: Yale University Press, 1979), argues that in Kleist's plays the verdict repeats the crime it condemns (245). Applied to "Michael Kohlhaas," this argument would find in the execution of Kohlhaas the necessity for mistaken interpretation that Kohlhaas himself embodies. De Man finds this necessity in the operation of language itself, a contention he also supports with reference to Kleist, especially to Kleist's essay on the marionette theatre (294). This argument is pursued at greater length in chapter 10 of de Man's *The Rhetoric of Romanticism*. For studies treating Kleist as a literary influence on Doctorow, see John Ditsky, "The German Source of *Ragtime:* A Note," *Ontario Review* 4 (1976): 84–86; Lieselotte E. Kurth-Voigt, "Kleistian Overtones in E. L. Doctorow's *Ragtime*," *Monatshefte* 69 (1977): 404–14; Peter Neumeyer, "E. L. Doctorow, Kleist and the Ascendancy of Things," *CEA Critic* 39 (1977): 17–21; Josie P. Campbell, "Coalhouse Walker and the Model T. Ford: Legerdemain in *Ragtime*," *Journal of Popular Culture* 13 (1979): 302–9; Marjorie Gelus and Ruth

Crowley, "Kleist in *Ragtime:* Doctorow's Novel, Its German Source and Its Reviewers," *Journal of Popular Culture* 14 (1980): 20–26. These studies do not directly take up the subject of narration. In "'Michael Kohlhaas' and *Ragtime*—the Hopeful Text and the Despairing Story," *Wissenschaftliche Zeitschrift der Wilhelm-Pieck* 31 (1982): 3–7, Duncan Smith calls attention to the contradiction in Kleist's story between the events narrated and the "fragile rigidity" of the narration through which optimism is achieved only "at the cost of what might be called human narrative tone" (6). While demurring on the subject of optimism, I think Smith's perception of a contradiction in Kleist's narrative deserves attention in discussions of the relevance of Kleist's story to *Ragtime*.

12. *The Marquise of O and Other Stories,* trans. Martin Greenberg (New York: Ungar, 1973), 87.

13. Bernard Rodgers, in "A Novelist's Revenge," *Chicago Review* 27 (1976): 138–44, argues that as an artist-figure Houdini represents the dilemma of a contemporary fictionist who feels the burden of his audience's demand for escapes but who cannot compete with the real world. This reading implies that the artist eventually becomes reconciled to providing escapes. For another discussion of Houdini as an artist-figure, see John Clayton, "Radical Jewish Humanism: The View of E. L. Doctorow," EC, 116.

14. Tateh's life in the tenements of New York is depicted as an imprisonment in suffocating tenement buildings that Jacob Riis would open up with air shafts (20–21). Tateh's escape from Lawrence, Massachusetts, on the train for Philadelphia is described as follows: "He clung to the railing, finally hoisting his knees to the platform overhang and clinging there with his head pressed against the bars like a man in prison begging to be set free" (146).

15. Saltzman, "Stylistic Energy," 97–98.

CHAPTER 6   *Loon Lake:*
            The World as Fiction

1. Discussions of the narration of *Loon Lake* have arrived at no consensus as to the identity of the narrator. Geoffrey Galt Harpham, in "E. L. Doctorow and the Technology of Narrative," *PMLA* 100 (1988), endorses the Joe-as-single-narrator hypothesis, but he also contends that the text is "the product of multiple voices" and "imperfectly 'efficient' in reconciling those voices" (93). Neil Schmitz, in "Three Novels," *Partisan Review* 48 (1981): 629–33, argues that there are two narrators, Joe and

Warren. On the other hand, Dean Flower, in "Fiction Chronicle," *Hudson Review* 34 (1981): 105–16, believes the "*real* point of *Loon Lake* is that fat poet Warren Penfield invented it. . . . And behind Penfield's hopelessly bad artistry lies a modern computer, printing out non-poems and raw data, the *real* real author no doubt of the book" (106). In "Restless Roads," *Christian Century,* 7 January 1981, 20–21, Douglas C. Runnels recognizes the importance of the novel's technical experimentation: "It is probably an exaggeration to say that Loon Lake is about narrative technique—but not much of an exaggeration" (21).

2. For the merging of the points of view, see Runnels, "Restless Roads," 20, and Jochen Barkhausen, "Determining the True Color of the Chameleon: The Confusing Recovery of History in E. L. Doctorow's *Loon Lake,*" DP, 137. For the identity of Joe and Warren, see John Clayton, "Radical Jewish Humanism: The View of E. L. Doctorow," EC, 116, and Jochen Barkhausen, "Recovery of History," DP,. 138.

3. Daniel L. Guillory, in "Doctorow as Poet," *A Writer in His Time: A Week with E. L. Doctorow* (Davenport, Iowa: The Visiting Artists Series, 1985), believes that the computer voice supplants the voice of the omniscient author (17). A similar argument is made by Pearl K. Bell, "Singing the Same Old Song," *Commentary* 70 (1980), 70–73: "The adventures of young Joe are repeatedly interrupted by mysterious computer printouts supplying biographical data on the various characters . . . the computer becomes the mechanical master" (72). In addition to these critics, Harpham, in "The Technology of Narrative," distinguishes the voice of the "data linkage escape" from Joe's (90–91), as does Robert Towers in "A Brilliant World of Mirrors," *New York Times Book Review* 28 September 1980, 46. As in *Ragtime,* the narrating entity cannot be named without error. Here it will be referred to as "the narrator" or "Joe," depending on the context.

4. E. L. Doctorow, "Loon Lake," *Kenyon Review* 6 (1979): 5–13.

5. There are a few changes in diction and numerous revisions in punctuation and line endings. The latter undo the distinction between prose and poetry just as the novel's use of blank space does. The most conspicuous change is the novel's elimination of four lines from the version printed in the *Kenyon Review*. These lines all concern the gangsters' horseback ride. Three lines that appeared between the words "know" (at the bottom of 63) and "they" (at the top of 64) are as follow: "And the gangsters looked around for guidance / but there was none not even from the best gangster among them / and nobody laughed."

This unacknowledged ellipsis in a source makes Doctorow resemble Daniel. The ellipsis unavoidably prompts an intertextual inquiry—a sterile one, like speculation about the meaning of "Korzienowski"—as to why the lines would be appropriate for Doctorow but not for Penfield.

6. Paul de Man, *Allegories of Reading: Figural Language in Rousseau, Nietzsche, Rilke, and Proust* (New Haven and London: Yale University Press, 1979), 125.

7. In an insightful article, Alan Nadel, in "Hero and Other in Doctorow's *Loon Lake*," *College Literature* 14 (1987): 136–46, argues that the novel points to a necessary rivalry between reader and writer and that Doctorow locates that rivalry "within an Oedipal paradigm" (144). In "The Cry of Power Once Heard: Patterning in Doctorow's *Loon Lake*" in *A Writer in His Time* (Davenport, Iowa: Visiting Artist Series, 1985), 1–12, Susan Brienza points to a Freudian component of the father-son competition between Joe and Bennett.

8. Schmitz, "Three Novels," 630.

9. For a discussion of further parallels between Joe, Bennett, and J. P. Morgan, see Herwig Friedl, "Power and Degradation: Patterns of Historical Process in the Novels of E. L. Doctorow," DP. Friedl links Joe to the tradition of the Emersonian man and discusses the "quasi-Nietzschean" wisdom Bennett shares with him (38).

10. For the relevance of Conrad's titles, see Harpham, "The Technology of Narrative," 95. In "Types Defamiliarized," *Nation* 27 September 1980, 285–86, George Stade connects the novel's depictions of struggles between surrogate fathers and sons with this recurrent problem in the novels of Joseph Conrad.

11. In "Hero and Other," Nadel's discussion of the allusion to Conrad sums up well the sense in which it undermines expectations of meaning: "Allusions suggest some form of parallel, some extra-textual point of reference from which to identify similarity and/or difference. By making 'nothing' of this allusion, by withholding it until the last page of the book, Doctorow creates one more unfulfilled expectation, something like giving us one parallel line" (142). For a discussion of the way pure allusiveness in the visual arts undermines notions of originality, authenticity, and presence, see Douglas Crimp, "On the Museum's Ruins," in Hal Foster, ed., *The Anti-Aesthetic: Essays on Postmodern Culture* (Port Townsend, Washington: Bay Press, 1983), 53.

12. In "Power and Degradation," Friedl mentions William Carlos Williams in his discussion of Paterson as the "all-American place" (38).

13. The most sustained discussion of the influence of *Walden* is Sam B. Girgus's, in *The New Covenant: Jewish Writers and the American Idea* (Chapel Hill and London: University of North Carolina Press, 1984). Girgus, too, observes that the "loon seems to mock Thoreau's attempts to understand him." Girgus argues that the novel valorizes the Indians' view of nature in contrast to the corrupt "current uses of the lake" epitomized in Bennett (179).

14. Henry David Thoreau, *Walden and Civil Disobedience* (New York: W. W. Norton, 1966), 157.

15. Ibid, 157.

CHAPTER 7   The Intertextuality of *Lives of the Poets*

1. Some rhetoricians identify antimetabole as a scheme rather than a trope. See Edward P. J. Corbett, *Classical Rhetoric for the Modern Student* (New York: Oxford University Press, 1971), 477. An overview of the troubled distinction between these terms is provided by Richard A. Lanham, *A Handlist of Rhetorical Terms* (Berkeley and London: University of California Press, 1969), 101–3. Lanham himself considers antimetabole a trope (130).

2. In "Light and Lively," *New York Review of Books*, 6 December 1984, Robert Towers called "The Writer in the Family" a "miniature novel of Jewish family life" (34). Bruce Bawer, in "The Human Dimension," *Nation*, 17 November 1984, argued that "Lives of the Poets" should not be identified as a novella at all (517). Doctorow himself added to the uncertainty with two remarks: first, that the "novella is the story of the stories" (quoted in Benjamin De Mott, "Pilgrim Among the Culturati," *New York Times Book Review*, 11 November 1984, 42); second, that the collection as a whole should be regarded as a "novel about a guy who has written six stories" (quoted in James Wolcott, "Rag Time," *New Republic*, 3 December 1984, 31). Doctorow's second remark proposes a redefinition of the generic category "novel"; the critical commentary suggests that generic identification may not be wholly a matter of authorial choice.

3. Paul De Man, *Allegories of Reading: Figural Language in Rousseau, Nietzsche, Rilke, and Proust* New York and London: Yale University Press, 1979), 124. De Man's doubt about the principle of contradiction resembles Wittgenstein's questions about the principle of identity. For a discussion of the latter, see Henry Stein, *Wittgenstein and Derrida* (Lincoln: University of Nebraska Press, 1984), 131–34.

4. J. Hillis Miller, *The Linguistic Moment: From Wordsworth to Stevens*

(Princeton: Princeton University Press, 1985), xix. Miller adopts the term from a passage in Nietzsche's *Daybreak*.

5. The phrase "after the first" is in quotation marks to indicate skepticism about whether a pure "first reading," unmediated by another, is possible. My own view is that reading is always intertextual, a value expressed in the metaphor of the palimpsest, which of course appeared in Doctorow's first novel.

6. See Doctorow's remarks quoted in Wolcott's "Rag Time," in note 2, but other readers disagree. Robert Towers disputes the interpretation put forth on the dust jacket (34). Adam Mars-Jones, in "Boosting the Status of the Text," *TLS* 5 April 1985, 376, finds the idea of Jonathon's authorship of "The Foreign Legation" only an "implication" or "hint" that is not "carried through." Would "true" hermeneutic criticism accept the author's word as final on this subject? My argument is that the author of the second through sixth stories in the collection cannot be established with certainty. If this is so, then Doctorow's remarks exemplify the idea that an author may be the first misinterpreter of her own work. The discussion that follows finds that idea is also exemplified in "The Writer in the Family."

7. The idea that authors are misreaders of their own works is explored by Miller in his analysis of the prefaces of Henry James in J. Hillis Miller *The Ethics of Reading* (New York: Columbia University Press, 1988).

8. An influential reading of Poe is Jacques Derrida's "The Purveyor of Truth." That essay and discussions of its relevance to larger issues of critical theory are included in *The Purloined Poe: Lacan, Derrida, and Psychoanalytic Reading*, ed. John P. Muller and William J. Richardson (Baltimore: Johns Hopkins University Press, 1988). Poe's importance to *The Book of Daniel* is discussed at the end of chapter 4. It is also worth noting that Doctorow was named after Poe. See Carol Iannone, "E. L. Doctorow's 'Jewish' Radicalism," *Commentary* 81 (1986), 53. For readings of Kafka and Kleist which stress their undecidability, see, respectively, Miller's *The Ethics of Reading* and de Man's *Rhetoric of Romanticism*.

9. Towers, "Light and Lively," 34.

10. The concept of the *grand récit* or "master narrative" is developed by Jean-Francois Lyotard in *The Postmodern Condition: A Report on Knowledge*, trans. Geoff Bennington and Brian Massumi (Minneapolis: University of Minnesota Press, 1984). Lyotard argues that the fictional patterns inspired by such narratives govern the orientation of knowledge in all fields but most conspicuously in the social sciences. Doctorow makes a similar point at the end of his essay "False Documents."

11. Willi is thirteen when the events of the story take place in 1910. At the time of the narration, Willi is "older than my father when he died, and to whom a woman of my mother's age when all this happened is a young woman barely half my age" (29). If Willi was born soon after his father married his mother, who was just "out of the gymnasium" (35), his mother would be about 30 at the time of the story. If the story were written in 1957, Willi would be sixty and his mother's age at the time of the story, thirty.

12. Lionel Trilling's "Freud and Literature" appeared in 1940 and was revised in 1947 for inclusion in *The Liberal Imagination* (New York: Macmillan Co., 1950), which also contained the essay "Art and Neurosis." Norman O. Brown *Life Against Death* (Middletown, Conn.: Wesleyan University Press, 1959). Simon Lesser *Fiction and the Unconscious* (Boston: Beacon Press, 1957). David Perkins, in *The Quest for Permanence: The Symbolism of Wordsworth, Shelley, and Keats* (Cambridge: Harvard University Press, 1959), discusses the linking of man and nature and "the Wordsworthian withdrawal" in terms of Wordsworth's repression of feeling. See also David Ferry, *The Limits of Mortality: An Essay on Wordsworth's Major Poems* (Middletown, Conn.: Wesleyan University Press, 1959). M. H. Abrams, "Introduction: Two Roads to Wordsworth," in M. H. Abrams, ed., *Wordsworth: A Collection of Critical Essays* (Englewood Cliffs, N.J.: Prentice-Hall, 1972), 7. Harold Bloom, *The Visionary Company: A Reading of English Romantic Poetry* (Garden City, N.J.: Doubleday and Co., 1961), 21. Robert Towers's paraphrase of "Willi" aptly summarizes its conflation of Wordsworth and Freud: "The story begins with the thirteen-year-old boy's 'oceanic' experience of a mystical union—and communion—with nature, an ecstatic condition promptly shattered by a 'primal scene'" ("Light and Lively," 34).

CHAPTER 8 Models of Misrepresentation in *World's Fair*

1. The closest we can come to establishing Edgar's date of birth is Rose's remark that in 1931 or 1932 "you were an infant, about a year old" (116). We also know that there is an eight-year difference in ages between Donald and Edgar (106) and that Donald was fifteen and a half in the winter-spring of 1937 (185). On the other hand, Edgar says that he and Meg were nine years old (296) in the spring of a year that is most probably 1941 (although no precise date is given). This technique teases the reader and mocks efforts to erect a signified history for what are, in the end, arbitrary signs and numbers. It was first introduced in *The Book*

of Daniel (see note 1 of chapter 3) and continued with new complexity in "The Writer in the Family," in *Lives of the Poets* (see note 15, below). In *Billy Bathgate* the homology between letters and numbers becomes a central concern of the text.

2. For the elaboration of this argument in a famous work of retrospective fiction, see my analysis of the narrating and narrated Pip in "The Bad Faith of Pip's Bad Faith: Deconstructing *Great Expectations*," *ELH* 54 (1987): 941–55.

3. For a discussion of pronouns and locative adverbs as "Dasein-designations," see Martin Heidegger's *Being and Time*, trans. John Macquarrie and Edward Robinson (New York: Harper and Row, 1962), 155–56. Roman Jakobson discusses shifters in "Shifters, verbal categories, and the Russian verb," Russian Language Project (Cambridge: Harvard University Press, 1957).

4. The effect is similar to the one created by the forced substitution of "Joe Korzienowski" for the previously accepted "Joe [of] Paterson" in *Loon Lake*. Moreover, Dave's nickname for Edgar may be equally intertextual. It may refer to his morning smile, as Edgar thinks, but maybe also to "Sunny Jim" Sherman, Taft's running mate in *Ragtime*, 219.

5. The "double gestures" of the novel's cover are multiplied even more when the title's puns are taken into account. T. O. Treadwell writes: "Multiple meanings, it turns out, reside in Doctorow's title. *World's Fair* . . . is also much concerned with questions about the fairness of the world in terms of both beauty and equity" (*TLS* 14 February 1986, 163). "World's Fair" is an example of the trope syllepsis, the use of a word understood differently in relation to two or more other words that it modifies or governs. The undecidability of these meanings is discussed on pages 169–72.

6. Heidegger, *Being and Time*, p. 297.

7. Ibid.

8. In "In the Shadow of the War," *Newsweek* 4 November 1985, Walter Clemons wrote that some "thrills would be welcome—a faint trace of a plot, maybe, to pep up the glacierlike progression of Edgar's days" (69). See also the review of *World's Fair* by Rhoda Koenig in *New York*, 25 November 1985, 96–97.

9. Freud returns to this subject in many works, but one important account is the analysis of "omnipotence" of thought in *Notes upon a Case of Obsessional Neurosis*, in *The Complete Psychological Works of Sigmund Freud*, trans. James Strachey (London: The Hogarth Press, 1955), 19:233. For a discussion of the difficulty of sustaining the distinction between

such superstitious beliefs and the "normal" enterprise of psychoanalysis, see Jacques Derrida, "My Chances/*Mes Chances:* A Rendezvous with Some Epicurean Stereophonies" in *Taking Chances: Derrida, Psychoanalysis, and Literature,* ed. Joseph H. Smithy and William Kerrigan (Baltimore: Johns Hopkins University Press, 1984). Derrida argues that the hermeneutic compulsion is common to superstition and to "normal" psychoanalysis (22, 25). The narrating Edgar is obviously also prompted by such a compulsion. It is noteworthy that Derrida finds that "some sensitivity to superstition is perhaps not a useless stimulation for the deconstructive desire" (26), thereby refusing to exempt his own discourse from the sorts of errors committed by hermeneutics. Derrida's gesture is consistent with de Man's "secondary deconstruction," discussed in *Allegories of Reading: Figural Language in Rousseau, Nietzsche, Rilke, and Proust* (New Haven and London: Yale University Press, 1979), 205. That this book also commits these errors is clear from its personifications of Doctorow, from its inability to ignore endings, and its inevitable "taking" of Doctorow's texts, even as models of misrepresentation.

10. Here I concur again with the view advanced by Derrida in "Signature Event Context," in *Margins of Philosophy,* trans. Alan Bass (Chicago: University of Chicago Press, 1982).

11. Whitney Balliett particularly noted the novel's "catalogue of the everyday detritus of the thirties" in "Mel-O-Rols, Knickers, and Gee Bee Racers," *The New Yorker,* 9 December 1985, 158.

12. Like other signs, photographs may aspire to meaning but in all cases they defer or withhold it. The picture of Edgar on a tricycle cannot reveal the circumstances that motivated the photographer (86–87, 88); home movies depict mute gestures (28–29, 63); the photograph of Dave and Donald in similar suits is uninterpreted (172), as is the snapshot of Don and his girlfriend (287). That photographs can also function as misunderstood evocations of *Sein-zum-Tode* is suggested by Edgar's otherwise unelaborated mention of the sepia photographs of his grandmother's relatives in Russia (125). In *Camera Lucida: Reflections on Photography,* trans. Richard Howard (New York: Hill and Wang, 1981), Roland Barthes argued that the signified of photography is always death. However, as in the case of the other "signifiers of death" discussed earlier, to attribute even this minimal ontology to photography would, paradoxically, restore signification. Edgar's apparent obliviousness to the deferred presence of death in photography func-

tions in the same way that his *méconnaissance* of death functions elsewhere.

13. John T. Irwin, "The Dead Father in Faulkner," in Robert C. Davis, ed., *The Fictional Father: Lacanian Readings of the Text* (Amherst: University of Massachusetts Press, 1984), 147–68.

14. This interpretation of the novel's epigraph is made possible only by the "traditional" reading of Wordsworth and romanticism that see in both the valorization of the poetic imagination. Of course this traditional view has been challenged in many quarters. For this book's argument an important challenge is Paul de Man's in *The Rhetoric of Romanticism* (New York: Columbia University Press, 1984). A de Manian interpretation of Book VII of *The Prelude* might stress the figural character of the "hubbub" condemned by the poem's "I." Following this line of argument, the raree-show epigraph would diminish the apparent claims for selfhood in both *The Prelude* and *World's Fair.*

15. The character Aunt Frances retains her name in each work. Other characters are renamed in *World's Fair,* although the details of family history in each work are nearly identical. The temporal setting is changed. In "The Writer in the Family" Jonathon is of school age in 1955. The main action of *World's Fair* ends in 1941, when according to the novel's contradictory chronology, Edgar is either nine or eleven. Some attempt to reconcile the chronologies of the two texts probably occurs to readers of them; the experience of counting, then renouncing when the fictionality of a chronology becomes apparent, is an analogue to the process of reading itself.

CHAPTER 9   Selected Essays and Interviews

1. In "E. L. Doctorow and the Technology of Narrative," *PMLA* 100 (1988), Geoffrey Galt Harpham credits Joseph Valente with this observation.

2. Jean-Paul Sartre, *Literature and Existentialism,* trans. Bernard Frechtman (Secaucus, N.J.: Citadel Press, 1980), 57. This work was originally published in 1949 under the title, *What Is Literature?* The work consists of three parts totaling 160 pages. It is odd that "False Documents" refers to it as an "essay," but perhaps that usage calls up the etymological meaning of "try."

3. Walter Benjamin, *Illuminations: Essays and Reflections,* ed. Hannah Arendt (New York: Schocken Books, 1969), 87.

4. Reversals of critical judgments have been associated with modernist diminutions of the status of literature. See Louis Menand's analysis of T. S. Eliot's many critical reassessments—as portending dissociation from literature itself—in his *Discovering Modernism: T. S. Eliot and His Context* (New York: Oxford University Press, 1987), 156–63.

5. Victor S. Navasky, "E. L. Doctorow: 'I Saw a Sign,'" *The New York Times Book Review* 28 September 1980, 44.

CHAPTER 10 *Billy Bathgate:*
Reading as Larceny

1. Two obvious tropes are polysyndeton (phrases linked by the conjunction "and") and alliteration.

2. Other details in the novel suggest Billy's narrative duplicity. Billy concedes that he lied when at first he claimed not to have noticed the gangsters' cars arriving while he juggled (26). He also admits temporarily withholding from Berman the identity of the man from Cleveland (80). Although this information is eventually becomes known to Berman (85), Billy never tells us how. This omission and Billy's failure to comment on it raise further questions about his motivation and loyalty. Billy admits lying to Bo, "to make it easy for him" (163) about what he overheard while standing outside the cabin occupied by Schultz and Drew Preston. Billy never relates to the reader his telephone conversation with Harvey Preston, in which he warned Drew's wealthy husband not to bring the police when responding to Billy's plan to rescue Drew at the racetrack (241). In his first report to Berman about Hines's refusal of the bribe, Billy withholds details (278). Later, Billy begins his account of his disclosure to Schultz that Drew was recognized by the "bad-skinned man," in this way: "I will talk about this moment, what I thought I was doing, or what I think now I thought I was doing, because it is the moment the determination was made" (290). His apparent equation between historical truth and a present reconstruction of that truth is of a piece with the undecidability of his narration. Billy admits lying to Schultz about the timing of this revelation about Drew (291). Billy introduces his account of Abadabba Berman's dying words as follows: "And I will say here now what he said" (304). He admits, however, that his account cannot render the dying man's arduous effort to speak.

3. Of course "Bathgate" is Billy's self-baptism. His father's surname is never disclosed. The discrepancy between maiden names and married names once more calls attention to the arbitrary nature of all "proper

names," a fact Billy acknowledges in his "license plate theory of identification" (138).

Afterword

1. Despite misgivings, editors of anthologies of world literature retain periodization. For example, although the editors of *The Norton Anthology of World Masterpieces* consider the term postmodernism "unhelpful" (2450), they also characterize a great deal of contemporary literature as prolonging the modernist experiment (2449). See Mack, et al., editors, *The Norton Anthology of World Masterpieces*, 5th ed. (New York: W. W. Norton, 1987). In *Literature of the Western World*, Vol. 2: *Neoclassicism Through the Modern Period* (New York: Macmillan, 1988), Brian Wilkie and James Hurt see modernism and postmodernism as a continuum but distinguish them as follows: "Postmodernism's principal extension of Modernism is in the direction of a preoccupation—sometimes it seems an exclusive one—with the text itself" (1513). In Nina Baym et al., eds., *The Norton Anthology of American Literature* (New York: W. W. Norton, 1989), period definitions are retained for earlier American literature.

2. Although he distinguishes "postmodernism" from "Modernism," Mas'ud Zavarzadeh complains that the former term is "too general to catch the nuances" among works published after the modernist movement. See *The Mythopoeic Reality: The Postwar American Nonfiction Novel* (Champaign: University of Illinois Press, 1976), 3. In his discussion of Doctorow as a novelist who unites the central concerns of both modernism and postmodernism, Arthur Saltzman writes: "Whereas the Modernists concerned themselves with what art should aspire to (the transcendent, the mythical), the Postmodernists resign themselves to what art can manage: in Robbe-Grillet's words, 'a way of speaking'" ("The Stylistic Energy of E. L. Doctorow," EC, 74). For Zavarzadeh and Saltzman, the distinction between modernism and postmodernism may be of only limited use.

For the argument that feminism is essential to postmodernism, see Craig Owens, "The Discourse of Others: Feminists and Postmodernism," in Hal Foster, ed., *The Anti-Aesthetic: Essays on Postmodern Culture* (Port Townsend, Wash.: Bay Press, 1983), 57–82. Owens's argument is both endorsed and questioned by Susan Rubin Suleiman, in *Subversive Intent: Gender, Politics, and the Avant-Garde* (Cambridge: Harvard University Press, 1990), in her chapter 8, "Feminism and Postmodernism: In Lieu of an Ending."

On the other hand, David Gross's discussion of Doctorow as a postmodernist places him in a context similar to the one used in this study: Doctorow is "in the forefront of postmodernism, a movement preoccupied since Nietzsche and especially now, since Jacques Derrida, with the deconstruction of all historical narrative claiming any direct, naive relationship to truth." See David Gross, "E. L. Doctorow," in Larry McCaffery, ed., *Postmodern Fiction: A Bio-Bibliographic Guide* (New York: Greenwood Press, 1986), 341. My principal disagreement with this point is that I do not believe that the "movement" Gross refers to began with Nietzsche. It is equally possible to believe, as de Man does, that this movement is inherent in language from the beginning. See note 6, below.

3. The difficulties of distinguishing "modernism" and "postmodernism" are multiplied in any attempt to define a purely American postmodernism. One attempt is Harold Bloom's *Agon: Toward a Theory of Revisionism* (New York: Oxford University Press, 1982), which celebrates Emersonian "resistance" against European, especially French, emphasis on text. It is likely that, for Bloom, "resistance" is an extraliterary, psychological entity, although he does not discuss what makes it a peculiarly American trait.

4. The concept of play in my hypothetical definition of postmodernism recapitulates its importance in Derrida, Heidegger, and Bakhtin (see chapter 2, note 14), but play is also crucial to the aesthetics of Jean-Francois Lyotard. See his *The Postmodern Condition: A Report on Knowledge*, trans. Geoff Bennington and Brian Massumi (Minneapolis: University of Minnesota Press, 1984), chapter 3, and, with coauthor Jean-Loup Thebaud, *Just Gaming*, trans. Wlad Godzich (Minneapolis: University of Minnesota Press, 1985).

5. Harold Bloom's analysis of intertextuality argues for the existence of a variety of "revisionary ratios" between poets and their precursors. These ratios explain intertextuality in terms of the oedipal struggle, the images used in literature, and the psychic defenses of authors. See Harold Bloom, *A Map of Misreading* (New York: Oxford University Press, 1975). To the extent that these ratios are discovered in "post-Enlightenment" English and American poetry, they serve to define a single, very long, literary period, one that would deny any specific content to postmodernism. On the other hand, Bloom's few remarks about "pre-Enlightenment" literature make it unclear why, and whether, the

revisionary ratios should characterize only the later period. The contradictions evident in the attempt to define and apply the term "postmodernism" make more plausible Paul de Man's contention that literary history be understood in terms of rhetoric, not chronology. De Man sees literary history as the effect of an alternation between ironic and allegorical modes which is inherent in the nature of language. See *Blindness and Insight,* 2d ed. (Minneapolis: University of Minnesota Press, 1983).

6. "Ragtime Revisited; A Seminar with E. L. Doctorow and Joseph Papaleo," *Nieman Reports* 31 (1977), 6.

Appendix

1. For existentialist interpretations of *Sein-zum-Tode,* see Michael A. Slote, "Existentialism and the Fear of Dying," *American Philosophical Quarterly* 12 (1975): 17–28, and W. B. Macomber, *The Anatomy of Disillusion: Martin Heidegger's Notion of Truth* (Evanston, Ill.: Northwestern University Press, 1967), 45. Existentialist interpretations persist even in commentaries that propound Heidegger's attack on both representation and the Cartesian subject. For example, in Jacques Lacan, *The Language of the Self: The Function of Language in Psychoanalysis,* trans. Anthony Wilden (Baltimore: Johns Hopkins University Press, 1968), Anthony Wilden interprets *Sein-zum-Tode* in existentialist terms.

2. In 1935 Heidegger delivered a series of lectures on the relation between aletheia and physis. The lectures were revised for publication as *Einfuhrung in die Metaphysik* (Tubingen: Max Nieeyer Verlag, 1953) and translated into English by Ralph Mannheim as *An Introduction to Metaphysics* (New Haven: Yale University Press, 1959). Heidegger's 1943 lecture "Aletheia" further develops the notion of truth as unconcealment.

3. Martin Heidegger, *Being and Time,* trans. John Macquarrie and Edward Robinson (New York: Harper and Row, 1962), 305.

4. See for example section 52 of *Sein und Zeit,* at the conclusion of which Heidegger questions whether an authentic *Sein-zum-Tode* has yet been ontologically defined, and section 53, in which he distinguishes *Sein-zum-Tode* from expecting (*Erwarten*) death.

5. "Die Sprache," originally delivered as a lecture in 1950, collected in *Unterwegs zur Sprache* (Pfulligen: Verlag Gunther Neske, 1959), 9–34. The original passage appears on pages 12–13. The English translation in my text is from Albert Hofstadter's "Language" in his collection *Poetry, Language, Thought* (New York: Harper and Row, 1971), 190–91.

6. Heidegger, "Die Sprache," 19; Hofstadter, "Language," 197.
7. Heidegger, "Die Sprache," 14; Hofstadter, "Language," 192.
8. The essay was formed from three lectures, delivered in 1957 and 1958, and published under the title "Das Wesen der Sprache," in *Unterwegs zur Sprache,* 157–216. The original passage appears on page 215. The English translation in my text is from Peter D. Hertz's "The Nature of Language" in his collection *On the Way to Language* (New York: Harper and Row, 1971), 107–8.

Index

Abrams, M. H., 144
Actaeon, 17, 103, 127, 241 *n*8
Allison, David B., 227 *n*6
Alliteration, 252 *n*1
Anacoluthon, 202
Antanomasia, 159
Antimetabole, 87, 133–34
Arnold, Marilyn, 29, 36, 231 *n*12, 232 *n*14
"The Art of Fiction" (interview), 20, 186–87
Ashbery, John, 228 *n*11

Baker, Carlos, 188
Bakhtin, Mikhail, 61, 235 *n*17, 254 *n*4
Bakker, J., 39
"The Ballad of W. C. Fields (2:20)," 77–78, 174
Balliett, Whitney, 250 *n*11
Barkhausen, Jochen, 244 *n*2
Barth, John, 62, 177, 218
Barthes, Roland, 69, 178, 250 *n*12
Bawer, Bruce, 246 *n*2
Bell, Pearl K., 244 *n*3
Benjamin, Walter, 178, 179
Bevilacqua, Winifred Farrant, 237 *n*12
Big as Life, 13, 15, 19, 22, 41–65, 68, 71, 77, 81, 88, 93, 114, 120, 124, 134, 150
Billy Bathgate, 15, 16, 17, 22, 70, 78, 199–215
"Billy's Dream of a Dead Friend (3:40)," 76–77
A Bintel Brief, 239 *n*20

Bloom, Harold, 144, 254 *n*5
The Book of Daniel (Old Testament book), 81, 86–87, 91, 95–96
The Book of Daniel, 7, 12, 14, 15, 16, 19, 22, 68, 69, 79–97, 110, 119, 123, 124, 141, 161, 162, 163, 167, 169, 180, 183, 202, 208, 212, 236 *n*5
"Braver Than We Thought" (review essay), 20, 187–89
Brienza, Susan, 240 *n*4, 245 *n*7
Bruns, Gerald, 7, 227–28 *n*11, 234 *n*14
Budick, Emily Miller, 241 *n*10
Busby, Mark, 240 *n*4

Camus, Albert, 146, 150, 152
Caputo, John D., 229 *n*18
"A Citizen Reads the Constitution" (essay), 192–95
Clayton, John, 39, 229 *n*22, 243 *n*13, 244 *n*2
Clemons, Walter, 249 *n*8
Conrad, Joseph, 13, 130–31, 134, 137, 200
Cooper, Barbara, 80, 232 *n*1, 234 *n*15, 240 *n*4, 241 *n*10
Corbett, Edward P. J., 237 *n*13, 246 *n*1
Crimp, Douglas, 245 *n*11

De Man, Paul, 4, 8–9, 11, 14, 20, 23, 40, 69, 90–91, 111, 125, 126, 134, 222, 228 *n*14, 230 *n*29, 242 *n*11, 246 *n*3, 251 *n*14, 254 *n*2, 255 *n*5; blindness and insight, 15, 22, 63, 64, 74, 78,

De Man, Paul (*cont.*)
  90, 91, 101, 107, 111, 123, 130, 131, 139, 143, 145, 173, 183; primary and secondary deconstruction, 90, 102, 197, 206, 250 *n*9
Derrida, Jacques, 4, 9–11, 20, 23, 44, 46, 53, 58, 61, 127, 222, 228 *n*15, 229 *n*16, 230 *n*29, 231 *n*5, 233 *n*6, 234 *n*14, 247 *n*8, 254 *n*2
Diana, 17, 76, 103, 127, 240 *n*8
Dickens, Charles, 27, 31
Dostoevsky, Fyodor, 177, 184–85
Dreyfus, Hubert, 229 *n*16
Drinks Before Dinner (play), 5, 19

Ellipsis, 38, 81–83, 85–86, 87, 92–93, 96, 116, 123, 124, 145–46, 178, 179, 180, 181–82, 203, 204, 211–13, 237 *n*13, 239 *n*20; unmarked, 96–97, 182, 245 *n*5
Epistrophe, 87
Estrin, Barbara, 80, 239 *n*3
Eternal Return/Eternal Reiteration, 5–7, 14, 17, 18, 27, 32, 38, 54, 65, 75, 76, 88, 91, 92, 95, 96, 99, 106, 109, 111, 112, 113, 114, 116, 118, 127, 139, 142, 162, 169, 172, 174, 177, 185, 188, 189, 194, 206, 209, 210, 215, 219, 226 *n*5, 227 *n*6. *See also* Nietzsche, Friedrich
"Even and Odd in the Garden of Adding (5:15)," 74–76, 85, 238 *n*16

"False Documents" (essay), 17, 20, 63, 78, 174, 177–83, 195, 202, 208
Fleming, Thomas J., 232 *n*1
Flower, Dean, 244 *n*1
"The Foreign Legation" (story), 137, 146–49, 153, 154
Forrey, Robert, 80
Foucault, Michel, 52
Freud, Sigmund, 64, 173, 249 *n*9
Friedl, Bettina, 240 *n*4
Friedl, Herwig, 226 *n*5, 245 *n*9

Gasche, Rudolphe, 226 *n*3
Ginsberg, Allen, 91–93
Girgus, Sam B., 80, 246 *n*13
Grand recit ("master narrative"), 143, 151, 152, 172, 219, 247 *n*10. *See also* Lyotard, Jean-Francois
Graves, Robert, 16, 76
Gross, David S., 230 *n*1, 231 *n*11, 254 *n*2
Guillory, Daniel, 244 *n*3

Halliburton, David, 234 *n*14
Harpham, Geoffrey Galt, 19, 80, 100, 236 *n*5, 238 *n*14, 243 *n*1, 244 *n*3, 245 *n*10, 251 *n*1
Hattmann, John W., 232 *n*1
Hawthorne, Nathaniel, 4, 140, 151, 153
Heidegger, Martin, 4, 5–7, 32, 43–44, 49–51, 58, 61, 152, 162, 166, 227 *n*10, 234 *n*14, 238 *n*15, 249 *n*3; *Sein-zum-Tode*, 83–84, 95, 163, 165, 185, 221–23, 250 *n*12, 255 *n*1
Heller, Joseph, 125
Hemingway, Ernest, 4, 17, 20, 177, 186–89
Hopkins, Gerard Manley, 93
Humm, Peter, 236 *n*1
"The Hunter" (story), 137, 145–46
Hurt, James, 253 *n*1
Hyperbole, 87, 141, 162, 180, 183

Ianone, Carol, 39, 229 *n*22, 247 *n*8
Irwin, John T., 4, 168

Jakobson, Roman, 233 *n*12, 249 *n*3
Johnson, Samuel, 134, 135, 136, 173, 200
Joyce, James, 161, 162, 168, 170

Kafka, Franz, 17, 140
King, Richard, 5, 6, 226 *n*5, 239 *n*2, 240 *n*4

Index 259

Kleist, Heinrich von, 12, 106, 107, 121, 140
Klossowski, Pierre, 227 *n*6
Kloeb, Clayton, 242 *n*11
Krell, David Farrell, 228 *n*11

Lacan, Jacques, 4
Lanham, Richard A., 246 *n*1
"The Leather Man" (story), 15, 137, 149–52, 154, 158
Levine, Paul, 42, 45, 61, 230 *n*2, 232 *n*1, 242 *n*11
Lives of the Poets (collection), 9, 12, 14, 15, 19, 22, 27, 62, 68, 90, 98, 126, 131, 133–56, 171, 173, 176, 236 *n*4
"Lives of the Poets" (novella), 15, 136, 137, 144, 152–56
Loon Lake (novel), 9, 12, 13, 15, 16, 17, 22, 62, 68, 69, 70, 98, 115–32, 134, 136, 137, 149, 158, 159, 169, 173, 176
"Loon Lake" (poem), 120, 244 *n*5
Lorsch, Susan E., 80, 83
Lyotard, Jean-Francois, 254 *n*4. *See also grand recit* ("master narrative")

Macomber, W. B., 255 *n*1
Mars-Jones, Adam, 247 *n*6
Menand, Louis, 252 *n*4
Metonymy, 170
Michigan Quarterly Review interview, 20, 195–98
Miller, J. Hillis, 4, 11–13, 23, 35–36, 134, 180, 222, 229 *n*19, 231 *n*5, 238 *n*16, 242 *n*11, 246 *n*4; on prosopopoeia, 11, 35–36; "varnishing," 12, 14, 22, 71, 73, 76, 108

Nabokov, Vladimir, 62, 178
Nadel, Alan, 245 *n*7
Navasky, Victor, 195
Nietzsche, Friedrich, 4–6, 14, 32, 58, 61, 112, 129, 134, 178, 227 *n*6, 234 *n*14, 254 *n*2. *See also* Eternal return/eternal reiteration

"The Orphans' Home (3:12)," 16, 69–70
Owens, Craig, 253 *n*2
Oxymoron, 74, 117–18, 180

Parks, John G., 17–18, 231 *n*11, 235 *n*17, 241 *n*10
"The Passion of Our Calling" (essay), 183
Poe, Edgar Allan, 4, 80, 140, 247 *n*8
Polysyndeton, 252 *n*1
Prolepsis, 160, 164, 170
Prosopopoeia (personification), 45, 55–56, 137, 140, 161, 166, 167, 171, 190, 220
Pynchon, Thomas, 109, 218, 228 *n*11

Ragtime, 7, 9, 12, 13, 14, 15, 16, 17, 19, 21, 22, 70, 78, 80, 98–114, 120, 124, 127, 138, 167, 169, 173, 196
Rodgers, Bernard, 243 *n*13
Rovit, Earl, 225 *n*1
Runnels, Douglas C., 242 *n*2

Salinger, J. D., 12, 94
Saltzman, Arthur, 29, 42, 111, 230 *n*2, 239 *n*3, 242 *n*10, 253 *n*2
Sartre, Jean-Paul, 150, 152, 178, 181–82, 251 *n*2
Schmitz, Neil, 129, 243 *n*1
Shapiro, Gary, 228 *n*15
Shelley, Percy Bysshe, 100, 241 *n*8
Shelton, Frank W., 29, 31, 230 *n*1
"She's Too Good For Me (2:04)," 72–73
"Short Order Cook (2:35)," 70–72
Sica, Alan, 228 *n*15
Slote, Michael, 255 *n*1
Smith, Duncan, 243 *n*11
"The Songs of Billy Bathgate," 15,

"The Songs of Billy Bathgate" (*cont.*)
 16, 17, 19, 66–78, 88, 89, 107, 120, 134, 136, 137, 167, 174, 182, 208
"Song to the Leaders of the World (3:26)," 73–74
Stade, George, 245 *n*10
Starr, Kevin, 231 *n*11
Stark, John, 80
"The State of Mind of the Union" (essay), 189–92
Stein, Henry, 246 *n*3
Strout, Cushing, 225 *n*1, 242 *n*10
Suleiman, Susan Rubin, 253 *n*2
Syllepsis, 249 *n*5
Synathroesmus, 205
Synechdoche, 38, 62, 63, 68, 116, 120, 123, 134, 147

Tanner, Stephen, 39, 225 *n*1
Thoreau, Henry David, 4, 12, 131–32, 246 *n*13
Tokarczyk, Michelle, 236 *n*4, 239 *n*2
Towers, Robert, 142, 244 *n*3, 246 *n*2, 247 *n*6, 248 *n*12
Treadwell, T. O., 249 *n*5
Turner, Frederick Jackson, 29, 31
Turner, Joseph, 16, 225 *n*1, 236 *n*1

Updike, John, 152, 190

Valente, Joseph, 178
Varnishing. *See* Miller, J. Hillis

"The Water Works" (story), 7, 137, 140–42, 153, 163, 165, 208
Welcome to Hard Times, 5, 6, 7, 8, 9, 12, 13, 14, 16, 18, 19, 20, 22, 23, 25–40, 54, 55, 61, 62, 63, 65, 68, 69, 71, 75, 77, 80, 83, 85, 93, 113, 131, 141, 158, 161, 162, 163, 238 *n*16
Wilkie, Brian, 253 *n*1
White, David A., 227 *n*10
White, Hayden, 236 *n*5, 237 *n*12
Wilden, Anthony, 233 *n*12, 255 *n*1
"Willi" (story), 135, 136, 142–45, 173
Williams, William A., 237 *n*12
Williams, William Carlos, 131, 137
Wordsworth, William, 12, 143, 172, 173
World's Fair, 7, 9, 12, 15, 16, 17, 22, 31, 78, 90, 98, 110, 126, 157–75, 180, 182, 208, 209
"The Writer as Independent Witness" (interview), 177, 183–86
"The Writer in the Family" (story), 15, 137, 138–39, 152, 168, 173

Zavarzadeh, Mas'ud, 235–36 *n*1, 253 *n*2
Zins, Daniel L., 237 *n*12